Quality and Power in Higher Education

SRHE and Open University Press Imprint
General Editor: Heather Eggins

Current titles include:

Catherine Bargh et al.: University Leadership
Ronald Barnett: The Idea of Higher Education
Ronald Barnett: The Limits of Competence
Ronald Barnett: Higher Education
Ronald Barnett: Realizing the University in an age of supercomplexity
Tony Becher and Paul R. Trowler: Academic Tribes and Territories (2nd edn)
Neville Bennett et al.: Skills Development in Higher Education and Employment
John Biggs: Teaching for Quality Learning at University
David Boud et al. (eds): Using Experience for Learning
David Boud and Nicky Solomon (eds): Work-based Learning
Tom Bourner et al. (eds): New Directions in Professional Higher Education
John Brennan et al. (eds): What Kind of University?
Anne Brockbank and Ian McGill: Facilitating Reflective Learning in Higher Education
Ann Brooks and Alison Mackinnon (eds): Gender and the Restructured University
Sally Brown and Angela Glasner (eds): Assessment Matters in Higher Education
John Cowan: On Becoming an Innovative University Teacher
Gerard Delanty: Challenging Knowledge
Chris Duke: Managing the Learning University
Gillian Evans: Academics and the Real World
Andrew Hannan and Harold Silver: Innovating in Higher Education
Norman Jackson and Helen Lund (eds): Benchmarking for Higher Education
Merle Jacob and Tomas Hellström (eds): The Future of Knowledge Production in the
    Academy
Peter Knight: Being a Teacher in Higher Education
Peter Knight and Paul Trowler: Departmental Leadership in Higher Education
Mary Lea and Barry Stierer (eds): Student Writing in Higher Education
Ian McNay (ed.): Higher Education and its Communities
Elaine Martin: Changing Academic Work
Moira Peelo and Terry Wareham (eds): Failing Students in Higher Education
Craig Prichard: Making Managers in Universities and Colleges
Michael Prosser and Keith Trigwell: Understanding Learning and Teaching
John Richardson: Researching Student Learning
Stephen Rowland: The Enquiring University Teacher
Maggi Savin-Baden: Problem-based Learning in Higher Education
Peter Scott (ed.): The Globalization of Higher Education
Peter Scott: The Meanings of Mass Higher Education
Anthony Smith and Frank Webster (eds): The Postmodern University?
Colin Symes and John McIntyre (eds): Working Knowledge
Peter G. Taylor: Making Sense of Academic Life
Susan Toohey: Designing Courses for Higher Education
Paul R. Trowler: Higher Education Policy and Institutional Change
Melanie Walker (ed.): Reconstructing Professionalism in University Teaching
David Warner and David Palfreyman (eds): The State of UK Higher Education
Diana Woodward and Karen Ross: Managing Equal Opportunities in Higher Education

Quality and Power in Higher Education

Louise Morley

Society for Research into Higher Education
& Open University Press

Published by SRHE and
Open University Press
McGraw-Hill Education
McGraw-Hill House
Shoppenhangers Road
Maidenhead
Berkshire
England
SL6 2QL

email: enquiries@openup.co.uk
world wide web: www.openup.co.uk

and
325 Chestnut Street
Philadelphia, PA 19106, USA

First Published 2003

A catalogue record of this book is available from the British Library

ISBN 0 335 21226 3 (pb)   0 335 21227 1 (hb)

Library of Congress Cataloging-in-Publication Data
Morley, Louise, 1954–
    Quality and power in higher education / Louise Morley.
      p.   cm.
    Includes bibliographical references and index.
    ISBN 0-335-21227-1 – ISBN 0-335-21226-3 (pbk.)
    1. Education, Higher–Great Britain–Administration.   2. Education, Higher–
Standards–Great Britain.   3. Quality assurance–Great Britain.   I. Title.

LB2341.8.G7 M67 2003
378.1′00941–dc21

                                                                    2002030368

Typeset by Graphicraft Limited, Hong Kong
Printed by Bell & Bain Ltd, Glasgow

Contents

Introduction   vii

Abbreviations   xiv

1   The Policy Context of Quality in Higher Education   1
Globalization: opportunity and/or exploitation?   1
The risk society: manufacturing moral panics   5
Brain sells: the knowledge economy   6
Liquifying higher education: new sites of knowledge   8
Democratizing discourses: the learning society and lifelong learning   10
Continuous improvement: to travel hopefully, but never to arrive   13

2   How Quality is Assessed   15
The genesis of the quality assurance movement   15
Jeux sans frontiers: quality internationally   18
Thought lakes and word mountains: measuring research productivity   21
Reinventing teaching and learning   26
The professionalization of university teachers   29
Scores and league tables: the comfort of numbers   34
Classifying chaos: standards, benchmarks and qualifications
frameworks   41

3   Managing Quality   47
New managerialism and old organizational cultures   47
Accountability, autonomy and the audit culture   53
Performance indicators: measuring creativity   57
Never mind the quality, feel the cost!   60

4   The Psychic Economy of Quality   67
Identity: the professional is political   67
Trust me, I'm a doctor!   69

Performativity and the power of discourse   70
Job satisfaction: alienation and 'counterfeit' reflexivity   76
Unhealthy organizations and occupational stress   78
Naming and shaming: post-modern torture   87

5   Changing Employment Regimes   91
De- or re-professionalization? Scholars or knowledge workers?   91
Increasing workloads and the long hours' culture   93
Split focusing   100

6   The Micropolitics of Quality   105
The everyday life of power   105
Collegiality   107
Peer review: outsiders within or insiders without?   111
Gulliver and the Lilliputs: reinforcing the binary divide   123
The methodology of quality assurance in higher education:
modernization or a return to modernism?   126

7   Reconstructing Students as Consumers   129
Delighting the customer!   129
From change agents to consumers?   131
Words, words, words: writing risk reduction   132
Educatainment and student evaluation   137
Radical pedagogy or teaching and learning?   143

8   (E)quality   146
Quality and equality   146
Joining the procession   148
Quantitative signifiers and qualitative differences   150
Globalizing inequality   152
The gendered division of labour   155
Gendering performativity   157

9   Desiring Changes   160
Long-term effects: supply, stratification and surveillance   160
Quality otherwise   164

References   172
Index   190
The Society for Research into Higher Education   201

Introduction

This book explores the relationship between quality and power. It is an examination of the power relations that organize and facilitate quality assurance in higher education. It interrogates power in terms of macro-systems of accountability, surveillance and regulation, and also in the microprocesses of organizational life, that is, how quality assurance influences culture, relationships, subjectivities and identities in the academy. Quality has become a universalizing metanarrative. The definition of quality in quantitative terms in the public domain is one of the ways in which discursive regulation takes place. In Britain, higher education institutions, subject areas and departments become totalized by the scores that they receive. It is an installation of power, with monolithic notions of what constitutes quality. Quality parades as a universal truth and therefore continually extends its domain.

Quality assurance can be like a prism through which other aspects of contemporary academic life are examined. Quality procedures translate particular rationalities and moralities into new forms of governance and professional behaviour. As such, quality is a political technology functioning as a regime and relay of power. Political technologies, with their norms and common-sense assumptions, disguise how power works. There has been a re-formation of the academic *habitus* itself. Quality in the academy has involved significant rehabilitation of the labour force. Yet there has been a lack of a sociological imagination in quality assurance. An aim of this study is to begin to uncover some of the ways in which quality, as a regime of power, is experienced by academics and managers in higher education.

The academy is encountering challenges to its epistemological presumptions. Limits are being set and prescribed by a wider range of actors. There are strong arguments in favour of holding an elite professional group and dominant organizations of knowledge production to account. Power has always been exercised in the definition of expertise and in academic judgements. Now, the dominant have become the dominated. Quality assurance has acquired a discursive orthodoxy in higher education, with material and symbolic consequences. There are those who believe that quality assurance is at the very epicentre of the debate about the future of higher education in Britain (Alderman, 1996). The central legitimating idea of higher education is changing, with questions about the type of public mandate the university now has. The rise of academic management, together with the rise of consumerism and political concerns with the exchange and use value of higher education have produced new organizational cultures and professional priorities (Deem, 1998). While quality assurance is concerned with fitness for purpose, a question arises as to whether quality technologies themselves are fit for academic purposes. Complex organizations are granularized, i.e. reduced to a myriad parts and reconstituted to represent a 'pure' whole, containing certain knowledge about processes and practices (Guile, 2001). Universal pragmatics have begun to emerge which justify the development and application of quality assurance practices to the academy. Quality, like 'community', 'empowerment', 'partnership' and 'flexibility' has become a hooray word or, to use Williams' (1976) term, a keyword in the public services. As such, it is suffering from conceptual inflation. However, it is important to remember that quality audits are essentially relationships of power between observers and observed. An important part of the power relations is the way in which norms are created and maintained. Norms can constitute an invisible web of power because the norms become internalized and more difficult to recognize and contest (Shore and Wright, 1999). The psychic operation of the norm can offer a more insidious route for regulatory power than explicit coercion (Butler, 1997a).

The insertion of the quality discourse into higher education is an example of the changing relations between universities and the state. In one sense, it represents a challenge to the medieval achievement of separating the idea of intellectual authority from political authority (Finch, 1997). Quality assurance could also be perceived as the state asserting its responsibility. The state has shifted from a promoter of intellectual activity to a controller of it (Dominelli and Hoogvelt, 1996). It also represents change in relations with diverse stakeholders, including employers, the international donor community and indeed, students and their families.

Higher education has been re-engineered. Quality assurance is perceived as part of the modernization process. As such, critics can be accused of golden ageism. However, as Scott (2000: 5) reminds us: 'Three-quarters of the extant universities – even of universities in Europe, its ancient heartland – have been established since 1900; half since 1945'. As one of the great institutions of modernity and the Enlightenment, the university is being interrogated. It seems burdened with a sense of its own history and its formations for professionalization and credentialization are increasingly perceived as archaic (Scott, 2000). The traditional model of the university appears to be adjusted to a now vanishing world. The monopolistic, or privileged role of universities in the creation of values and production and dissemination of knowledge is being challenged and contested by other agencies. Higher education has been metaphorically floated on the stock exchange and its once exclusive properties have been deregulated, privatized and challenged (Bauman, 2001a). Resistance to change is perceived as an incapacity for readjustment and redeployment in a rapidly changing social and economic world.

I am also interested in how quality intersects or collides with equality issues, and whether quality regimes reproduce or challenge gendered, classed and racialized hierarchies in the academy, and expose difference and inequalities. If quality assurance is about standards and conformance, what place is there for difference and diversity? I question whether quality assurance procedures are producing new systems of power and reinforcing gendered power relations in the academy (Morley, 2001a). There is a powerful rhetoric of inevitability and macrodeterminism in quality assurance procedures, or a TINA effect (there is no alternative) (Bauman, 2001b). The common-sense logic means that resistance is hard to mobilize. Terms that are used to describe organizational life in the academy are also active forces shaping it. There is an idealization embedded in quality assurance, and as Benjamin (2000: 232) argues, every idealization defends against something. Quality assurance could be perceived as a collective defence mechanism. What is exteriorized or performed relates to fear of being inscribed in the negative end of the quality continuum (Butler, 2000). Some questions are: What is being acted out and occluded in the performance of quality assurance in the academy? What signs of quality are being performed and valued? What does quality assurance allegorize? What losses, fears and anxieties are activated by the procedures? How does quality assurance invade interior spaces, silence opposition and promote conformity and ontological complicity? Is the culture of excellence resulting in mediocrity?

This book considers theories as to why the quality discourse was introduced at a particular social and political moment. The policy context of the Learning Society, Lifelong Learning, the knowledge economy and the shift from an elite to a 'mass' higher education system has been well-documented (Association of University Teachers, 1993; Scott, 1995), although the implications and effects of this expansion for university staff are still fairly under theorized. The growth of the higher education system in Britain (and elsewhere) has been rapid and extreme. Two-thirds of British universities were created after 1960. The majority of the remainder were founded in the three decades prior to the First World War (Delanty, 2001). After the 1992 Further and Higher Education Act, with the abolition of the binary divide, the number of universities in Britain increased from 46 to 112. The number of students has doubled, as has the student:staff ratio across the entire system (Watson and Bowden, 1999). There is a target to increase participation to 50 per cent of the under-30 population by 2010. The trend for massification is noticeable on a global basis, with international organizations citing increased access and participation as major policy objectives (UNESCO, 1998).

Quality, in the public services, invariably relates to performance, standards and output, rather than to inputs such as employment conditions. However, new organizational regimes demand temporal investment, emotional labour, and commitment to cultural change (Trowler, 1998). There is a psychic economy of quality assurance. Quality procedures require the activation and exploitation of a range of feelings such as guilt, loyalty, desire, greed, shame, anxiety and responsibilization, in the service of effectiveness and point-scoring (Ozga and Walker, 1999). There are profound ontological issues at stake in the scoring of organizations. The translation of higher educational activities into cash terms and league tables with exchange value establishes new relations of power (Bowden, 2000). Pedagogical, social and interpersonal relations are changing as a consequence of the introduction of the customer-care revolution, new competitions between individuals and organizations for research funding and student numbers. The two accounting systems in the UK can also lead to split focusing for academics who have to be increasingly multiskilled. This book documents the genesis and policy context of quality assurance in higher education. It includes voices of academics and managers relating how quality has been interpreted and experienced in the academy.

As a feminist academic, I am accustomed to the practice of attempting to situate myself in the discourse. As both an academic manager and scholar of higher education studies, I find myself having to operate inside and outside the discourse. The culture of compliance in the UK means that I, like countless other colleagues, have to suspend critical faculties and perform within regulatory frameworks. However, the hybridity of my position means that I have to struggle to ensure that I am not co-opted and incorporated into practices and ideologies which are fundamentally in opposition to my beliefs. Hence, my drive to make quality assurance an object of inquiry, rather than an internalized *modus operandi*. I attempt to recycle the corrosive and contradictory experiences and discomforts of being subjected to quality regimes into data for policy analysis, thus embodying the radical feminist mantra of 'the personal is political'!

Methodology

First, I wish to state that this project was not funded by any of the research councils. They turned it down, largely on the basis that they could not see its relevance as quality assurance procedures are in transition. I found this strange as when I gave papers at conferences in Britain and overseas, I 'played' to packed rooms of students, academics and managers. There seemed to be an intense desire to discuss, analyse and debate the issues. Furthermore, while mechanisms and structures for assessing quality might change, the ideology continues. Convinced of the value of such a study, I decided to fund it myself from my international consultancy work and a grant of £750 from my institution. I wrote this book in the cracks and fissures between teaching, managing, applying for funded research, and international work. I exemplified the split focused academic – always working with interruptions, always feeling that I should be doing something else.

My potent internalized critic worried that the findings would be easily dismissed as a small sample size always provokes questions about generalizability. In the same way as early women painters were forced to paint bowls of fruit as they were not allowed out of the house, or women writers focused on domestic dramas, I was forced to scale down my sample. Hence, I make limited, cautious and modest claims.

The empirical field is quality in the rapidly changing academy in Britain. My theoretical field includes the sociology of higher education, organization studies, feminist and post-structuralist theory. This is a qualitative study, or theorized narrative of quality. My sample of 36 comprises 18 women and 18 men in 35 higher education institutions in England, Scotland and Wales. Twenty-two informants are from old universities and 15 were from new/post-1992 universities. Nineteen informants are academic members of staff and 17 are administrative. Academic staff comprise 4 professors, 1 reader, 3 principal lecturers, 5 senior lecturers and 6 lecturers. Administrative staff comprise 1 pro-vice chancellor, 2 registrars, 4 assistant registrars, 3 heads of department and 12 quality assurance managers. If these figures do not always add up, it is because some of the administrators doubled up as academics! The disciplines include philosophy, French, Spanish, English, economics, education, international studies, technology, applied science, social policy, sociology and veterinary medicine.

Semi-structured interviews were used to elicit the views of people with a range of engagements in quality assurance. Some co-ordinated the entire organization's arrangements while some worked at departmental or course level. There were critics, product champions and those who occupied both positions simultaneously. I struggled not to get positioned by my informants who frequently introduced their statements with 'I'm not sure if this is what you want to hear . . .' Furthermore, as performativity is such a central feature of presenting quality, I had to be conscious of when I was getting a performance, or the party line. I asked for details, feelings, critical incidents – probing beneath the surface presentation. I sought the hidden transcripts – voices of those (I would not dare to say 'authentic') that had been involved in the performative utterances of quality assurance.

Chapter overview

Chapter 1 examines the policy context and policy drivers behind the development of quality assurance in higher education. In asking why quality is assessed, it considers globalization, the risk society, the knowledge economy, new sites of learning, the learning society and lifelong learning and continuous improvement. It explores the underpinnings of the quality assurance discourse including fear, risk and the threat of chaos and misrule in globalized mass systems of higher education.

Chapter 2 focuses on how quality is assessed. It examines the genesis of the quality assurance movement, international dimensions, the two accounting systems of research and teaching quality. It raises questions about the professionalization of university teachers, and the use of league tables and benchmarks.

Chapter 3 interrogates how quality is managed. It explores links between quality assurance, new managerialism and changing organizational cultures. Questions are raised about the industrialization of quality and the costs of audit. The concepts of accountability, autonomy and the audit culture are examined, as well as performance indicators and resistance. It analyses ideas about the evaluative state, accountability, and consumer empowerment. It explores the power relations involved in human accounting and audit (Power, 1997; Strathern, 1997). Questions are raised about the values behind the seemingly neutral evaluative technologies, and the mechanisms employed to manufacture consent.

Chapter 4 focuses on the psychic economy of quality. It includes discussion on identity, trust, performativity, job satisfaction, alienation, and reflexivity. It examines the range of emotions manipulated and unleashed in quality audits such as fear, greed, desire, anger, powerlessness, pride and shame.

Chapter 5 considers changes in employment regimes in terms of increasing workloads, split focusing, multiskilling, and the de- or re-professionalization of academics. It examines how the two accounting systems relate and collide.

Chapter 6 is concerned with the micropolitics of quality, that is the everyday life of power. The relay of power is explored via concepts and practices including collegiality, peer review, the binary divide and the methodology of quality assurance in higher education. This chapter poses questions about how quality is experienced in the quotidian life of organizations.

Chapter 7 highlights the changing construction of students. It traces the shifting social identity from change agents to consumers and raises questions about changing pedagogical relations, and how the student voice has been incorporated into the quality project via evaluations rather than protest. It traces the contours of changing power relations between academics and students as a consequence of the discourse of entitlements and consumer rights.

Chapter 8 raises questions about the relationship between quality and equality, and the gendered division of labour that is reinforced by quality assessments. It is questionable whether equity has been displaced or promoted via concerns over quality. Are socially excluded groups benefiting from the quality movement? Do the managerial demands of quality assurance appear to have gendered implications with the quality movement a new form of hegemonic masculinity?

Chapter 9 focuses on changes. It summarizes the research findings and raises questions about the long-term effects of quality on the academy and offers insights into how quality can be assured while promoting healthy and intellectually creative working environments.

Acknowledgements

First of all, many thanks to all the informants who shared their experiences, insights and views with me – all of whom are made anonymous for reasons of confidentiality. Thanks to colleagues at the Institute of Education who support and inspire me, including Stephen Ball, Ron Barnett, Debbie Cameron, Jenny Corbett, Jan Derry, Dave Gillborn, Anne Gold, David Guile, David Halpin, Val Klenowski, Diana Leonard, Sally Power, Elaine Unterhalter, Gareth Williams, Geoff Whitty, Michael Young. Thanks to my doctoral students and the students on the MA in Higher and Professional Studies for all the stimulating discussions on quality in the academy. Thanks to my network of feminist academics including Miriam David, Rosemary Deem, Mairead Dunne, Meg Maguire and Naz Rassool. Thanks to Simeon Underwood for sending me his extensive personal archive of newspaper articles on quality assurance. Thanks to John Skelton at the Open University Press for his editorial advice. Thanks to Sophie Kemp and Sue Cranmer for helping with data collection and to Katy Evans and Leanne Guillen for transcription. Thanks also to the Dean of Research at the Institute of Education for the grant towards the cost of data collection.

Abbreviations

AUT	Association of University Teachers
CNAA	Council for National Academic Awards
CPD	continuing professional development
CVCP	Committee of Vice Chancellors and Principals
DES	Department of Education and Science
DfES	Department for Education and Skills
DfEE	Department for Education and Employment
EC	European Commission
HEFCE	Higher Education Funding Council for England
HEQC	Higher Education Quality Council
ILT	Institute of Learning and Teaching
NUS	National Union of Students
OECD	Organization for Economic Co-operation and Development
OfSTED	Office for Standards in Education
QAA	Quality Assurance Agency
RAE	research assessment exercise
SPR	subject provision review
SRHE	Society for Research into Higher Education
THES	Times Higher Education Supplement
TQA	teaching quality assessment
TQM	total quality management
UFC	Universities Funding Council
UGC	University Grants Committee
UNESCO	United Nations Education, Science and Cultural Organization

1

The Policy Context of Quality in Higher Education

Globalization: opportunity and/or exploitation?

Globalization is affecting the rise of the quality industry. Globalization is a heavily contested concept, theorized as both process and ideology with material and discursive influence. It is economic, political, technological and cultural. Values, cultures and capital flow in new networks, partnerships and coalitions. The features of globalization that are often expounded are (Burbules and Torres, 2000):

- new exchange relationships;
- the internationalization of trade;
- the restructuring of the labour market;
- the decrease in capital–labour conflict as a consequence of opportunities for the mobility of plant;
- the international division of labour, the movement from Fordism to increased flexibility;
- new forces of production and new technologies;
- capital-intensive production;
- the increase in the number of part-time and female workers;
- the increase in the size and importance of the service sector;
- the financial gap between more developed and less developed countries.

The themes of chaos and control permeate debates on globalization. The global is multivocal, heterogeneous and unpredictable. Risk has been globalized. Quality assessment is seen as the antithesis to the chaos of global expansion of higher education. It is a way of ensuring that systems and structures can process ever-increasing numbers of students.

The power of the nation state is supposedly reduced while that of the market is enhanced. Quality is critical to the functioning of the market. Global consumers are thought to require condensed and reliable information about the product that they are purchasing. Globalization has provided a justification for the restructuring of the workplace and for organizational priorities. Material changes produce new subjectivities, as global citizens are encouraged to internalize shifting reference points. Global competition determines domestic economic behaviour. Workers are told that they have to be more flexible, self-managing, entrepreneurial and responsive to a rapidly changing environment. Academics are being propelled towards the global at the same time as their day-to-day domestic pressures are under greater pressure than ever (Marginson, 2000).

Like many dominant concepts and theories, there are dichotomous accounts, with critics and champions, and discussions of enhanced risks and rights. The politically neutral representation of globalization as the compression of time and space (Robertson, 1992) contrasts with the notion that globalization is an economistic discourse embedded in market values (Marginson, 1999). Globalization is perceived as both homogenizing and heterogenizing in so far as it increases similarities and differences (Vidovich and Slee, 2001). Arguments tend to be polarized into those suggesting that globalization enhances opportunities, while others believe that it intensifies possibilities of exploitation and cultural imperialism. For example, Bauman (1998a) suggests that social exclusion is the inevitable consequence of globalization. Social exclusion and poverty today are reproduced by lack of human capital, rather than lack of natural resources, and globalization can promote inequity due to differential technological opportunities (Gorostiaga, 1999). In the context of globalization, there are multiple lines of power and decision-making mechanisms. Luke and Luke (2000: 288) believe that the exploitation discourse casts the local 'in a victim narrative, robbed of agency, stripped of authenticity, and reduced to nothing more than a hapless consumption machine'.

Proponents argue that globalized competition will lead to improved service (McBurnie, 2001). Globalization is also seen as an opportunity for networking, inclusion and the expansion of democracy and human rights. While others see it as yet another variety of colonialism, exploitation and domination, giving rise to structural unemployment and poor labour relations. Currie and Newson (1998) politically locate globalization within the framework of neoliberalism. This philosophy supports free trade and the operation of market mechanisms, including their application to traditional public services. This includes reduced government funding of the public sector, the marketization of public services, the privatization of state activities and/or their exposure to competition from private providers, and the removal or reduction of regulatory barriers to free trade. For Pels (2000: 135) auditing and accounting have become the operational signs of the global spread of neoliberal values. Audit, with all the momentum of a cultural movement, holds out the possibility of a global professional consensus (Strathern, 2000a).

Globalization impacts on higher education and *vice versa*. The obvious connection is that expansion of higher education across national boundaries demands more rigorous and robust measures for quality assurance. Deem (2001) argues that changes in funding regimes, organizational and cultural changes, new forms of educational provision through the internet or the inclusion of new groups of students are the central effects of globalization on higher education. Academics have also extended their global reach via conference, offshore courses and international networks (Luke, 2001). Slaughter and Leslie (1997: 31) see globalization as a set of political and economic changes and argue that 'These changes are putting pressure on national higher education policy makers to change the way tertiary education does business'. Universities have become more prominent in their contribution to the globalized knowledge economy. Reich (1991) believes that governments now want to shape higher education in relation to the needs of technological societies. He has divided work into three main categories: routine production services, in-person services and symbolic analysts. He believes that the most productive workers in a global economy are the 'symbolic analysts'. However, a global trend is emerging as more knowledge-based occupations develop, the greater the demand for more places to be created for people to gain initial and in-service qualifications. Scott (2000: 5/6) believes that the university is challenged by globalization in three main ways:

> First because of the University's close identification with the promulgation of national cultures; second, because of the standardisation of teaching through the impact of communication and information technology, and the emergence of global research cultures and networks; and third, because global markets have undermined high public expenditure welfare states on which universities depended for the bulk of their income.

In addition, opportunities for policy borrowing have been greatly enhanced by the various information flows of globalization. Convergence is one of the core aspects of globalization. University managers are drawn together as a global power elite. To be outside that consensus is to be marginalized or excluded. However, quality assurance might unearth global challenges, but contingencies of context suggest that local solutions are also required, a fact that is frequently overlooked by influential organizations. This process is sometimes known as 'glocalization' – the 'nexus or intersections of global forces with local sites, uptakes, and historical contexts' (Luke, 2001: 19). While globalization appears to be isomorphic, it also means that the same systems and structures are being applied to a diverse set of local and organizational settings, with unequal outcomes and consequences.

Lingard (2000) points out how international organizations including the OECD (Organization for Economic and Cultural Development) and the World Bank function as instruments of policy as they act as institutionalizing mechanisms for the new global educational policy consensus. There are particular policy networks and traffic flows, for example the European Union, Commonwealth countries, Anglophone regions. The World Bank

(1994) report on higher education suggested that countries should shift from one source of funding for higher education and should attempt to raise funds from student fees, endowments and consultancies. The report actually stated that higher education globally should resemble the United States model more closely. This raises questions about the locus of power in globalized discourses.

The nation state being out of control is a common theme in globalization. The emphasis is on the transnational and the network society (Castells, 1996). Open structures, mobilities and flows of information rather than closure, stasis and boundaries are key features. This leads some critics to argue that this process of deterritorization results in an absence of a centre. For example, Burbules (2000: 345) asks 'where are you when you are online?' The disembeddedness is part of the liquification process. Others argue that the centre is firmly located in the West. Jarvis (1999: 252) observes that the structures of higher education in the West are pointing the direction for less economically developed countries. Higher education is forming its own powerful multinationals. In higher education, new partnerships, coalitions and strategic alliances are emerging. Universitas 21 is an initiative run from the University of Melbourne. It comprises a group of elite universities from the UK, Canada, Australia, New Zealand, Singapore and the United States to accredit each other and share external examiners (Sadlak, 1998).

Another feature of globalization is that of more permeable boundaries between nation states. This is currently being reflected in the phenomenon of borderless universities (Middlehurst, 2000; Tapsall, 2001). Borderless higher education includes e-learning, forms of transnational provision and new providers, for example for-profit universities (Ryan, 2002). Learning is leaking into every crevice of the social world. The university is becoming liquified (Bauman, 2001a).

Questions can be posed about whether the expansion of distance learning and the rise of mega-universities offer opportunity or exploitation, a new organizing principle or the potential for chaos. In Britain, the e-university has been ostensibly designed to enhance participation while simultaneously expected to increase export revenues. Morrow and Torres (2000: 42) remind us how the 'diploma mill' universities in the US, unable to convince suitable numbers of US citizens of the value of their product, have expanded overseas. Transnational companies relocate their production to areas that are more likely to generate greater returns on their capital investment. The 'first world' has become a knowledge society, while a great deal of the actual manufacturing has been relocated to lower and middle-income economies. Morrow and Torres (2000: 34) argue that there has been an analytical shift from post-industrialism to information-alism, or training now means learning less about more. Foucault (1972) equated knowledge with discourse, power and ideology, rather than with permanent truths. However, disposable (shallow), or just-in-time knowledge is legitimated via the compression of time and space associated with globalization.

The risk society: manufacturing moral panics

There is a powerful discourse of crisis, loss, damage, contamination, and decay in higher education. There are images of the university in ruins (Readings, 1996), the 'degradation' of academia (Nisbet, 1971), the university 'in crisis' (Sommer, 1995), the death of autonomy (Dill, 2001) and proletarianization (Dearlove, 1997). Massification, industrialization and the more overt linkage of higher education with the needs of commerce and industry have polluted the purity of elite organizations of knowledge production. The university is now one provider in a learning market. Universities now have to open their doors to new constituencies, new competitions and new risks. One of the emerging functions of higher education has become the aversion of risk. Readings (1996) argues that increased risk in society at large has led to more authoritarian and exploitative forms of capitalism. Like other neoliberal discourses, for example choice and consumer empowerment, quality assurance appears to be client-focused and democratizing, whereas it has deeply conservative underpinnings. However, the rational agenda is that higher education plays a pivotal role in many societies. If it is purified at source, this will cascade into more reliable professional practices inside and outside the academy.

The academy, like other public services, has become a site of social anxiety and fear. Institutions no longer connote safety. The construct of trustworthiness is being associated with standardization, competence, continuity and reliability. Professional contexts today are characterized as low trust/high risk cultures. The risk society has resulted in the decline of trust in professional conduct. Quality assurance in industry aims for zero defect and error reduction and prevention. The same principle is being applied to the public services. Eraut (1994) points out that whereas at one time, professional bodies existed to protect the public from unqualified non-professionals such as 'quack' doctors, now they also function to protect the public from the professionals themselves. Issues of trust, authority and expertise have been disaggregated. Routine, rather than deviant practices, have been subjected to scrutiny. Academics have lost some of their authoritative power. The advantage is that powerful groups are being held more to account. The disadvantage is that success criteria for complex public services are being reduced and manipulated into over-simplistic classifications. A new defensiveness is emerging.

Quality assurance is a model of panic creation or a 'synthetic panic' (Jenkins, 1999: 8/9). The moral panic over standards could be said to have originated in a speech made by John Pattern when he was the Secretary of State for Education in 1994, to the CVCP. He called on the Higher Education Quality Control Council (HEQC) to place more emphasis on broad compatibility in the standards offered by different institutions. In 1994, the HEQC set up a Graduate Standards Programme to develop threshold standards for degrees. A review was also commissioned and in 1996 it reported that degree standards varied significantly between universities and even within one institution (HEQC, 1997; Lucas and Webster, 1998).

Quality assurance links the micro-world of the organization with the public world of policy and politics. It is questionable whether policy is a response to existing conditions and problems, or a discourse in which both problems and solutions are created (Bacchi, 2000). Quality assurance is a policy domain with material and ideational implications. It is a response to the moral panic over standards, massification, wealth creation and globalization. Heightened concern is a prerequisite for panic. There is political potential in crises and catastrophes. Politicians can demonstrate their effectiveness via quantitative measures of 'improvement' in the public services. With moral panic, authorities, including politicians and managers, either play a central role in initiating it, or are likely to join ongoing arrangements and derive some benefit from them, such as a more docile workforce. Beck (1997: 265) explains:

> In an age of uncertainty, discourses that appear to promise a resolution to ambivalence by producing identifiable victims and blameable villains are likely to figure prominently in the State's ceaseless attempts to impose social order.

Goode and Ben-Yehuda (1994) identified five crucial elements of moral panic:

- concern;
- hostility;
- consensus;
- disproportionality;
- volatility.

Certainly, this model would describe the trajectory of assuring quality in teaching and learning in Britain.

McRobbie (1994: 199) identifies two main responses to panic. The first is the 'fortress mentality that is characterized by a feeling of helplessness, political powerlessness and paralysis'. The second is the 'gung-ho' approach, the 'something must be done about it' mindset. The latter could exemplify the quality mongers (Hart, 1997). This is the group of people from which the pool of peer assessors, quality assurance officers and managers is drawn. This group can be driven by paradoxical and contradictory aims. On the one hand, they subscribe to processes that are profoundly undemocratic and authoritarian. On the other hand, there is a democratizing driver. They want a better deal for students – more information, product specification and risk reduction in a knowledge-driven economy. The values of the consumer society are now firmly embedded in educational relationships.

Brain sells: the knowledge economy

Quality assurance is linked to the knowledge economy. Whereas once the theory of knowledge was confined to philosophy departments, now it has entered the public arena. Knowledge and understanding are being made more visible as objects of inquiry. Clark (1996) stressed that the expansion and complexity in the knowledge with which universities now deal is one of the salient forces for change in higher education. James (2000: 42) identifies two separate and distinct categories of knowledge in modern universities. First, the disciplinary knowledge at the heart of the teaching, research and consultancy enterprise. Second, there is 'intricate operational knowledge that is held in a university's values, policies and practices'. However, changes in policy and the labour market mean that this is constantly in flux.

Whereas the United States of America has had a tradition of vocational education, the elitist distinction between education and training is now beginning to disappear in Europe. Scheffler (1965) suggested that there are three ways of legitimating knowledge: rational, empiricist and pragmatic. The latter is concerned with instrumentalism, which according to Jarvis (2000) lies at the heart of capitalist enterprise. Increasingly, the mercantization of knowledge and education means that higher education knowledge is being evaluated for its pragmatic value. According to Gibbons *et al.* (1994) a new model of knowledge, called Mode 2, is replacing the Mode 1 of organized modernity. It is characterized by the proliferation of many knowledge producers working in the context of application, which is increasingly linked to problem solving. Knowledge becomes utilitarian, rather than an end itself.

Change in higher education is being driven, in part, by the needs of large transnational companies and related knowledge-based industries. Partnerships between universities and knowledge-based industries are being formed and carefully nurtured. Polster (2000: 19) calls this the 'corporatization agenda'. Boundaries between the academy, government and business have been loosened and reformulated in what is sometimes known as the 'triple helix' (Etzkowitz and Leydesdorff, 1997). Corporate interests play a more powerful role in determining the purposes of higher education. While higher education is largely dependent on state funding, it is expected to meet the requirements of the private sector economy. Increasingly, higher education is being framed as a source of labour market training. There is a more explicit concern with universities producing new workers. The performance indicator in quality assessments of graduate employability suggests that more vocational outcomes are required (Morley, 2001b). There are multiple linkages between the different stakeholders in the economy and universities are being increasingly encouraged to work with industry and commerce to generate knowledge, wealth and regional and national economies (Coaldrake, 2000; Coate *et al.* 2000). Today, boundaries between disciplines and professional knowledges are continuing to shift.

Professional knowledge has become unstable. The old notion of banked knowledge, whereby professionals acquire a body of knowledge in their youth and then practice throughout their careers, is changing. There is increasing emphasis on disposable, transferable and just-in-time knowledge. The focus is increasingly on learning how to learn, rather than on acquiring a reservoir of lifelong disciplinary knowledge. This notion is not entirely new. Lyotard (1984) argued that all knowledge is narrative because it changes so rapidly. Continuing professional development (CPD) is seen as the systematic maintenance, improvement and broadening of knowledge, understanding and skill, and the development of personal qualities necessary for the execution of professional duties throughout an individual's working life (Eraut *et al.*, 1998). In the wake of many well-publicized cases of professional misconduct, a growing number of professions are introducing mandatory CPD as part of the licence to practise or practising certificate. This is a strong part of the lifelong learning agenda, to which national and European governments and policies have a major commitment.

The relationship between work and education is currently a dominant policy discourse. There is growing interest in professional education and how people learn in the workplace, how they learn from others and how they apply abstract knowledge to professional situations (Eraut, 1994). The trend is now for many public service professionals to make their own practice an object of inquiry. Action research, while highly problematic for its linear, input/output methodologies, is becoming attractive to employers. There is a growing inclination for 'professionalization' of all educational activities in many professions. Professionally-related programmes in Britain such as the National Professional Qualification for Headteachers (NPQH) have been introduced. There is a related need for the development of robust systems for the recognition of creativity, effort and scholarship in professional activities, and for overt reward of creativity, effort and scholarship. Hence the rise in credentialism, with professionals wanting more evidence of their development in the form of accreditation. All this frenzied activity in higher and professional education suggests an even greater demand for stable indicators of quality and standards.

Liquifying higher education: new sites of knowledge

The university has traditionally been a place, albeit a large cognitive network segmented into disciplinary tribes and territories (Becher and Trowler, 2001). Now, with distance learning and borderless education it is increasingly becoming a space – one space amid many others. There is a distributed knowledge production and consumption system. Knowledge is diffused, configured and reconfigured. New sites include virtual, for-profit, open, corporate, technical, consortia, franchise, offshore, museum, diversification (Newman and Couturier, 2002). For example, in Britain, higher education is sometimes delivered in mixed economy colleges which are predominantly further education, but which also deliver degree, subdegree and professional courses (Baron, 2000). In the USA 35 states now have a virtual university (Keegan, 2000). In Europe, the Bologna Declaration's (1999) statement that universities are autonomous institutions at the centre of society appears rather outdated and nostalgic. Fuller (1999) suggests that the idea of contained knowledge, or the university as a microcosm, originated in medieval times, when the physical universe itself was held to be bounded. Higher education today is no longer confinable within a marked terrain. It is exterritorial and it travels and oozes into every crevice of professional and social worlds. To use Bauman's metaphor (2001a), it has become liquified, or as Scott (1998) observes, it has become de-institutionalized. The dematerialization process demands more tangible tracking mechanisms.

New sites of higher education are proliferating. Most of Western Europe tends to be dominated by public universities, with over 95 per cent of students attending them. However, internationally, private higher education is 'one of the most dynamic and fastest-growing segments of postsecondary education at the turn of the 21st century' (Altbach, 1999: 1). Massification in some countries refers to the increase in number of higher education institutions, as well as in the number of students. In the United States of America, there are 400 higher education institutions and over 15 million students. Over half of the HEIs are private. The growth of private higher education is noticeable in countries in transition. For example, Moldova has a population of approximately 4 million. It has 18 state universities and over 36 private universities. In Poland, more than 180 private institutions have captured a third of the student body (Newman and Couturier, 2002). One explanation is that in former Soviet countries, private education is not driven solely by profit, but also by a form of resistance and commitment to de-ideologization. That is, private universities are thought to allow greater autonomy than those regulated by the state. In many Eastern European countries, higher education is accredited by the state and private institutions must pay for this service. For societies in transition, quality assurance, in the form of accreditation, offers some global benchmarks.

Private education is well established in several South-East Asian countries including the Philippines, Thailand, Japan, and South Korea. In this region, over 80 per cent of students attend private institutions. The expansion of private education is linked to massification. In Asia alone, it is estimated that the demand for higher education will grow by 48 million students between 1995 and 2020 (Newman and Couturier, 2002). More recently, there has been a noticeable shift from public to private provision in Latin America and Central and Eastern Europe. In countries and regions where governments are unable to provide sufficient funding for higher education, for example the former Soviet Union, and Sub-Saharan Africa, private education is flourishing. This global explosion is accompanied and facilitated by a conceptual shift that suggests that higher education is a private, rather than a public good (Singh, 2001). It is a product one buys, rather than a process one enters.

The new borderless market has provided new opportunities for the development of private sector distance higher education. Jones University in the USA was the first online university to be accredited by one of the six US regional accrediting agencies (Coaldrake, 2000). The University of Phoenix, a subsidiary of the Apollo Group, now has over 40,000 students in 25 different countries (Manicas, 1998). The University of Maryland University College is an accredited public institution in the USA which offers 24 complete online courses to over 35,000 students (Ryan, 2002). Sadlak (1998) estimates that there are approximately 300 colleges and universities worldwide offering virtual degrees with a total of more than a million students online.

The overt market forces, profit motives and commodification of private sector higher education means that the concept of best value is paramount. Quality assurance claims to be a means of verification of the standards being purchased. There is a constant monitoring of performance in private higher and professional education. For example, at Keller in the US, Center Directors sit in on classes at least once a term. McDonald's has one-way mirrors and the University of Phoenix holds transcripts of all online courses to be reviewed if students complain that they have not received value for money (Coaldrake, 2000).

Corporate training has also grown significantly. Eighty per cent of all corporate training in the USA is now undertaken inhouse (Jarvis, 2000). By 1995, corporate training budgets in the USA totalled 52 billion dollars and there were over 1000 corporate universities (Rowley *et al.*, 1998). Burger King alone has opened 'academies' in 14 US cities (Burbules and Torres, 2000). In the United States, General Motors has its own university in Chicago. In Britain, there is the University for Industry (UfI).

Franchising, as a form of distributed or subcontracted educational delivery, is another test for quality assurance mechanisms. Between April and June 1996 Britain's then named Higher Education Quality Council visited and audited 20 overseas partner institutions in Greece, Hong Kong, Malaysia, Singapore and Spain. The audit teams found what they believed was *prima facie* evidence that the quality of some UK programmes being delivered abroad was not fully assured (Lee, 1999).

While universities are no longer the only sites of knowledge production and consumption, they continue to occupy a pivotal role in credentializing and validating knowledge. As such, they also confer and withhold cultural capital and social status. The economic exploitation of knowledge is leading to more standardized and globalized systems to assure the quality of the higher education product and the credentials of graduates.

Democratizing discourses: the learning society and lifelong learning

Learning is a huge new market. Internationally, the number of students in higher education increased from 51 million in 1980 to approximately 82 million in 1995, representing an increase of 61 per cent. Policies for expanding participation exist in national locations throughout Eastern

Europe, South-East Asia, Northern Europe, the Middle East, Sub-Saharan Africa and Latin America. The World Bank (1994) correlates the participation rate in higher education with economic development. OECD countries currently have an average of approximately 51 per cent participation rate compared with 21 per cent in middle-income countries and 6 per cent in low-income countries (Sadlak, 1998).

The learning society is currently an international policy discourse. Both economic and democratic imperatives are embedded in the ideology. Lifelong learning is not new. Indeed, Yeaxlee wrote on the subject in 1929. There has been some linguistic slippage from continuing education to lifelong learning and the learning society. Ostensibly, there appears to be a critique of class monopolization of knowledge and education. There is an avowed commitment both to social inclusion and citizenship and to the changing skills base of the global economy (Day, 1997). There have also been growing demands for more advanced educational opportunities for larger segments of the population.

The learning society is a consumer market. Consequently, in many societies, change in higher education has taken the form of massive expansion of students numbers from 5 to 20–30 per cent participation in some European countries over the last 30 years, with resulting changes in student demographics (Gellert, 1993; Scott, 1995; Morley, 1997). Growing demand for enhanced access to higher education also reflects the European Union's alleged commitment to democratization and to the principles of lifelong learning (Avis *et al.*, 1996; Dearing, 1997; Duke, 1997). It has been a European policy objective to increase opportunities for under-represented groups in higher education. European Union policy documentation has discursively linked poverty, mass unemployment and social exclusion with lack of opportunities for education and training (EC, 1993, 1995).

The concept of the learning society is influenced by human capital theory, suggesting that national prosperity depends on individual and collective cultural capital. Kenway and Langmead (1998) argue that universities are increasingly expected to contribute to state capacity-building. The emphasis is on wealth creation, rather than wealth distribution. Human capital is understood in terms of the stock of individual skills, competencies and qualifications. Yet it is a controversial ideology. Hughes and Tight (1998: 184) argue that there is little evidence to support the view that the total quantity of training is closely correlated to a country's economic performance, nor is there a necessary connection between stocks of skilled labour and productivity. Within the context of the changing relations between the state and universities, there is now an input/output mindset, with an algorithmic certainty and formulaic authority. This is in stark contrast to the influence of post-modernity which stresses a loss of certainty (Delanty, 2001).

While the momentum to enhance participation in higher education (HEFCE, 2001) is laudable, it has not been informed by the decades of research into equality and social justice in the academy (e.g. Edwards, 1993; Modood, 1993; Farish *et al.*, 1995; Morley, 1999). The Learning Society is based on a simplistic access model in which the wire is lifted to allow a small minority of members of under-represented groups to enter the academy. The onus of change is on those groups, rather than on the academy as an organization. It is a surface reallocation, rather than a transformation (Fraser, 1997). It is a gesture towards recognition, rather than redistribution. For example, in the policy context of increasing participation, there is little consideration given to inflation of certification. Hence, while strenuous and expensive efforts are made to assure quality and standards, questions also need to be asked about whether the same qualifications have different value for different social groups. According to Macrae, Maguire and Ball (1997) the learning society is grafted onto existing, historic oppressions and inequalities. It is a new basis on which social divisions are re-established and relegitimated. Gender, race and social class are often seen as background variables, rather than constructs embedded in learning processes.

Lifelong learning is related to the learning society and it represents a disaggregation of education and age. It is conceptually linked to continuous improvement, and to improving access. Scott (2000: 9) argues that 'Lifelong learning requires the breaking-down, certainly the transcendence, of traditional institutional boundaries . . .'. However, there are often contradictions between the goals of lifelong learning and performance indicators in higher education. In many national locations, course completion rates are seen as measures of effectiveness. But lifelong learning suggests that the educational process is never complete. There is no requirement for closure in a permanently open-ended arrangement.

Lifelong learning and the learning society have had profound structural influences on higher education. For example, new qualifications and new modes of delivery have developed. There have been pressures on universities to restructure courses, to make them part-time, modular, and sometimes delivered in the workplace, or technologically via distance learning programmes. Notions of continuity and the logic of knowledge acquisition have been disrupted or fragmented as new modes and packages are delivered to a widening client base (Trowler, 1998). Customer-driven packaged learning is proliferating. The university is perceived as a knowledge outlet, with students/customers browsing and selecting from marketing documentation. Assessment practices have also been adapted in many cases. Portfolio work and the successful completion of projects, action research studies and the accreditation of work-based learning are becoming increasingly popular.

In Canada, the United States of America and the UK there are more returning adults than undergraduate school-leavers in universities. A greater proportion of university teaching is becoming post-graduate and vocationally oriented (Jarvis, 1999). Many students are now learning and earning simultaneously. There are discursive links between current concerns with continuous professional development that underpin policy initiatives such as the learning society and lifelong learning and the continuous improvement rhetoric embedded in the quality discourse.

Continuous improvement: to travel hopefully, but never to arrive

The public services, initially in the USA, and later in Britain followed Deming's (1986) beliefs, that his total quality approach was equally applicable to manufacturing and to services (Billing and Thomas, 1998). However, higher education adopted management processes from the private sector long after they had been tried and abandoned by corporations (Birnbaum, 2000). The early 1990s saw a proliferation of literature in the USA berating total quality management (TQM) as too expensive, bureaucratic, and unreliable (Brigham, 1993; Harari, 1993; Keller, 1992). Shore and Selwyn (1998: 165) believe that in academia, TQA (teaching quality assessment) has become 'practically homonymous with TQM.' However, the concept of improvement in quality assurance can often seem under-theorized in the context of sophisticated analyses in the academy of measurement techniques. For example, Strathern (1997: 307) writes:

'Improvement' is wonderfully open-ended, for it at once describes efforts and results. And it invites one to make both ever more effective – a process from which the tests themselves are not immune: measuring the improvement leads to improving the measures.

Improvement is linked to commensurable increase. There is a question here about the endpoint in continuous improvement, with an underlying sense of the permanence of struggle, the elusiveness of satisfactory goals, and the ambiguity of measurement procedures.

As I have written elsewhere (Morley and Rassool, 1999), initial thinking about quality assurance, especially the body of knowledge known as Total Quality Management originated in the Japanese car industry. Such policy borrowing or technology transfer has meant that mindsets and dispositions have been imported as well as models for measurement and evaluation. For example, according to Imai (1986) the key to the overall success of Japanese business and industry lies first in the philosophical concept of *kaizen* which, he argues, provides the best means by which all aspects of Japanese production and management can be understood. *Kaizen*, literally translated, means continuous improvement 'involving everyone, including both managers and workers' (Imai, 1986: 3). It is a generic term that penetrates all aspects of Japanese life. Imai (1986: 3) states that '(t)he *kaizen* philosophy assumes that our way of life – be it our working life, our social life, or our home life – deserves to be constantly improved'. The concept of *kaizen* is imbued with a work ethic or work preparedness grounded in self-monitoring.

Continuous improvement has a surface agenda that is credible and desirable in the context of global changes and the risk society. However, continuous improvement also has a subtextual agenda that could be theorized in terms of the Foucauldian concept of govermentability. It is an example of capillary power. The language and ethos of quality assurance often appears to have quasi-religious connotations, implying lack, deficit, rescue and renewal. This is reminiscent of the Christian notion of original sin. It takes a professional lifetime to redeem oneself. Closure is infinitely deferred. There is interest in the utility value or 'just-in-time' rather than 'just-in-case' skills and competencies. Hence the rapid change agenda creates what Barnett (2000) describes as 'supercomplexity'. The sense of tumultuous urgency can create panic and feelings of inadequacy for those struggling to keep on top of changes. The individual is in perpetual motion, never allowed to stand still. Workers have to internalize the demand for flexibility.

An aspect of the modernization of higher and professional education is the attempt to link the work and aspirations of individuals with the goals of the organization. Barnett (2000) believes that knowledge is now less important for the professional than attitude and the disposition to respond to change. There is a complex relationship between the individual and the collective. Professionals are being encouraged to develop individual learning strategies, and increasingly, to practice the art of self-observation. Sennett (1998) argues that higher education is rapidly becoming the ally of a ruthless economic system in which individuals are expected to re- and up-skill with no continuity of identity, security or purpose. Another argument is that higher education helps individuals to survive in changing settings. Whereas the locus of change appears to be the individual, the individual is now also more accountable to the collective via quality procedures and scores. Teaching quality and research productivity have been converted from individual professional responsibility to the collective interests of institutions and departments (Henkel, 1999). Quality assurance, as part of new managerialism, involves the responsibilization of every organizational member. The organization, or unit of analysis, becomes the reflexive project for which all organizational members are responsible. This is reminiscent of the Japanese car industry.

Quality assurance itself is producing the need for more professional development. The quality agenda and the culture of continuous improvement in public services have resulted in the need for professionals to evaluate and represent their practice and organizations within new modes of description. The debate on standards, accountability, customer care and transparency of decision making in the professions is demanding enhanced skills relating to representation, measurement, resource management and evaluation. A culture of evidence-based practice and an economic climate of best value are emerging. Quality assurance and continuous improvement are powerful policy condensates, demanding consensus and orthodoxy. They exemplify the steering-at-a-distance trend in public policy whereby education is more overtly tied in to national economic interests while giving the appearance of site-based and/or individual autonomy (Ball, 1998).

2

How Quality is Assessed

The genesis of the quality assurance movement

Quality assurance is not new. It was originally an integral part of craftspersonship and professionalism. More recently, it has been disaggregated from the professions, formalized and transformed into an object of inquiry (Hart, 1997). In Britain, quality assessment exists 'to ensure that all education for which the Higher Education Funding Council provides funding is of satisfactory quality or better, and to ensure speedy rectification of unsatisfactory quality', the main aim being to 'inform funding and reward excellence' (HEFCE, 1992, 1993). Universities have possessed various forms of internal and external mechanisms for assuring the quality of their work. The external examiners system has traditionally been a form of quality assurance. Silver (1993) researched peer assessment in higher education, and found that it was a fairly haphazard business, with no clear demonstration of common standards. While the external examiners system could have been characterized in terms of Cameron and Ettington's (1988) concept of *adhocracy*, there is little evidence to demonstrate that the development of quality systems was in response to *serious* quality problems in the sector (Trow, 1994).

A more cynical view is that quality assurance was introduced as a regulatory device for the process of production rather than as a check on the quality of the product itself. The education reform of the schools sector in Britain in the 1980s was soon followed by political concerns over the regulation of quality and standards in higher education. Kogan and Hanney (2000) argue that perhaps no area of public policy has been subjected to such radical changes over the last 20 years as higher education. In 1983 the Reynolds Committee was set up to consider academic standards in higher education. It reported in 1986 with formal codes of practice covering external examiners and post-graduate studies (Hodson and Thomas, 1999). Between 1992 and 1994 there were 14 influential reports published about the future of higher education. The content of these reports addresses both immediate requirements for change caused by a mass higher education system (HEFCE, 1993), a changing student population (NIACE, 1993) and longer-term requirements arising out of economic and social imperatives.

In 1991 the government's White Paper *Higher Education: A New Framework* set out the audit procedures for quality assurance and the new government agency, and recommended that new funding councils should be given the responsibility of ensuring the quality of teaching and learning in higher education (DES, 1991). In 1992, the Further and Higher Education Act brought about the redesignation of polytechnics as universities and the abolition of the CNAA and the Higher Education Inspectorate. The Act also led to the establishment of higher education funding councils in England, Scotland and Wales, which were required by statute to monitor the quality of the programmes that they funded and to ensure value for money. Each funding council set up a quality assurance division which, from 1992–93 onwards began, on a subject-by-subject basis, an assessment of funded programmes. Also, in 1992, the Higher Education Quality Council (HEQC) was established. This was a UK-wide body owned and funded by all HE colleges and universities. Its principal tasks were to undertake quality audit of each HE institution over a five-year cycle and to promote quality enhancement.

In 1993, the Conservative Government in Britain published a further White Paper on higher education, *Realising Our Potential* stating that all universities in Britain were to have the quality of their education provision 'assured' thanks to the introduction of rigorous systems of monitoring, inspection and assessment. The White Paper also called for 'a key cultural change' that would 'enforce accountability' to the taxpayer (DES, 1993: 5). In the early 1990s, HEFCE required university departments to submit bids or claims that their teaching standards were excellent, satisfactory or unsatisfactory. They then sent teams of senior academics into universities to assess and grade the departments. Any provision graded as unsatisfactory had twelve months to rectify the problems, or funding would be withdrawn. The audit of subjects was first called teaching quality assessment and later subject review.

In 1997, the National Committee of Inquiry into Higher Education, chaired by Lord Dearing, recommended a number of interventions relating to standards and quality. These have contributed to the terms of reference for the Quality Assurance Agency (QAA) which was set up in 1997 to co-ordinate the review and report of the performance of higher education institutions. The QAA is contractually linked to the government-controlled funding councils rather than universities. Following the publication of the Dearing Report a second agency was also established – the Institute of Teaching and Learning. This aims to provide professional development and accreditation of teachers in higher education.

Governments have achieved greater power and control over universities via a series of accountability polices between the 1980s and 2000s, using funding and status levers as drivers (Vidovich and Slee, 2001). It is interesting to note that these policy developments came at a time when university vice-chancellors, professional associations and staff were warning of a funding crisis in higher education. The Association of University Teachers (1996: 1) warned that the crisis posed 'a serious threat to the economic future of the UK'. The policy solution was to focus attention inwards on the micro-practices of higher education institutions in a more systematic and tabulated form. The belief is that quality can be assured through measurement of performance, productivity and customer satisfaction.

Whereas the Quality Assurance Agency oversees the quality assurance of teaching and learning, as well as developing benchmarks, qualifications frameworks and programme specifications, subject assessors and institutional reviewers are recruited from the academic community. In England, subject review was first introduced in 1993. From April 1995 to December 2001 six aspects were audited: learning resources, curriculum development and organization, teaching, learning and assessment, quality management and enhancement, student progress, and achievement and student support. There was an aspect group meeting for each area in which assessors interrogated staff. Often, staff were required to produce further documentary evidence, at short notice, as a consequence of concerns raised by assessors in aspect group meetings. Each aspect was scored out of four. The highest score for an institution was 24. There were three sources of data: observation of teaching sessions, interviews with students, staff and employers and scrutiny of documentation. The latter was housed in a base room. This contained volumes of information about courses, quality assurance procedures, organizational policies, samples of student work, minutes of meetings, information to students etc. For some, subject review was viewed as a valuable opportunity for organizational development and reflection. While others experienced it as a highly corrosive form of performance and regulation.

A movement from quality control to quality assurance and enhancement is noticeable in the evolution of formal arrangements. Whereas control implies inspection at the end of the production line, assurance involves auditing mechanisms and systems for quality management embedded in every stage of the production process. The aim is to interrogate the regulatory mechanisms through which quality is assured and enhanced. The QAA ostensibly focuses on organizations' own systems of quality assurance and their own aims and objectives. Discrepancies between declared and actual agendas of assessors, as many of my informants have noted, is one of the most significant forms of tension in the process, as I shall explore in Chapter 6.

There are now two major accounting systems: teaching, and learning and research. In Britain, research is assessed through the research assessment exercise (RAE). This is a mechanism for distributing funding. It operates by the bestowal and withdrawal of resources. The assessment of teaching and learning has moved from subject review (known as TQA – teaching quality assessment – until 1995) to institutional audit. Subject review involved the inspection and scoring of 42 disciplinary areas out of a total score of 24. The emphasis in the new system of institutional audit is on the institution, rather than on subject areas. The assessment of both research, and teaching and learning have been highly controversial enterprises in Britain. Pressure from the CVCP/Universities UK, elite organizations and letters to the media coagulated to produce the need for political action in relation to subject review. On 22 March 2001, the Secretary of State for Education announced in parliament that changes were to be made in the way quality is audited. He announced that the number of review visits would be cut by 40 per cent. University departments that had received good scores, that is 21 or over in subject review, were to be exempt from external review in the next round. In August 2001, John Randall, the director of the QAA, resigned in protest, as he was unable to accept that the methodology adopted in the new policy was sufficiently rigorous.

In the transition period from subject review to institutional audit, two consultation documents were published. The first was *Quality Assurance in Education* (QAA, 2001). The second, *Information on quality and standards of teaching and learning: proposals for consultation* (HEFCE, 2002a), was published by a committee chaired by Professor Ron Cooke, to investigate what public information on quality and standards could be made available to the public. More controversy raged in early 2002 as Margaret Hodge, the higher education minister, refused to endorse new proposals for institutional audit, as she disagreed with a 'lighter touch' and felt that new proposals were 'insufficiently rigorous to ensure public accountability' (Baty, 2002). The issue of what constitutes appropriate measures of rigour remains highly contested in the policy domain of quality.

In Britain, quality assurance procedures themselves have been subjected to continuous improvement over the years. Over the past 20 years, higher education has been regulated by at least three forms of external scrutiny. First, in the late 1980s, the Committee of Vice Chancellors and Principals (CVCP) established an Academic Audit Unit. This later became incorporated into the Higher Education Quality Council. Second, the Further and Higher Education Act of 1992 dissolved the Council for National Academic Awards (CNAA) and invested funding councils with statutory responsibility for quality assessment of the educational provision that they funded. A third strand relates to the arrangements for accreditation of programmes of study leading to professional 'licence to practice'. In this case, higher education has continued to operate in partnership with professional bodies such as the Royal College of Nursing, the British Psychological Society, the Royal Institute of Chartered Surveyors etc. Stakeholders are proliferating as higher education is now operating in wider professional and international markets.

Jeux sans frontiers: quality internationally

Quality assessment is an international phenomenon. While the British system is currently the most audited in the world (Cowen, 1996), other countries have not escaped new modes of regulation. There are commonalities across national boundaries. A general model of quality assessment in higher education has emerged in several European countries:

- a national co-ordinating body
- institutional self-evaluation
- external evaluation by academic peers
- published reports

(Brennan and Shah, 2000: 11).

Quality assurance, via the globalization of accountability, is spreading rapidly across national boundaries. It represents a major form of policy borrowing and policy learning. Brennan and Shah (2000) mention how, in 1990, only France, the Netherlands and the UK possessed quality agencies. The European Union has enthusiastically supported the development of quality procedures and now almost all European countries, including Eastern Europe, have followed suit. Brennan and Shah (2000: 28/9) note how the European Union issued a recommendation to its member states in 1997 to 'establish . . . transparent quality assessment and quality assurance systems' (European Commission, 1997). These systems were to incorporate the following three aims:

1. To safeguard the quality of higher education within the specific economic, social and cultural context of their countries while taking due account of the European dimension and of international requirements.
2. To help higher education institutions use quality assurance techniques as steering mechanisms to promote organizational flexibility for permanent improvement in a rapidly changing environment.
3. To underpin European and worldwide co-operation in order to benefit from each other's experience for the accomplishment of the two foregoing tasks.

The Danish Centre for Quality Assurance and Evaluation in Higher Education (Evalueringscenteret, 1999) undertook an official review of quality assurance developments in Europe. The study reports that 11 of the 15 member states had established national evaluation procedures for their higher education systems.

In some countries, for example, the USA, quality assurance takes the form of accreditation. The components of accreditation are self-study and peer review by external colleagues. However, the emphasis is on no-fault change and improvement rather than scores and league tables in the public domain. In several Eastern European countries, accreditation takes the form of external peer review, certification and recognition of the qualifications. It is linked to validation of particular programmes, rather than to scoring institutions.

There appears to be some synchronicity in critical comments about the process and outcomes of quality assessments. Fredericks *et al.* (1994) report how quality management has been an issue in Dutch higher education since the 1980s. The procedures are similar to those employed in Britain, that is universities are visited and have to prepare a self-evaluation in advance. The visiting committee produces a report. However, Fredericks *et al.* (1994) are highly sceptical about the use of the evaluation results in organizational development. They believe that a central variable in whether organizations act upon the reports relates to the status, or 'reputation for power' of the evaluators. Like commentators in the USA, Britain and Australia, they conclude (Fredericks *et al.*, 1994: 196) 'we cannot say that the large amount of resources invested leads immediately to an equally large improvement in the quality of education; measures are not taken in response to every recommendation, nor are the measures taken drastic measures'.

An assistant registrar in my study had experience of the Dutch system for quality assurance and noted how the size of the country made audit consistent and how policy convergence was moving the Dutch model closer to the British one:

> The number of universities – 14, I think, is sufficiently small to mean that they can have the same review team which goes around all the universities and therefore, is in a position to compare them. Mostly the subject they're looking at isn't offered in all the institutions so, you know, they're looking at something like seven and so they keep together as a team and they do all the reviews. . . . And they interestingly have for many years not had a scoring system but they've introduced one recently and I can't remember the exact date. But I think possibly under influence from the British system because they're quite in touch with the QAA process.

Fillitz's (2000) commentary on the transition to an audit culture in Austrian higher education from 1996 outlines some of the major tensions between mass higher education and a required market orientation of teaching and research. Gefou-Madianou (2000: 259) describes how in Greece, academics who had once been 'informed, politically enlightened, action-oriented public servants' came under the bureaucracy of European Union actions to introduce an audit culture.

Frazer's (1997) study of 38 European countries found that while agencies for external evaluation differed significantly in different locations, there were some common challenges. For example, if accountability is over-emphasized, then self-evaluation may be an exercise in self-promotion, and the document produced, an exercise in self-concealment. Another challenge, particularly in small countries with few universities, was to find 'genuinely disinterested' peers (Frazer, 1997: 355). When academic networks are small, it is sometimes difficult for assessors to come 'fresh' to an organization (Cizas, 1997). A vice provost in my study comments:

> They have a real problem in Slovakia because they only have two really good universities and how do you show in such a tiny country that they are really international standard?

The director of academic affairs in a new university observes a similar problem:

> I mean Mauritius has got three institutions, so you know, the notion of peer review is a bit different, they don't really have any. You know the notion of benchmarking within a national sector, which is for example the UK system, is obviously very difficult there. In other countries what they want to do is benchmark against the UK or America.

The synchronicity or policy convergence is no accident (Perellon, 2001). Whether it is classified as globalization or colonization, UK consultants are often involved in the development of quality systems across the globe. Billing and Thomas (2000) outline how current British practice, funded initially by the British Council and then by the World Bank, was applied to establishing a system for quality assessment in universities in Turkey. Lim (2001) outlines how quality assurance is being imported and interpreted in developing countries. He reports that a key issue in developing/lower income countries is that employment conditions in universities are often poor, for example lack of facilities, lack of staff development, poor remuneration, lack of academic freedom. Hence there are different benchmarks for assessing quality such as staff qualifications. What all these studies demonstrate is that quality assurance is totalizing. In time, no university in any national location will be able to escape the gravitational pull of the quality assurance discourse.

Thought lakes and word mountains: measuring research productivity

In Britain, research is currently audited via the research assessment exercise (RAE). The University Grants Committee first established this system in 1985. The first RAE was undertaken in 1986, followed by similar exercises in 1992, 1996 and 2001. The aim is the norm-referenced assessment of research against a standard ranging from international excellence to below national excellence. One of the reviewers who rejected my application for research funding disagreed with me that the RAE is self-evidently a form of quality assurance. S/he argued that it was a 'selective funding mechanism, or an incentive to carry out certain kinds of research' and that the HEFCE website describes the RAE as 'a form of assessment designed to guide the distribution of funding' (private correspondence, 8 October 2001). However, I argue that the scoring implies kitemarking that operates as a signifier of excellence to stakeholders.

The system relies on peer review. A committee or panel of researchers from the disciplinary field evaluates the intellectual quality of a piece of research. The assessment process employed is a largely subjective judgement of worth (Whittington, 1997). Assessors read the work submitted and grade it on its quality. A common complaint is that the appointment of assessors and decisions about the composition of the panels are not transparent or democratic (Lee and Harley, 1998). Furthermore, the emphasis on disciplinary classifications can place interdisciplinary writers at a disadvantage. The concept of excellence is also seen as unstable, or a 'floating signifier' (Lawson, 1998). Another aspect of the RAE is the quantification of the number and proportion of 'research active' staff. The results determine the allocation of funding to individual institutions. Hence, there is considerable managerial pressure exerted to make staff more research active as this has tangible financial rewards. The individual writer/researcher has been reconceptualized as an economic agent. Scholarship has been reduced to income generation.

The RAE is both a mechanism for the allocation of funding and a system of kitemarking. It functions to rationalize the stratification of research resources and the stratification of universities (Henkel, 1999). It also aims to maximize and reward research output. Talib and Steel (2000: 68) argue that the Research Assessment Exercise is a 'budgeting exercise tool to measure past performance benchmarked against other "units" upon which future budgets are based'. The method of budget allocation is a compromise between autonomy and public accountability. The stakes are high! In 1992 the highest rated department received 4.0 times the amount of funds awarded to the lowest funded department for the same volume of research activity, while in 1996 they received 4.05 times more (Talib and Steele, 2000).

The funds allocated to higher education institutions for research by the Funding Councils are almost entirely determined by the RAE gradings of departments. The budget allocation process is a zero sum game. In 1996, 192 institutions submitted 2896 individual assessments to the 69 subject area panels (Baimbridge, 1998). In 2001, 2598 submissions were received from 173 HEIs, listing the work of 50,000 researchers (HEFCE, 2002b). Fifty-five per cent of researchers are currently in 5 or 5* rated departments, compared to 31 per cent in 1996 and 23 per cent in 1992. Formula funding models serve policy objectives. Furthermore, policy objectives are affecting the construction of the labour force and employment regimes. The McNay (1997) Report on the 1996 RAE showed that institutions are focusing on whom they should recruit for research, and how they should reward and retain existing staff. His staff survey results had 12 per cent of the recent appointees, i.e. those less than one year in post, say that the RAE was the most dominant factor in their appointment.

At the time of writing this book, a dispute over the allocation of funding as a result of the 2001 RAE was raging. The designation of more 5 and 5* rated departments meant that funding had to be stretched further. A lecturer in sociology explains how this reinforces inequalities:

> And I mean some of it, I think, is symbolic. Well an interesting issue is that, you know the current discussion at HEFCE, about what's going to happen with RAE money for example, and you know the goal posts have been changed as it were. You know it looked like universities that

had done much better than they'd done previously would be rewarded. Whereas now it increasingly looks like in order to safeguard the more prestigious and elite universities, who are doing well anyway, the other universities that have come from nowhere as it were are going to, yet again, be disadvantaged. . . .

The RAE has considerable symbolic power (Henkel, 1999). Priorities have provided new descriptions and signifiers. For example, academics are described as 'research active' or 'research inactive' in line with the language of the accounting system for research productivity. Some staff are not entered in the RAE as their research contributions, if any, are not considered by their colleagues to be of the required standard. If too many staff are recorded as research inactive, this not only influences the financial allocation, but also calls into question the existence of a research culture in the organization as a whole.

The RAE, as a funding mechanism, influences employment regimes and material conditions. It also surfaces and creates interpersonal tensions, competitions and hierarchies, and reinforces individualistic, rather than collaborative projects as a lecturer in English literature indicates:

This particular person who came in for trouble, he had his five windows but some of the department felt that they weren't of sufficient quality and so it wasn't even a sort of simple, 'Well, we like you but you've only got three of the four'. It was, 'You've got four and they're no good'. And so it became a very poisonous episode indeed . . . what we need to do is collaborative research, 'get together with your colleagues and do something together'. But then in another way we're told, 'Okay, you're all individuals in a sort of Darwinian nightmare, go and fight it out with each other for anything that there is going really. Up to and including your jobs.'

Henkel (1999: 106) also notes how the RAE has been 'a vehicle of professional and personal humiliation'. It has also been a vehicle of aggrandisement, with those fortunate enough to carve out time and space for research disproportionately rewarded in terms of career development. The RAE has reinforced new and more formal demarcations between teachers and researchers. It has created new roles and relationships. There is a danger that the research 'inactives', individually and collectively acquire the status of pariahs in higher education. Hence a problematic task ensues of 'converting' existing staff into active researchers (Baimbridge, 1998; Harley and Lowe, 1998). This transition can be viewed as a manifestation of the continuous improvement discourse. Talib and Steel (2000: 84) argue that the greatest value will be created by team players who can act as mentors, that is those who can add value to others (the inactives). However, in order to become research active in the first place, academics may have had to focus on their individual, rather than collective interests. As one informant in McNay's (1998: 20) study observes:

The 'stars' were focused on their own work and on personal external reputation; they tended to give little support to developing others.

The 'stars' also have their value enhanced by the sizeable transfer market that has developed. Cash rich universities are able to buy in the 'big names' to increase their scores in the RAE (Dominelli and Hoogvelt, 1996). Hence a new form of circulating elites has emerged. A reader in social policy felt that the transfer market was operating against new blood in the academy and reinforcing existing hierarchies:

> . . . because we've got these ratings now we only recruit people who are, already have international reputations, publishing records. . . . The reality is, when you're faced with people who come with a long list, and they tend to be the older people obviously, then they're the ones who are getting the jobs. . . . So I think it's stifling potential, where is the new talent going to come from if you have to come in with a string of publications?

This view was contradicted by a (young) lecturer in English literature who comments that the RAE has shaped her career:

> I'm 31, I was appointed to my first full-time job when I was 26 and . . . they were appointing on the basis of people who might have stuff for the RAE for the future. . . . So, I mean I think without the RAE my career would have had a completely different shape.

Research productivity has become a performance indicator for all higher education institutions regardless of their excellence in other fields. For some, this is seen as a positive development. A professor in a new university notes:

> . . . for people working in what's still called, after ten years, a new university, the push towards publication came particularly with the gaining of university status. In a way the RAE has reinforced that so I would say it's sort of added to dynamism that was already there. Sort of enhanced or reinforced an existing momentum.

Multiskilling is a feature of contemporary professional life. Some informants from new universities commented on the split focusing involved in the two accounting systems and how the RAE was a distraction from teaching and learning. A director of quality and learning support in a university college notes:

> . . . certainly the RAE has tended to distract staff, I think, away from learning and teaching. Those that are research active want to be more research active, and that's got a lot to do with the funding associated with research activities, that comes out of RAE. . . . And so a lot of energies get devoted on that. And that sometimes students miss out . . . because people are so busy doing their research and publishing their books and so on.

The research assessment exercise has produced a coercive creativity. Like Scherezade in the *Arabian Nights,* life in the academy is prolonged with the production of words that please external assessors, confusing whether academics write and research from anxiety, rather than intellectual curiosity (Morley, 1995). Formal relays of power such as the appraisal system reinforce research productivity. A professor in a new university describes how:

> We have a formal appraisal system and it enables quite a clear statement of objectives and targets in an appraisal. Typically I can say to somebody . . . 'Between now and this time next year, I want you to produce so many articles in refereed journals' – two, three, four, whatever we're talking about articles in refereed journals. And if we can agree that and agree some time allowance to let the person do that then, you know, that benefits all round really. He or she is doing what they want to do and the university is benefiting from a better RAE in the long run.

A head of department in a new university believes that measuring research output is antithetical to scholarship:

> The idea that you've got to keep producing this stuff on a constant drip feed rather than undertake a life's work and transform a discipline by some huge paradigmatic shift. I mean I just think that that trivializes and travesties the whole process of research. . . . So the regulation of research, I think, is inimical to knowledge, real knowledge production . . . it's the output of clerks rather than the output of thinking academics and scholars.

A lecturer in Spanish also comments on how the RAE encourages short-termism in research:

> I do find aspects of the research assessment exercise to be flawed as it is not conducive in encouraging those very long-term projects that simply can't be turned around in a very short time . . . I think it has to a certain extent conditioned some of the research projects that I take up because you take a project that can be turned around quickly and projects that involve years and years and years of scholarship are set aside.

My informants had far less to say about the RAE than subject review. One explanation was that the former is assessment at a distance, whereas the latter is experienced as more invasive. A reader in social policy observes:

> I suppose in a way the research assessment exercise feels a bit distant. It's not immediately people coming in and being present. Although there is a big build up to it, and there is pressure of how many articles have I got, and counting them, and that sort of idea, quite early on.

A director of quality in an old Scottish university contradicted this view noting how the RAE took management priority over the assessment of teaching and learning:

It [the RAE] does of course dominate life. It's given far higher, far greater visibility within the university and affects people far more and the university has put much more resources into preparing for it than it does for institutional review because, of course, so much money hangs on it.

A philosophy lecturer felt that the scoring of research output disguised resource inputs and the power relations that facilitate and impede research productivity:

... a high score for the RAE masks and disguises a whole number of factors in the working conditions and working environment. . . . Such as, well the sort of department that can afford teaching assistants can cut down the teaching hours, can release the academic to do further research. And there are spirals and spirals here. So that if you cut funding of departments that are scoring three, or three b, now, then all they can do is to increase their teaching to make up the funding, which means that they can't do any research.

A director of quality in a university college also comments on the inequalities embedded in the process:

We haven't got five star departments here, you know, never will have. I mean we just haven't got the funding to be able to do that. So it's always quite a struggle to get a research profile when you're at the lower end of the research profile naturally. It's because you can't get the funding.

The RAE, according to these two informants is reinforcing the binary line. With academic capitalism money makes money and those organizations with the resources to invest in research development receive more research funding. Research productivity became a priority for many British universities by the early 1990s and teaching was downgraded as the refuge for research inactives. A senior lecturer comments on the research cultures in old universities:

In the past teaching was seen as, somewhat of an inconvenience . . . and the priority of people who took their work seriously was always research. People who didn't do research, but were excellent teachers were seen as sort of somehow stupid or incompetent.

However, research-poor organizations have been offered the consolation of a second accounting system to scrutinize the quality of teaching and learning. New opportunities now exist to demonstrate newly valued competencies.

Reinventing teaching and learning

Traditionally, there was a belief that disciplinary knowledge automatically led to pedagogical excellence. The academics in Henkel's (2000) study were more closely allied with their disciplines than with pedagogical processes in their organizations. Strenuous efforts started to be made to 'improve' the overall quality of teaching in learning throughout the higher education sector in the 1990s (Gibbs *et al.* 2000; Rowland *et al.*, 1998; Samuelowicz, 2001). In anticipation of the findings of the Dearing Report (Dearing, 1997), the HEFCE commissioned a draft of 'A Teaching and Learning Strategy for Higher Education' (Gibbs, 1997). A proposal in this strategy was the use of funding, not to reward, but to encourage institutions to develop and implement comprehensive learning and teaching strategies. Incentive funding was also part of higher education policy in the USA and in Australia.

The concept of learning, rather than education, has become more popular in recent years. There is a putative certainty that 'effective' learning automatically follows 'excellent' teaching. There are two broad strands of argument. One is that there has been a conceptual shift from the sociology of education to a preoccupation with the cognitive structures of how people learn. Formulae, theories and models of effective learning have replaced consideration of the socioeconomic context. Indeed any social contextualization is discursively constructed as part of the 'culture of excuses'. Another is that higher education has never seriously concerned itself with pedagogical theory and is now appropriating the language and concepts of liberatory pedagogies, without the political and transformatory underpinnings.

Whereas teachers in the compulsory sector have been thought to require professional training in many national locations, this has not been the case with teachers in higher education. In McInnis's (2000) Australian study just over one third (34 per cent) of academics surveyed had received training in teaching methods at the start of their careers. Even today, the majority (56 per cent) do not receive any form of professional training for teaching. The issue of the *ad hoc* professionalization of university teachers has been a major policy driver in the introduction of new measures. In her Australian study, Adams (2000: 68) notes how:

> The academics of most Australian universities have usually learned their craft on the job, have modelled their practices on those observed when a student, or have tried to teach differently from how they were taught (a homeopathic model). None has admitted to changing their practice as a consequence of university policy.

A new culture is emerging and the professional aspects of higher education teaching are surfacing. Gudeman (1998) argues that previously uncounted aspects of teaching are now converted into identifiable units of currency. However, this currency is being perceived as an over-simplification of pedagogical complexities. A head of department believes that Taylorizing teaching detracts from the intellectual excitement:

> When you talk to students about their experience you have to say it's the, I hesitate to call them academic waccos, but it's the people that have really off the wall enthusiasm, that are the most intellectually

infectious if you like.... And the idea that all of that is somehow submerged under some endless specification of the curriculum. You know you've got to have, you've got to write 10 outcomes, then you've got to show how all those are delivered across the curriculum, you've got to be able to demonstrate an internal coherence, and so on, and so on. Yes, but what's really important is the sense of intellectual excitement, it's catching that intellectual excitement, and willingness to think the unthinkable, and you know, question ideas. And you could get a perfect QAA score, and not do any of it.

The atomization of teaching consists of an attempt to make the tacit more knowable and calculable. It also enables teaching to move into the public domain, as a senior lecturer in economics notes:

In the past teaching in universities . . . was seen as the responsibility of the individual and if they did an appalling job, it wasn't really seen, only if it was a really appalling job, was it seen as the responsibility of the department to intervene. The teaching is now seen very much more as the responsibility of the department to ensure not only it is good, but in some sense according to some sort of definition, is actually improving.

The audit of teaching quality suggests an element of recognition for an undervalued set of responsibilities and competencies. Yet the extent of the recognition is open to debate – particularly in terms of promotion. A study by Moses (1986) supported the view that job dissatisfaction among academics included the misrecognition of teaching in promotion decisions. Halsey and Trow's study (1971) also found that while teaching offered a considerable degree of satisfaction, academics who were primarily oriented towards teaching rated their promotion chances lower than those primarily oriented towards research. The promotion system in the academy has traditionally rewarded research and publication. Research productivity is the main criterion for academic career success. Research by Gibbs (1995) found that where 96 per cent of all UK universities included excellence in teaching as a criterion promotion but it was apparently ignored when only 11 per cent of promotions were on the grounds of teaching excellence and in 39 per cent of institutions no-one had ever been promoted on their teaching contribution. There have been moves to validate teaching via promotion. This has created some resentment in both directions, as a senior lecturer in an old university relates:

. . . our school is very research based, that's why there's a certain hostility to teaching and learning, pedagogy, etc. People want to just do and not talk about it, and not write about it. And there's also a certain hostility to other bits of the university where they say those people don't research, why should they get a senior lectureship. . . . And they also, those bits of the university, bring in far bigger student numbers than we do, so you know they're really valuable too.

The two accounting systems appear to jostle for ascendancy. Teaching suffers from severe misrecognition even though effort is invested in 'improving' teaching quality and pretending that excellence in teaching counts as a performance indicator for career success. This can produce a moral dilemma. Academics who focus on their research are likely to be successful in career terms, whereas those who focus on teaching gain some moral high ground, but significantly lose out on career development. Hence the aspect of progress has been introduced into teaching with the coming of more structured professional development and accreditation for university teachers.

The professionalization of university teachers

The Institute of Learning and Teaching (ILT) was established in Britain as a result of recommendations made by the Dearing Committee (Dearing, 1997). It has been highly controversial, perceived as both the de- or re-professionalization of academics. The Association of University Teachers (AUT), a trade union, advised their members to boycott it. For them, it represents a vote of no confidence in academic pedagogical ability. For others, the emphasis on developing teaching and learning skills is seen as a long overdue innovation (Nicholls, 2002). For teachers in the state school system, professional credentialization is an essential licence to practice. However, there has been no such requirement in the academy. The reconstruction of students as consumers suggests that they have entitlement to quality pedagogy. Quality teaching is no longer perceived as a gift, but as a right. In my study, informants held a range of views about the move to 'professionalize' and accredit university teachers. For some, it was a healthy challenge to the elitism in the sector. For others, it was seen as more regulation and interference. Some applauded the theory, but were critical of current practices. A registrar in an old university relates it to new market relations:

> It hasn't had an enormous impact here. My personal view is that I think it's certainly right that there needs to be an element of professionalization because one cannot assume that someone who comes out of university with a first class honours degree and then a PhD is thereby qualified to be a good teacher of university students. You do need some training . . . it's going to become probably more and more important because students will simply not accept poor quality teaching in the way that perhaps they have in the past. . . . And since students are now, some of them, and their parents, paying for the higher education they get, they're entitled to get a quality service I think.

There is an implication that the ILT will weed out the bad and plant the good. Its existence signifies the possibility of poor teaching. An academic development officer in an old university comments on consumer empowerment and information:

I think for too long the British students have had to sort of endure, you know, second rate teaching. I don't think that's global, but you know too much of it has gone on or, you know, it's something, you know that staff have done because they've had to, and I don't know what percentage I'm talking about here. I'm not talking about the majority, but you know too much of it has gone on, and I think it's unacceptable. So I think if the ILT can, can raise teaching, the status of teaching and learning with respect to research, then I think that can only be a good thing from the student point of view.

The ILT is also positioned as a performance indicator in the context of market competition. A professor in an old university mentioned how membership of the ILT was used to strengthen the potential of the organization's position in league tables:

> We have a policy here that everyone should be a member of the ILT, because, I mean to be frank the reason for that we suspected that it would be brought in to a league table at some stage. . . . And students will think 'Ah but they're not very high in the league tables of ILT membership, therefore they're not interested in learning and teaching'.

Membership is also seen to enhance promotion prospects, as it provides benchmarks for what is considered good practice, as an academic registrar in a new university notes:

> I personally am very positive about ILT and ILT membership and certainly a lot of our staff who are teacher trainers have done very well out of it. We have a promotion to PL on excellence of teaching and we do it on the basis of a portfolio and because it's very close to what they do for ILT, we've had a lot, a significantly higher number of our teacher trainer staff who've got that PL promotion, which I think is positive.

A lecturer in Spanish comments on the ritualistic aspects of accreditation of professional practice:

> I've taught continuing professional development to teachers like myself and I have reservations about, you know, a required clocking on of a certain number of hours and credits or whatever. They don't always necessarily map onto the actual development of that person to do the job better. Quite often they are clocking up numerical credits or whatever.

A head of department in a new university describes how membership of the ILT is another performative ritual to reassure auditors and consumers that some type of reflective practice is in operation.

> I'm cynical about it. I don't think the ILT has got much more than a name behind it. I mean I know they hold workshops but I can't imagine any of my colleagues going. It was a bit of window dressing basically . . . for the SPR. I shouldn't be so negative and cynical should

I? We were doing it for window dressing at one end . . . and I tell you how easy it is to do, is you photocopy 20 application forms and you sit people in a room and you say 'We've got one hour, write something'. And then you swap over, everybody reads each other's, sort of thing, and away they go off in the post . . . and then you get your membership, right.

This functional engagement is reminiscent of Clegg's (1999) observation about 'counterfeit reflection'. That is when practitioners have to feign concern, care and rigour within prescribed parameters. However, a director of learning and teaching in a new university cites reflection as a selling point for the ILT:

I found the procedure for applying membership quite useful in some respects, although I thought it was rather onerous at the time, it was the first time, I think, in 15 years that I'd actually been forced to reflect on my teaching practice, I found that useful.

A professor in an old university also supports the idea of bringing university teaching more in line with requirements for state schoolteachers:

I think the universities went far too long without having any professional teaching qualifications. So yes, as I say, I agree with it.

Initiatives to professionalize university teaching often rely on different codes from those traditionally associated with academic endeavour. For example, there is considerable attention paid to 'good practice' – a concept that is embedded in consensus, certainty and orthodoxy in pedagogical practices. The over-simplification of the modernist technicization of teaching and learning can bore and irritate academics. The director of quality in an old university discusses the conceptual gulf that exists between the policy makers and members of the profession. He also comments on the low intellectual level of materials produced by the ILT:

Well, no, we have a statement . . . that the university supports in general the ILT but cannot be persuaded it's to the advantage of any particular member of the university to join it. Which I think is true; you pay a lot of money, you get virtually nothing for it . . . they give you access to these journals which are, on the whole, articles and which are, on the whole, not very good and not very interesting journals that most people aren't going to read.

A senior lecturer in economics dismisses the generality and lack of disciplinary focus of the ILT:

No one in our department has joined the ILT. Most people in the economics professions see it as a waste of time. We can't see how some generic body could be useful for a subject teacher. They can see the use of economics teaching and a teaching support network. They can't see how some independent generic institute can be of much use.

In these accounts, the ILT appears to be failing in intellectual, pragmatic and market terms. It is not offering value for money. Indeed, it is questionable if it is offering anything to its members other than a type of kitemarking. A professor in a new university also commented on the poor value for money and the low level of intellectual and professional debate:

> I don't think that many people in the sector would say they got much out of their 70 quid.... At the moment it's simply just a source of information and gives you examples and details, or whatever, somebody's most recent paper on lecturing to large groups in small rooms, or something. Or is it the other way round? But, frankly, I don't think it's very helpful.

A philosophy lecturer argues that the ILT is regulation posing as professional development. She thinks that the introduction of such initiatives is laden with value-judgements about academic professionalism:

> I think it [the ILT] confuses assessment, staff development, and training, and it was a very cheap way of answering questions that only a few people were asking.... The ILT is the perfect solution to audit, or assessment of individual lecturing performance. The actual process that you go through, the actual portfolio acquisition, is really fairly vacuous but still couched in this new educational-agenda speak. But it does assume that lecturers need to be, need to have their performance assessed, and monitored, either by their peers or by somebody external. And I think it's a huge shift in terms of what an academic is supposed to do, and this sort of, the nomenclature, calling this professionalism, is to assume that we weren't professionals before we went through the process, and that we're demonstrating our professionalism or acquiring our professionalism.

A pro-vice chancellor in an old university also sees the ILT as an affront to university teachers' professionalism. She argues that it overlooks all the staff development provisions already in operation in the academy.

> I think we are professional, I don't think the ILT has made any difference what so ever.... We've always had some kind of introduction to teachers, to teaching.

The head of academic affairs in an old university believes that there has been a type of ontology-as-epistemology approach to professional practice in the academy – 'I am or was, therefore I know how' way of teaching and supervising. She also points out how new student constituencies, in a mass system, cannot be relied on to be self-directing and highly motivated. They need to be *taught*:

> I think a lot of the reasons why we need quality assurance and these kinds of things, is that the system is changing. It's much, much bigger, and we can't make the same assumptions about our students and the

world that we work in. So in the past a lot of things were assumed. I mean if you were actually to ask perhaps a member of academic staff how they were prepared to do a certain job, the answer would be 'Well I was a research student myself' and so on . . . and then they were more or less chucked in. But they were chucked in to a group of cultured sort of 18 year olds, with lots of A-levels and so on, and that worked, and that was the function, and also the groups weren't too big

A senior lecturer in an old university comments on the professional confusion that is caused by universities promoting membership of the ILT, while a major trade union condemns it:

I'm a bit confused . . . our university is pressing us to join ILT but the AUT is telling us not to . . . I see the level of professionalism in schools, as opposed to what I think of the lack of it sometimes in universities.

Support for the ILT is often more apparent outside the elite universities. It appears promotion of teaching and learning quality is validating some new universities. A director of quality in a university college observes:

Oh I'm in favour of it . . . I'm a member of it myself . . . and I think they're getting their act together now. It was a bit iffy in the early stages, but they've got a reasonable act together now, a decent website, and they're getting moving and they're getting quite a lot of members so it's looking quite positive really. And given that they're about learning and teaching, and that's part of my brief then I'm all in favour of it.

The head of a quality assurance unit in a new university supports the idea of professional development, but expresses concerns about the new cadre of professionals who are being recruited as specialists in teaching and learning:

I am in favour of that. What I'm not so much in favour of . . . is this kind of bringing in people as principal lecturers in learning and teaching, and people who are sort of generic academics whatever . . . I think that's a bit of a resource that we possibly can't really afford, and I'm not sure that they actually do the things that they might wish to do, I just don't know.

The creation of lecturers in teaching and learning rather than in subject disciplines seems to support Ozga's (1998) idea that now it is about knowing how, rather than knowing that. Even academics who make a living out of 'knowing how' can get caught out in quality audits. A principal lecturer in a new university relates an ironic tale of how a wing that specializes in teaching and learning and accredits ILT members only received 21 out of 24 in a subject review.

We have a commercial wing that goes out and does a lot of ILT training, and they were . . . inspected along side us. They ended up with a 21 . . . they really should have got a 24.

This incident could expose some of the many flaws embedded in subject review. However, it also suggests that excellence in teaching and learning cannot always be easily predictable, knowable and transferable.

Scores and league tables: the comfort of numbers

There has been an elision of quality with truth, even by members of the academy who are sensitized to the power relations embedded in positivism. In the chaos of marketization, quality scores provide a point of identification. Complex information about quality is scored and organized into at-a-glance league tables that are widely published in the popular press (Berry, 1999). Categoric ratings are converted into numerical variables. Subject review scored out of 24, but the institutional audit that replaces this uses linguistic classifications of commendable, approved and failing. Reviewers will state whether they have confidence, limited confidence or no confidence in standards. Reports list action points that are essential, advisable or desirable.

For the RAE, research is defined as 'original investigation undertaken in order to gain knowledge and understanding' (QAA, 2001). Research assessments are made by panel members selected for their record as practising researchers in their subject. The panels rate each department's research on a seven-point scale: 5* at the top, then 5, 4, 3a, 3b, 2 and 1. The QAA (2001) argues that the scores inform funding decisions of higher education councils and industry, commerce, charities and other organizations that sponsor research. Segal Quince Wicksteed's (1999) report claims that the RAE now has a high profile outside as well as within the sector. They believe that this partly reflects the length of time it has been in existence and also the fact that it determines funding. They also argue that it reflects the fact that the grades for all subjects and all institutions are published at one time, giving greater impact in the non-specialist press. Subject review scores were all published at different times.

The stratification of institutions has become more visible and more precisely differentiated, and the consequences more tangible (Henkel, 1999). Tomlin (1998: 204) argues that 'league tables hold a morbid fascination'. Scores and league tables travel the world and can sometimes inform decision making and choice of organizations and courses. They contribute to reputation and international status. The literature abounds with sporting metaphors. Tight (2000) compares higher education with football and Tomlin (1998) compares it with rugby.

Scores are meaningless unless they come from a trusted source. A senior lecturer in education refused to disclose the score that her department had achieved in a subject review, as she felt that disclosure validated a fraudulent process:

I sort of don't really want to tell you our number . . . I met a colleague from another university who said 'Oh what did you get?' And I said 'Well I don't think I want to play their game by telling you the number, because we got through, we survived, and I feel very sorry for anybody who doesn't, because it's such a hit and miss affair. It tells you nothing about yourself, it tells you nothing about other institutions, it tells you how well you jumped through their hoops, that's all. And if we're going to now, glorify that, by passing numbers on to one another, then we are caught up in their discourses. We have been sucked in to it. We have accommodated their discursive terms, and so much so that we've normalized it, and we're reproducing it by saying to one another 'I got, we got', and I'm not going to play that game!

A lecturer in Spanish feels that league tables are misleading because the methodology of audit is flawed:

The use of the TQA scores was fairly misleading because of the nature of the exercise, the fact that departments around the country are not visited by the same people, and no matter how many guidelines you have for these assessments, people assessed in different ways and also people were being assessed against their own criteria, rather than departments who gave themselves criteria that were a little too hard to follow did badly. Departments that didn't have high criteria could have done relatively well.

A philosophy lecturer comments on how quality assessment involved a type of test sophistication and scores were getting higher as organizations learned to decode requirements. In her view, the score was also meaningless:

I suppose if we'd got 22 I wouldn't have been saying that. But because we did get 24 out of 24 it just made it feel completely apparent that it was nonsense. . . . Nonsense because even though we'd got the full marks we had, we'd created an endless amount of paper, and endless amounts of documentation. We'd imposed some fairly absurd rigorous regimes on ourselves and on the students. . . . I think what has tended to happen with the SPR is that people began to, departments began to learn, universities began to learn what sort of questions, how to approach it to get good marks, which meant that we've started now seeing that most scores are very high, and that's not a matter of lax auditing, it's a matter of people knowing what's in the auditing process.

High scores, according to an assistant registrar, can induce complacency:

I actually feel that attaching numbers to this is extremely negative. I think they only look at the numbers. It means that if they get a 24 they think they're perfect!

A frequent observation related to the way in which performance indicators construct organizational life to such an extent that they are no longer accurate measures. Scores for subject review got higher over a five-year period. In 1995–96 the average aggregate score was 20.05. In 1996–98 the average aggregate score was 20.45 and by 1998–2000 the average aggregate score had increased to 21.68. The head of an academic standards and support unit notes how preparation paid off in her old university:

> I mean the league tables, nationally, have had an effect on us too, we've wanted to do well in terms of subject review. And we didn't do well at first, we did quite badly, we were in the fourth division really . . . I don't think we prepared for the actual visits that carefully. I mean at one time all you had to do was write a report and you were just graded satisfactory or whatever . . . but because it's become increasingly important there has been more effort put in to it.

An assistant registrar comments on how performance indicators are inflating to accommodate more demands:

> I think there has been a kind of divergent movement, where on the one hand laws of diminishing returns have applied. And you can see that very clearly in the subject review scores . . . getting higher to the point where they're not particularly meaningful anymore . . . people have worked out what's needed. OK a lot of what's needed is good practice, but on the other hand, what's also happening, is by the nature of audit there is an accretion of functions. The QAA keeps on adding more and more things.

Only those recipients of high scores were socially sanctioned to speak out against the scoring process. Protest from low scorers would be perceived as sour grapes. Whitehead (1997: 10) observes that 'any power that men and women may exert is only made possible through the taking up of, and being in, dominant discourses'. It is as if individuals have to experience and perform well in quality assessments before they are allowed to comment on them. By then, the damage, loss and waste have already happened.

Criticisms of the league table approach sometimes focused on the validity of the methodology as well as the way in which they reinforce hierarchies and divisions in higher education, as a registrar discusses:

> It's one of those things where everybody finds fault with them . . . although we tend to appear virtually where we would want to appear in the top ten, top five, top three, depending upon which league table you look at. But the bad things about them . . . is that someone who doesn't know higher education very well, might treat this in the same way as you treat a football league table and think that everybody's playing on a level playing field . . . the most important thing in the higher education sector is that there is a recognition of the diversity of mission and the diversity of function.

These comments stress the diversity of the system and the problem of reading socially constructed statistics without insider knowledge. The diversity can also relate to national systems. Subject review was not numerically scored in Scotland, as an informant from a Scottish university indicates:

> It is universally felt in Scotland that we have suffered badly from the league tables because of the difficulty of translating the results of the TQA in Scotland into English terms. And I would have thought the absolutely undeniable grade inflation there's been in England in the last few years . . . for example, no institution in *The Times*' list of the top 25 teaching – no *Scottish* institutions in *The Times*' top 25 teaching institutions, which sort of seems to us counter-intuitive. Several universities in Scotland . . . have scored nought for the quality of their teaching, which is ridiculous, it's a translation problem between one thing and another. I'm not saying the teaching is wonderful, but it's not – to give them nought is just ridiculous. That's the kind of thing that has caused us a lot of concerns.

A sociology lecturer comments on the limitations of quantitative indictors to signify qualitative processes, and how outputs disguise variation in inputs:

> Well, again, I suppose I think that they accentuate the view about all universities are equal and some are more equal than others. . . . You don't get a qualitative picture of what has actually made up the score of them, and there are often you know, issues of resources in terms of people power, as well as resources in terms of kind of physical resources, are somehow kind of lost in the kind of the translation of the league tables, the numbers.

Similar views were also expressed by a director of academic affairs in a new university:

> . . . mostly misleading, most league tables that sum up everything are simply indications of research income, because actually the one thing that makes the difference on most of the league tables is research income. That's the thing that differentiates institutions most.

A deputy vice chancellor draws attention to the dangers of manipulation:

> . . . the system can be manipulated by inconsistencies of term, by occasionally people conscious of what to produce for a league table, and so hiding information which should be in the public domain . . . league tables can be devastating, you know, in the sense that it's what students can easily look at in a newspaper report. And you can suddenly find yourself dropping, you know many, many places, because some of the information which you think is important in a league table hasn't been included.

The manipulation can relate to resources invested in the accounting system as a professor in a new university comments:

Oh we, of course, have brought in people to work in the institution specifically to get better points on QAA . . . and so have many, many institutions by the way. And so these people who are, many of them are very able colleagues, are not involved in teaching or researching or doing anything other than presenting what we do in a way that will score higher when reviewed by the Quality Assurance Agency.

The issues of distortion and disproportionality are noted by an assistant registrar in an old (small) university:

In terms of league tables, which are across subjects, so they measure a university's average performance, this is extremely distorted in relation to small institutions. Because we've noticed that when one of our small departments dropped a point on a subject review, it changes the average to such an extent that we could move about 12 places in the league table. But that might be somebody that doesn't like two pieces of student work, you know. I mean you can get extremely distorted results in a small university.

The head of a quality assurance unit in a new university discusses lack of intertextuality between government priorities. She felt that this is a contributing factor to distortion in league tables:

They don't take into account institutional diversity, and mission. So some of my task has got a huge widening participation agenda . . . we just get hammered by doing what the government wants us to do . . . I think everybody is fed up with it.

An academic registrar in a new university observed how keeping standards high meant lowering students' grades. This then lowered their position in the league tables. The example that she gives suggested that the quantitative signifiers of excellence were socially constructed, and that it was in an organization's interests to inflate students' marks:

We have found it incredibly hard to get academic staff to take seriously the notion that if they go too far down the road of standards then they depress students' gradings unnaturally. . . . We have done a lot of study of league tables, comparing us with our peers in terms of 'A' level entry and then exit award. And we're depressing their marks massively

A controversial debate is whether league tables inform decision making by providing more information to stakeholders. A further point is the extent to which scores informed funding councils. An assistant registrar notes:

I said earlier that I don't think the scores under such review were particularly meaningful. They were not taken as meaningful by the funding council. They did not inform funding. The gaps between them were not moderated, except by the presence of the review chair, who would defer to academics on many issues of academic judgement. So to that extent the existing type of score is pretty unreliable. . . . We're not standing outside the whole project and looking for external comparatives. I believe strongly that we should be asking ourselves what kind of information demands are made on hospitals or schools. What kinds of systems are used in America, or Japan? . . . students have got an immense amount of information already, I think we are buying in to the kind of thing that says we need more information, we need more information without actually standing back to look at what information we've got already.

Floud (2001) argues that reporting on everything gives lots of out-of-date information. This raises questions about disposable and durable forms of knowledge about quality. League tables and scoring are part of the information society. Yet they are unstable and are driven by the media as a faculty manager suggests:

> . . . they're media driven. So the media will have its league tables no matter what length they have to go to to manufacture them. The trick is to waste a bit of time playing the game, according to the rules. In other words best practice in the manipulation of your statistics is necessary. Otherwise the league tables will be even more useless than they are at the moment. So . . . you have to play the game, if you took your eye off the ball you could do yourself serious harm, but there's very little way that you can do yourself a lot of good. . . . But they're not fantastically helpful, because they don't measure a single thing, they aggregate all sorts of different measures and it produces a single measure, a position in a table.

The naming of parts is perceived as a benefit to stakeholders as this practice provides information about fitness for purpose and the comparability of awards from different institutions (Brown, 2000). An academic development officer analyses the usefulness of league tables in the context of the choice discourse:

> I think if I was a student, a potential student, I would certainly want, you know, some sort of profile, of the institution I was joining. . . . I think you want something that goes beyond, you know, the glossy veneer of the other prospectus. . . . I can understand why, you know, they're popular with the media, and with the general public . . . it must be very difficult to understand what goes on in academia. And it gives them a very convenient handle, you know, some sort of basis on which to make some sort of decision on, you know, where they should go, and where sons and daughters should go.

A professor in a new university discusses the elitism embedded in the scoring processes:

> . . . the universities which do best in the teaching league tables by and large are the ones that do best in the research league tables. Which is, frankly, ludicrous. The implication is that you can do everything well

which I know you can't. So I think, by and large, they're judging quite different things. They judge resources; they're judging tradition. Snobbery is obvious . . .

Becher (1989) argued that, in academia, reputation is the most highly prized commodity. League tables cannot always override previous reputations and status as a lecturer in English literature describes:

I have a colleague at the moment who's in a – not a post-92 university – but a university that's traditionally been thought of as, you know, more technical than academic and she's applying for jobs at a range of other universities at the moment. And she is very much aware that there are prejudices about her institution, which are directly contradicted by the results that they're getting in subject review and in RAE. But that nonetheless don't seem to die in the face of that evidence.

A reader in social policy felt that performance indicators such as employability were not accurate tests of quality as they were context-specific and hence not open to organizational interventions:

Well I don't think, I mean they're all measuring different things aren't they? And they can be very prejudiced as well. I mean, I suppose I should say I like them because we're going up, but then that's not fair on other people and why are we going up, because I find them quite arbitrary, the criteria used for them. I mean it always strikes me that the teaching quality, the quality assessment thing, and various other things, when they come in and they judge how much employment the students get. We really have no influence on that at all, especially in the social sciences. I mean they go to engineering and they get a hundred per cent employment, well I mean we can't guarantee that for our students. . . . It seems unfair that we're judged on that when it's out of our hands.

This informant notes that she likes league tables because they are 'going up' in them, but then describes their potential for distortion. Academics and administrators have contradictory locations within the discourse of scores and league tables. They are both critical of the flawed methodology and reductionism, but, in the market economy, they are also under pressure to promote their exchange value. The director of academic affairs in a new university highlights the contradictions:

we became university of the year in [a Sunday newspaper] in 1999, and in 2000, because we happened to do particularly well in a set of league tables. And of course we used it in PR but what's wrong with that?

The contradictory consciousness is apparent in the celebrations for high scores. The most vigorous critics of the methodology have some professional pride and achievement activated when the results are favourable, as the head of a quality assurance unit relates:

Biology at X got a 24 . . . none of us thought they'd get 24. We thought they were going for the faculty average of 22, and they got a 24. And the head of the department took us back to the department . . . we proceeded to drink the departmental wine cellar dry. After about two hours he then decided that he'd take us all to dinner, so we went to this beautiful restaurant . . . and he paid for it all, about forty-odd people, everyone from the cleaner upwards.

A noticeable feature of this debate on league tables was that even when informants had sophisticated analyses of the methodological and ideological flaws embedded in current practices of scoring and league tables, shame and pride were activated. Scoring, it seems, can have both material and affective consequences that cohere to make the workforce more governable. There is a convergence between description and prescription as organizations develop strategies to achieve high scores. Scores represent symbolic, and in the case of the RAE, material capital. Their value is the extent to which they communicate and recognize shared meanings. The score is a form of gift exchange – a high score is a gift from outside. A low score is a counter-gift. The limited appeals' procedures mean that they are irreversible time capsules – imbued with authority and prescribed meaning. A question remains as to whether quality is a quantifiable object.

Classifying chaos: standards, benchmarks and qualifications frameworks

Quality assessment imposes a fiction of coherence and unity on an otherwise fragmented set of academic functions and services. Britain has a standards-based quality assurance regime. Subject benchmarks have been introduced as an attempt to define the content of degree programmes. They are statements expressing general expectations about the outcome standards of awards, primarily at honours degree level in 42 broad disciplinary areas. By attempting to provide statements of outcomes, that is what a student should know and be able to do and how well they should be able to do it, they aim to provide an indication of the meaning of 'graduateness'. In Britain, another major development has been the 'qualifications framework'. This aims to provide information about levels of achievement and attributes represented in the main academic awards. There is an aim of consistent use of the qualifications title across institutional boundaries. The central mechanism is the use of the qualification descriptor, which identifies general expectations about the purposes and outcomes of the main qualifications. Programme specifications exist to provide descriptions of intended learning outcomes from higher education programmes. Programme specifications attempt to clarify the nature and purpose of programmes in terms of knowledge, understanding, key skills, cognitive skills as well as subject-specific skills that a student will be expected to have gained upon programme completion.

Benchmarking is supposed to be a structured process of comparison, with opportunities for organizations to learn from each other (Jackson and Lund, 2000; Birnbaum, 2000). Benchmarks draw on a normative idea of what is considered useful, essential and evidence of standards. One justification for the introduction of benchmarks has been the development of a mass, international system of higher education, with considerable product variety across national boundaries. The internationalization of higher education has resulted in greater mobility. UNESCO (1998) estimated that 1.6 million people were enrolled in higher education outside their own countries at the end of the 1990s. Enhanced student mobility via national and international credit transfer agreements such as the Bologna Declaration (1999) means that qualifications have to be more knowable. 'Concerns over quality assurance are an integral part of international trade in professional services' (Mallea, 1999: 11). Harmonization has resulted in an application of disciplinary-based evaluation procedures to meet the demands for internationalization of professional standards.

Informants in my study had mixed responses to the introduction of benchmarks and descriptors. Benchmarking was seen to represent a movement away from knowledge and towards the acquisition of skills. They are also perceived as paving the way for a national curriculum in higher education. A philosophy lecturer comments on the reduction of autonomy:

> Even with the best will in the world, and a lot of the benchmarkers were honourable academics, and they attempted to deliver something that wasn't too contentious, but it sets out really the parameters of the national curriculum, what are the basics you would expect a philosophy student to have learnt? But it's a centralized approach to delivering teaching, which, as a first principle, is taking it away from the individual lecturer, and that was the one thing that academic life was supposed to be, was about, it was about the, having that autonomy. And so I think the benchmarking, the sort of centralized aspect, and it's introducing the skills agenda in a really sly fashion.

An academic registrar in a new university describes how benchmarking is yet another game for academics. Interpretations of benchmarks are linked to hegemonic assumptions about how disciplines are interpreted.

> It's a game for the academics, you know . . . I do think that's something for academics, amongst academics and it's about the way that they are choosing to define their subject areas. It's so varied across the board . . .

Dispute is healthy, according to a reader in social policy who fears that benchmarking is about induced conformity. Like the philosophy lecturer, she also sees it as the first stage to a national curriculum for higher education:

> . . . this sort of Benchmarking idea . . . can be damaging, because I'm not sure we want conformity to that extent, on different . . . I mean different departments have different strengths. . . . I think there's more and more

pressure to have a national curriculum in higher education, which I don't think is necessarily a good idea.

A head of department describes the process of developing subject benchmarks for education in terms of classifications and boundary setting. He describes how there was no place for uncertainty and ambiguity:

> But what we tried to write in to the benchmark, was this uncertainty principle . . . what we wanted to write was 'We don't really know what education is. It's a mixture of all sorts of stuff. It's going to change . . . ; Now QAA couldn't cope with that, actually the benchmarking group couldn't agree, almost couldn't agree what education was, because they couldn't agree where the boundaries lay . . . the QAA people started to get quite shirty, even the group of professionals they got together could not map the boundaries of the, of the so-called discipline. If you accept it's a discipline then it's a multi-discipline, and then what's it a multi-discipline of? And so on, and so on. . . . The QAA in its pursuit of routinization, and reduction to the lowest common denominator, was starting to construct a discourse of quality, which attempted to embrace all of these radically different notions of what knowledge, quality, education, higher education, were. And they just couldn't do it.

An academic registrar in a new university also draws attention to the difficulties of retreating into disciplinary descriptors in an age of inter- and multi-disciplinary approaches to knowledge acquisition and problem solving. She comments on the changing level of degrees in a mass system:

> One of the things it does do is it misses out a lot of higher education. There's a lot of multi-disciplinary, or inter-disciplinary work, that doesn't fit neatly in a benchmark. And also the benchmarks are written for the honours degree student. And at a time when this government is talking about 50 per cent participation in higher education in the future, a lot of students aren't going to get honours degrees, you know they're going to be with intermediate degrees, so it may not have much impact upon them.

These observations exemplify a major theoretical and ideological tension. Some parts of the academy began to open up, from the 1960s, to the transgression of borders, boundaries of traditional disciplines via new maps of learning incorporating multi-, inter- and trans-disciplinary approaches. There are concerns about the return to rigid disciplinary demarcations, and questions about the place of inter-disciplinary areas of studies including women's studies and cultural studies. The emphasis on learning outcomes can eclipse concerns with learning processes, and can fragment more complex experiential aspects of higher education.

Theorists including Bernstein (1996) drew attention to the social construction of disciplinary boundaries and the fragmentation that can result by dividing the world into arbitrary classifications. Disciplines, according to Bernstein (1996) represent strong classification and framing. Inter-disciplinarity and flexible learning represents a weakening of boundaries and classifications. Classification involves defining what can be considered knowledge. An ontological conception of knowledge relates to understanding, process and experience, whereas a collection approach suggests that knowledge is truth and is a product that can be tested, and measured. It appears that there is some theoretical tension between the way that knowledge is characterized in educational policies including lifelong learning and the learning society and how it is positioned in quality assessment. Current policies including lifelong learning stress the need for flexibility, innovation, problem-solving and inter-disciplinary investigation (Jarvis, 1999). However, current methodologies for quality assessment rely heavily on modernist descriptors and disciplinary boundaries. Benchmarking is a positivistic concept of knowledge based on objective truths to be communicated, memorized and measured.

For some informants, the process was fairly meaningless. The criticism was methodological, rather than epistemological, that is that *true* benchmarks were possible. A professor suggests that:

> The vast majority are so anodyne that it's almost impossible not to do as many, they're not very stretching frankly. . . . There's truth in many of the benchmarks, you know but they're so guarded and so inclusive in a way that they're really not very helpful in producing true benchmarks.

An aspect of quality that is frequently noted is just how tedious, de-energizing and demotivating processes can be. An assistant registrar in an old university comments on the user-unfriendliness of benchmarks:

> Well, benchmarks and specifications – I remember when they were first touted as a way of summarizing everything you need to know about a course and using it for a variety of purposes, which is all very laudable but then you actually look at them and see how tedious and unreadable they are. One of the suggestions that they be used for marketing purposes, and the very thought of putting out a document with a series of intricate maps of learning outcomes, development criteria and the like, to prospective students sends shivers down my spine!

The issues of regulation, closure and isomorphism also surface. The director of academic affairs in a new university observes that there needs to be an opportunity for interpretation rather than just compliance:

> I think the idea that there should be national debates and discussions and sort of active referencing of what should be a degree in English is a good thing. What's not good is if it becomes a sort of notion that there is one particular description one has to comply with, because that would just make everything go dead, backwards. . . . As it stands the benchmark statements are OK, providing you treat them in fact as a series of questions, not a series of statements.

For others, benchmarking had a high nuisance value in so far as they represented more bureaucracy. However, they were intellectually unsatisfactory too as they imposed directions, boundaries and hierarchies. A director of quality explains:

> . . . it has made bureaucratic and other demands that are unreasonable . . . you know, the benchmarks, the qualifications frameworks and all that kind of thing are generally viewed as being generally unhelpful, inamicable to diversity, forcing us down roads we don't necessarily want to go down and so on . . .

The issue of consensus and multiple readings permeates every aspect of quality assurance. Yet benchmarking suggests a type of harmony that does not easily exist in the academy. Some informants find benchmarks too narrow and restrictive, while others find them too vague. A professor in a new university commented on the universalizing tendency:

> Well the only benchmarking I've been closely involved with is in economics and frankly the benchmarking is so general as to be really much less than helpful.

A senior lecturer in an old university describes how English does not easily lend itself to benchmarking:

> . . . for English particularly it's such a sort of odd subject really it's not, to us anyway, it doesn't really map on to ideas of levels, and linear ideas of progression. And we're finding that very, very difficult.

A criticism of the benchmarking industry is that it trades in norms, threshold standards and peddles a reductive functionalism. It merely means conformance and the negation of difference (Bensimon, 1995). A faculty manager in an old university argues that benchmarking is often interpreted as threshold standards, and that this under-estimates the range and depth of the knowledge acquired:

> . . . explaining what a threshold-adequate engineer needs to be able to do would give a picture of a pretty feeble practitioner.

The 'lowest common denominator' criticism was also expressed by a registrar in an old university:

> I mean, if subject benchmarking means that you've got to establish a threshold which every university has got to be above if it's going to award degrees in a particular subject . . . the benchmark is going to have to be set at such a low level that it's not going to be very meaningful.

The argument used to justify benchmarks is that they provide a structure and set of organizing principles in the face of possible chaotic innovations. In these cases, the audience is the course development and validation team. A director of quality in a university college has some positive views about how benchmarks could be used for internal measurement of standards:

I think that's been quite a good initiative really. We've got most of our subjects lined up now with subject benchmark statements, and we require whenever a programme is validated here now, we require the subject, the relevant subject benchmark statements to be applied, to be considered by the validators. So we're bringing our provision into line with benchmark statements.

An assistant registrar in an old university draws attention to the rapidly changing priorities in what is seen as essential:

The question of updating benchmarks, I think, is something that hasn't been stressed. Because it's, it seems clear they would need to be updated very, very regularly, for them to have any benefit in the long-term.

In my research, product champions for benchmarking tended to come from new universities, or from those with designated quality posts in old universities. Their views can be summarized in terms of perfecting the systems design to reduce the margin of errors, deviations and distortions. For them, description is an essential part of the improvement process. Academics in both sectors tended to be more critical, often on the grounds that educational outcomes could not be easily measured. Conformance to requirements overlooks diversity, complexity and change and returns us to modernist boundaries and classifications.

3

Managing Quality

New managerialism and old organizational cultures

Quality assurance is a variety of technology transfer from private to public sectors. It is inextricably linked to new managerialism. Managing in universities today involves making educational provision and social organization compatible with the demands of the international economic system. The excellence literature (for example Peters and Waterman, 1982) gives 'paradigmatic status' to commercial enterprise as the model for all organizations (Du Gay, 1994: 659). Differentiation between public and private goals are swept away and the enterprising qualities of employees, for example risk-taking, flexibility, self-reliance, innovativeness are mobilized in the pursuit of improved economic performance (McWilliam et al., 1999). Being useful to business is interpreted as being like business (Marginson, 2000). Changes in the political economy forced radical structural readjustment in the public services from the early 1980s in Britain, with a move towards privatization, contract government, output-based funding and the marketization of services. The surface rationality used to justify the need for more structured systems of management in higher education is the increased size and complexity of the global higher education system, alongside the policy discourses and concepts discussed in the previous chapters. Elitist interpretations imply that quality was assured in the past by restricting admission practices. New constituencies, consumers, partnerships and rainbow coalitions of stakeholders threaten to make the whole system unwieldy. Hence an increasing emphasis on management processes in higher education and the functional management of intellectual labour (Dominelli and Hoogvelt, 1996).

New managerialism is defined as a 'generic package of management techniques' (Randle and Brady, 1997: 15). These techniques include an emphasis on productivity and output, sometimes reinforced by performance-related pay. New managerialism's hallmarks include: the pursuit of continuous improvement defined economically in terms of productivity and outputs; imposition of tighter financial accountability and quantitative measures of performance; the marketization of structural relationships, for example purchaser–provider models and the creation of a governmentable and flexible workforce (Case *et al.*, 2000; Trowler, 1998). Deem (1998) defines new managerialism as a complex ideology which informs ways of managing public institutions by advocating many of the practices and values of the private-for-profit sector in pursuit of efficiency, excellence and continuous improvement. The narrative of organizations has changed. For example, quality assurance incorporates a cluster of terms including transparency, efficiency, performance and good practice (Audit Commission, 1984; Shore and Wright, 1999). Demands for prescriptive performance, within established regimes of logic and reason, have intensified as the culture of excellence expands.

While the term 'new' is used to describe the introduction of management processes into the public services, there is a view that we are reverting to very outdated modes of management thinking. Dominelli and Hoogvelt (1996) argue that intellectual labour has become 'Taylorized', with new regulatory codes. Whereas Taylorism (Taylor, 1911), as a 'scientific' approach was once used to control manual labour, now it is being applied to intellectual labour. This concept derives from the mechanized industrial work practices supported by Frederick Taylor during the early part of the last century in which productivity was measured in time-and-motion studies with the ultimate aim of reducing gaps in the working day (Sabel, 1984).

Taylorism ensured the reduction of worker autonomy over the labour process placing them 'under a permanent surveillance and control in the fulfilment of their output norm' (Aglietta, 1979: 114). The quality movement also demands that every academic activity is broken down into simpler and more manageable parts. Hence a fragmenting or fracturing process results, with complex processes translated into empirically identifiable indicators, measures, competencies and outputs. A term that is used more today is that of 'granularization'. An entity is reduced to a myriad parts and reconstituted to represent a 'pure' whole, containing certain knowledge about processes and practices (Guile, 2001). This atomistic view of quality assurance reflects the tradition of abstracted empiricism. That is to say, it suggests that stable organizational structures and practices can be engineered, sustained and reproduced.

Quality assurance depends heavily on the responsibilization of every organizational member. This 'steering at a distance' (Kickert, 1995) approach is well-documented in Foucauldian analyses of employment regimes (for example Shore and Wright, 1999). The entire process is fraught with paradoxes. Regulation is achieved by deregulation and centralization by decentralization. Opposition to bureaucratization is positioned as anti-modernization. Opting out of quality assurance, for example, via fugitive or oppositional tactics, is dismissed as the extinct roar of the dinosaurs. Reform has been justified by constructing the object of reform as wasteful/inefficient/ irrelevant/incompetent/outdated. This strategy minimizes possibilities for resistance. Performance, as an action, contradicts any suggestion of inaction or inertia. Clegg (2001) draws attention to the irony that in the reframed language of new managerialism, academics who think that the purpose of education is to develop critical thought are framed not as radicals but as conservatives. Resistance involves standing outside the parameters, logic or frameworks that name, classify and value in the first place. The power relations are such that to name quality assurance as undesirable carries the risk of naming yourself as undesirable. Furthermore, with competition, the binary divide and sectoral diversity, it is questionable as to whether a political community to co-ordinate resistance exists in academia.

Miller (1998) asks what new managerialism is replacing in the academy. Ball's (1990a) observation that management is the linguistic antithesis to chaos still applies to higher education. The use of the term 'new' managerialism suggests renewal of an archaic system. For example, in one of his 'guru status' texts, Ramsden (1998) uses the term 'wilderness' to describe the pre-managerial university. Improving the performance of universities, according to Ramsden, lies in more effective leadership.

In the 1970s, influential theorists including Argyris and Schon (1974, 1978) conducted organizational case studies that led them to propose that organizational effectiveness was associated with dispersed organizational knowledge. Their findings influenced later work on 'the learning organisation', for example Senge (1990). Literature on learning organizations suggests that it is an adaptive, reflexive organization that both learns about itself and the dynamic context in which it operates. A learning organization develops via feedback. Feedback, audit trails and information loops are central to the assessment of quality in teaching and learning. There is a circularity in audit processes where policy is designed to meet indicators which reconfirm policy, and so there is no discourse outside this circle (Russell, 2002). The circularity is reinforced in the language of audit and feedback loops. Clark (1996: 429) has applied the concept of learning organizations to higher education claiming that 'we need to know more about universities as learning organizations in which self-assessment and self-regulation lead to cycles of self-enhancement'.

The use of the terms 'enhancement', 'development' and 'improvement' invest quality with a morality that is hard to contest. The language becomes self-propagating and disguises how circuits of power operate. A philosophy lecturer explains how the imposition of quality had more to do with managing mass higher education than with organizational and professional development:

> It was to do with management processes, it was to do with introducing a set of processes that could deal with large numbers of students effectively, but it was all couched in a sort of self-development language.

While the intention might be to use quality as a management tool, Newton (2000) discovered a noticeable implementation gap between quality in terms of management objectives and how quality was interpreted and managed by key staff. The majority of staff in his study interpreted it as spurious bureaucracy, impression management and a form of discipline. However, they persisted in performing, rather than resisting quality rituals. The issue of resistance, or lack of it, repeatedly surfaced in my study. Resistance is often dismissed as the fear of the new. Change theory stresses the importance of ownership. A principal lecturer describes the closure of the happy ending:

> A lot of my colleagues are very, very cynical about it, and very reluctant to change anything that they were doing, to meet the requirements of QA. There was a very strong political resistance to it at the beginning. Everybody came round eventually.

Skills in 'dealing' with resistance are now seen as essential components of management repertoires. An assistant registrar in an old university notes his strategies for dealing with resistance:

> When I was interviewed for the job I was asked three or four different ways, how do you deal with the academic who doesn't go along with the project? And my basic answer to that is 'Whatever you do, you don't give them a platform.' You don't, as it were, seek to discuss this with them in a departmental meeting. Because of the propensity to show off in those kind of fora. It's only by dealing, almost one to one.

The quality project involves correction and rehabilitation. A question is whether change is cognitive restructuring with an emphasis on a totalizing approach or habituation. Quality evokes a common language of aspiration. A professor in a new university comments on how pragmatism jostles with resistance. However, carefully orchestrated resistance by some universities has been of benefit to the whole system:

> There's a sort of resistance to the philosophy of it, but there's also a pragmatism in the sector and we've had to do this so we have. The fact that some universities have overtly come out opposed to the whole procedures and seem to be winning the argument, I think probably has just given everybody a bit of a pep really. And it improved our well being. . . . The institution, I would say if I had to summarize it, looks upon it as a necessary evil and tries to get as high a mark as possible.

Quality can be a powerful management tool. For example, an external 'threat' is cited to justify management interventions. An assistant registrar in an old university describes how QAA visits catalyse:

> . . . we do use the QAA quite a lot to get things done . . . I mean we try not to over use that, because we like to have good academic reasons for doing things. But as part of a series of arguments they can be quite useful . . . subject review . . . acts as a catalyst for actually getting things moving, so it does have some perks.

The management tool can be used in both directions. The head of quality assurance in a new university felt that findings from audit can be used as a leverage over management, particularly in relation to resources:

It [subject review] can serve a purpose to bring out problems, you know to highlight problems, which the institution may or may not already be aware of. . . . So if you get a low grade in learning resources, then hopefully the vice chancellor will prick up his [*sic*] ears and go 'Mm, better do something about that'. You know, the summing up. So I think they see it as, sometimes, not always, but occasionally as a good sort of management tool.

I am struck by the fact that most of the managers in my study who see the QAA as strengthening their position have been women. The authority of an external body strengthens their influence and leadership. A female pro-vice chancellor in an old university comments on the leverage that quality has given her management:

In terms of the leadership of this university, it, of course, gives greater power to my arm. There is no question whatsoever about that I can get people to listen more carefully to the need, for example, to have some kind of accountability framework . . . it's strengthened my arm. That's the difficulty we've got, you've got somebody like myself saying 'We do need these procedures, and the QAA has helped to allow me to be heard in an academic institution.'

Quality assurance can empower the structurally disempowered. It can also appear to be the conversion of existing naked power into legitimate authority. James (2000: 44) notes, how, in Australia, quality assurance has resulted in 'a tendency to look for "stronger" leadership and to strengthen centralized, top–down decision-making structures'. Adams (2000) comments that these strategies are necessary because there is a basic cultural clash between academe and management. The codes, values and processes of managerialism and academia appear to conflict. The imposition of quality is sometimes perceived as a power struggle or naked domination. However, the codes can also cohere. Strathern (2000a: 3) points out the dilemma for academics over quality:

. . . after all, it advances values that academics generally hold dear, such as responsibility, openness about outcomes and widening of access.

The blurring of codes can stifle protest. The association of quality assurance with highly desirable procedures such as transparency and accountability disguises the power relations and plays down the coercive and punitive implications. Transparency implies a challenge to the discriminatory practices of the hidden curriculum (Margolis, 2001). Yet it also implies a truth to be un-/dis- covered and conceals the way in which texts are socially constructed and are therefore read and interpreted in different ways. Disguising how power works is one of the key features of what Foucault called 'political technology' (Dreyfus and Rabinow, 1982). A philosophy lecturer believes that the government's sole purpose in introducing quality assurance was to make the academic profession more docile:

There are certain things this government have won with its money, and this is, it has now a higher education system where academics are prepared, are acquiescent, and are prepared to manage large student numbers and have changed their ideas of what counts as quality education. And for the government I think that was three hundred million well spent. I really don't think it was about finding under-performing departments . . . it's done that by academics doing it to themselves. So it didn't need to come up with any grand-scale schemes, it didn't need to introduce a very controversial education White Paper. It could just do it bit by bit, round the back door until it now has an education system vastly different from what it was when the process began.

A head of department in a new university theorizes the culture of compliance and disqualified discourses:

. . . academic life is dominated by compliance in my view. And where it's not dominated by compliance in a very direct way, it's dominated by the kind of compliance that is involved in the production, what I think is the production and reproduction of authorized knowledge. And I mean it has to do with the control of discourse and the way in which quality has been inserted into the dominant discourse, and therefore, even the way in which you challenge that discourse has to engage with the discourse itself and try to re-appropriate it. So there's no point in trying, in my view, to try to create a wholly alternative discourse, because it's actually disqualified. It's only by, by if you like, co-opting the discourse from within it and challenging its own internal inconsistencies etc., that you begin to expose some of its contradictions.

A lecturer in English literature berates the docility of academics. She describes how the entrepreneurial imperative relates to income generation, rather than to distribution:

I think it's extraordinary how quickly academics adjust to a situation which they've all been complaining about. I think we're very spineless in that regard. Or you could say adaptable but, you know, I feel that we accept more or less any kind of imposition that is made on us. For example, when we got the excellent in the last subject review, we were supposed to get, I think it was £92,000 from the funding body. And we sort of didn't because the university took it all and, you know, there were a few weeks of cross words all round but that was all it ever amounted to. And I think if we were running a business and somebody took £92,000 that we'd earned, you know, there'd be hell to pay. So it always surprises me how easily academics adjust to these kinds of things.

This observation exemplifies a central irony in the quality industry. While transparency and accountability have become hooray words, the accountability can often be a one-way gaze. In this study, I have noticed how quality procedures enable a type of displacement and distancing to take place in which power relations are simultaneously enacted and denied. The 'I'm only following orders' syndrome allows regulation without accountability. It also ensures that new managerialism is enacted in every-day practices.

Accountability, autonomy and the audit culture

Accountability and the audit culture combine powerful moral reasoning with the methodology of financial accounting. Accountability in higher education appears to be a democratizing discourse. However, it is value laden in so far as it privileges certain types of knowledge, pedagogies, outcomes and management processes over others. Accountability is a common-sense term that over-simplifies power relations. The moral implications overshadow political agendas. Ball *et al.* (1997) offer two broad categories of accountability – market and political. They outline a trend towards the privileging of market accountability over political accountability. Vidovich and Slee (2001: 432) distinguish four main types of accountability: professional accountability to peers; democratic accountability to the community; managerial accountability to governments and market accountability to customers. Accountability appears to be a type of penance that is now being paid for former autonomy.

In terms of higher education, Strathern (2000a: 2) observes that specific procedures have 'come to carry the cultural stamp of accountability, notably assessments that are likened to audit'. Audit is increasingly seen as a substitute for professional ethics and an infringement of professional autonomy. The word audit comes from the Latin word *audire* meaning to hear. Organizational members have to read their organization out loud to assessors who scrutinize, evaluate and judge. Audit is a relationship of power between auditors and auditees. A refusal to participate in the process of reading the organization out loud suggests that there is something to hide. Power (1994) argues that critics of accountability and audit always appear to be defending elitism, secrecy and privilege.

Delanty (2001) argues that accountability is part of a move towards market values. If everything is driven by profit motives, there needs to be an external form of regulation, as one can no longer rely on intrinsic commitment and motivation. Henkel (2000) discovered that her informants associated accountability with increasing student numbers and a declining resource base. Staff in some of the pre-1992 universities believed that it was an attempt to impose centralized systems similar to those in the post-1992 universities. Underlying this was an assumption that a mass system could not rely on intrinsic motivation. Professionalism was being replaced by external monitoring systems. Readings (1996) locates current constructions of accountability within the logic of contemporary capitalism. This logic is riven with norms and power operates by techniques of normalization. As such, accountability is a major form of power. Giddens (1984: 30) suggests that being 'accountable for one's activities is both to explicate reasons for them and to supply normative grounds whereby they might be justified'.

The norms are embedded in the taxonomies of excellence and in the myths justifying the need for quality interventions. A polarization that emerged in my study was the now and then binary. Now, the bureaucracy is onerous, burdensome etc., but the past was a cauldron of secrecy and inefficiency. Quality assurance is strengthened by the repudiations it implies. The consumer paradigm is demanding much greater transparency in performance data than before. A registrar of an old university observes:

> We keep being told by the government and the QAA that we've got to be transparent, we've got to explain to our stakeholders, customers – awful words – why we're doing things, how we're doing things and what is the justification for them. And I mean if you go back 20/30 years nobody had to justify themselves to the public at all for what went on at universities. And we use up large amounts of public money and it's reasonable to say, 'Okay, well tell us that we're getting value for money. How?' So I think that's a good thing.

The language of the criminal justice system is sometimes used to imply that elite groups were allowed to 'get away with it' in the past. An academic development officer (quality enhancement) in an old university perceives accountability as a new form of justice:

> I think there always will be, to an extent, because I don't think the great British public, and certainly the politicians, will accept anyone being sort of judge and jury in their own case anymore . . . you know I think there has to be an element of externality about it.

Elsewhere, the justice system is represented in terms of human rights. An assistant registrar in an old university describes how his quality management interventions were perceived as a threat to civil liberties:

> . . . there are still people there who seriously dislike the whole agenda . . . interference with academic autonomy. They know, you know, they are the judges, and they should, therefore, be the judge of their own performance. There is one senior professor who's, on the one time I've actually spoken to him, threatened to take me to the European Court of Human Rights . . . on grounds of interference with trade.

A further potent binary is the accountability/autonomy two-step. Barnetson and Cutright (2000: 289) argue that accountability is that which is exchanged for autonomy in an authority relationship. Studies on academic identity have emphasized disciplinary culture and academic autonomy (Clark, 1987; Becher, 1989; Fulton, 1996). Mourning the loss of academic autonomy raises questions about transitions to more relational *modus operandi*. Autonomy can be understood as lack of vulnerability to others, a kind of solipsism or lack of sociality or imperviousness that ignores community and proximity. Autonomy is also associated with the elite who can protect their boundaries.

For example, Trowler (1998) questions whether the culture of academic autonomy extended to the former polytechnics where there was local educational authority control, and indeed, a different client group.

Autonomy is unproblematically positioned as a neutral or potentially benign concept. However, a senior lecturer in English in an old university argues that increased accountability promoted equity issues and that autonomy enables discriminatory decision making and corruption to go unchecked:

> I've been happier and I've faired better . . . where there is transparency and accountability. . . . My experience is more accountable sort of cultures where people do think about quality and are made to think about it and are held more accountable have been fairer on me as a woman

In this analysis, autonomy is discursively linked to conditions that facilitate discrimination against women in the academy. There are other gender connotations too. Psychoanalysts including Benjamin (2000) and Baker Miller (1976) have pointed out that autonomy is a gendered concept. Benjamin suggests that traditional notions of autonomy are associated with maleness and difference, whereas notions of femaleness are associated with dependence and sameness. Baker Miller (1976) talked about male socialization encouraging agentic behaviour, that is acting for oneself, whereas female socialization promoted communal behaviour, that is being linked to others. These theories could be dismissed as essentialist, binaried and somewhat dated in today's workplace. However, in this study, many of the women informants supported quality as they believe that it is associated with an openness that furthers their interests in a system that has discriminated against them. This has made them more easily persuadable to assume management responsibility for quality assurance procedures.

Blackmore (2000: 143) believes that gender is central to the conception/execution divide within the policy process. Women, she argues, are more likely to be excluded from policy production but included in policy implementation as change agents. My research too has indicated a sexual division of labour, with women being more heavily responsibilized for quality assurance of teaching and learning (Morley, 2001a). In this instance, their autonomy is discouraged, as it is seen as non-corporate and too self-interested. I shall return to this in more detail in Chapter 8.

My study produced evidence that academics and managers tended to support the concept of accountability but found the cumbersome bureaucratic requirements unacceptable. A pro-vice chancellor in an old university discusses the contradictions:

> There is no doubt whatsoever that the QAA procedures meant that we considered carefully our masters courses and found them lacking, and did something about it. However, the impact that it had on us as academics, was that it just stopped us in our tracks for somewhere, I would estimate, somewhere in the region of about six months, because

of the bureaucracy. So while it was an absolutely essential thing it was also one of the biggest time-wasters that I've been involved in as an academic. Something has got to be done and I think we are now seeing the fruits of so many people like myself saying, very loudly and clearly, keep the accountability framework but get rid of the bureaucracy!

The bureaucracy emerges for some in the form of unboundaried overkill and replication of procedures. Accountability can sit ill with professional ethics. A senior lecturer in education comments on over-regulation:

> . . . I feel very caught up in very complicated and contradictory process, because on the one hand I think that if taxpayers pay us money to do a job, at a certain level I think that we need to be accountable. Now I actually think I'm already accountable, I'm accountable to my line managers here. We fill in enormous amount of details about the work that we do. I'm accountable to the RAE for my publication rate. I'm accountable to my mentor here, for my teaching. I have annual appraisal in which I'm also made accountable. So I actually feel that while I think it's fair enough to be accountable, I sort of think there comes a point at which enough is enough.

Shore and Wright (1999: 557) argue that a particularly disabling model of accountability has emerged – one that elides it with policing, reductive inspectable templates and disciplinary mechanisms linked to neoliberal governmentality. For some, the 'policing' element is connected to the reduction of trust in the academy and the need to link all activities to the two major accounting systems. Berdahl (1990) argued that academic freedom and institutional autonomy are not the same thing. Informants in Kogan and Hanney's study (2000) believed that the power of institutions has grown at the expense of individual academic freedom. A reader in social policy in an old university comments on how all academic activities must now be quantified and calculable:

> . . . we have sabbaticals, which is great, it used to be that you just had to fill out a form to say what you were going to achieve from your sabbatical, now they're doing it in boxes. So you have to put down how many research applications you would put in, how many articles you would publish . . .

Regulation is passed down the line. The transparency exercise in the UK requires universities to quantify the amount of time their staff spend on different types of activity (Becher and Trowler, 2001). Transparency of operation, according to Strathern (2000a: 2), is 'endorsed as the outward sign of integrity'. We are asked to trust the measures, rather than the professionals delivering the service. Paradoxically, transparency invites concealment. Creative retrospective archiving is rife. While transparency is discursively linked to a notion of truth, a principal lecturer in a new university notes how transparency can be socially constructed:

... I mean I'm not saying that we told lies, but we cemented over certain issues and those weren't picked up. ... So the whole process wasn't quite as transparent as it might have been. ... The language that people use to write the self-assessment reports, and it really is quite fascinating, how we wrap up facts in management speak, and actually disguise the real issues, and I think that's what we did ... we just fudged it. We wrote policy two weeks before, and presented them, and we did lose one mark for it, but we should have lost a lot more!

A further paradox in the quality industry is that while accountability and transparency are lauded, there is little evidence of them in audit procedures, as a head of the quality assurance unit, in a new university observes in relation to subject review:

I think because the process itself is designed to be transparent, but actually it isn't ... I mean the grading, and how that survived that, you know – it's closed doors. The institution facilitator is not allowed to stay in the base room when they're talking about grades ... There is no right of appeal ... I think it's appalling that something which goes in to the public domain, and you are held publicly accountable for, you have no right of appeal to.

These observations highlight the one-way gaze of objectification, as the values, credentials and belief systems of the assessors are rarely called into question. There is a morality of visibility, with transparency a keyword in quality assurance. However, Strathern (2000b: 309) cautions that 'visibility as a conduit for knowledge is elided with visibility as an instrument of control'. She asks what visibility also conceals. The relationship between the known/visible and the unknown/invisible is rarely examined.

Performance indicators: measuring creativity

Performance indicators translate macro-policies into micro-practices. Accounting systems have been invented to calculate individual academics' and academic units' research and publication productivity and 'effectiveness' in teaching quality. These accounting systems represent an encodement of values and priorities. They also structure and construct desires, aspirations and ambition. Regulatory regimes structure desire through the instruments of suppression. While purporting to provide consumers with a basis for selection and funders with evidence of output, performance indicators also provide powerful managerial imperatives. They combine description with prescription and mediate between outcomes and goal setting. Performance criteria tend to be centrally determined. The task of university managers is to facilitate a culture of commitment to them (Taylor, 2001). There has been a marked trend towards internalizing audit functions and increasing an organization's and individual's capacity for self-inspection. A new disciplinary grid has been imposed (Shore and Wright, 1999).

Financial instability tightens the grip of performance indicators. Barnetson and Cutright (2000: 281) note the use of financial rewards and punishments to 'manipulate institutional behaviour'. Performance indicators are often allied to competitive bidding procedures. The evaluative information generated by performance indicators can be linked to funding, as with the research assessment exercise in the UK. Hence, performance indicators actively structure rather than simply measure the academy. Regulation can produce the object that it claims to discover. Barnetson and Cutright (2000: 277) believe that performance indicators are 'conceptual technologies' in so far as they shape what issues we think about and how we think about these issues by embedding normative assumptions into the selection and structure of those indicators. They are omnipresent and are part of new managerialism's dispersed responsibility (Clarke and Newman, 1997).

Performance indicators and taxonomies of effectiveness are often little more than socially constructed floating signifiers (Morley and Rassool, 1999; Ball, 2000). For example, priorities shift geographically and historically. Performance indicators capture panics, prejudices and fears at any one particular political and historic moment. The certainty of such taxonomies denies any consideration of alternatives. Kaufmann (1988) argues that there are five elements to which performance indicators can be applied: inputs, processes, products, outputs and outcomes. There is an assumption that so-called 'causal' factors are '. . . independent, universal and additive; that is, they do not interfere with each other and are uninfluenced by contexts' (Hamilton, 1998: 15). While they appear neutral, for example student completion rate, they are policy instruments to advance a political agenda. Performance monitoring is driven by external requirements for accountability and also by internal mechanisms linked to institutional performance. Forms of action are normatively and communicatively achieved via staff development and employment conditions, for example appraisal and the use of short-term contracts.

Performance indicators are part of the risk society. They are potent signs offering some sort of order and certainty in complex organizations. They are also linked to the principles of consumer entitlement. Nowadays, the public are deemed to be at as much risk from a failing public service organization as they are from faulty engines on aircraft. Middleton (2000: 542) argues that performance indicators 'are firmly established as a tool of strategic state-managerial control and the assumption is that if universities fail to provide public assurance of quality and standards, more stringent government intervention can be expected'.

An argument in favour of performance indicators is that they summarize complicated processes in at-a-glance information for consumers. Laurillard (1980: 187) observes that performance indicators 'reduce a complexity of subjective judgements to a single objective measure'. Strathern (2000b: 314) argues that there is a translation across domains – from service to assessment, and the language of the indicators eventually takes over the language of the services. Polster and Newsom (1998) suggest that performance indicators make it possible to replace substantive judgements with formulaic and algorithmic representations. However, feedback on performance is frequently incomplete, partial, situated and open to a range of interpretations. Normative obligations are interpreted, conveyed and justified via language and particular terms have been identified to signify complex processes, for example transparency. The observers and the observed have to learn how to exchange information within prescribed signifiers in order to justify claims to authenticity. It is questionable what opportunities there are for interpretative and evaluative differences.

Quality is defined in ever changing configurations. A common complaint in this study relates to policy fatigue. As soon as academics and managers learn to decode one set of performance indicators, they change. The transience produces a sense of erasure and negation. Achievement is easily undone. Herein lies a paradox – quality assurance is meant to regulate chaos but it ends up producing it. Turbulence is a relay of power encapsulated in economic theories promoted by the Austrian school, for example. Hayek is one of the theorists who celebrates the benefits of permanent disequilibrium (Middleton, 2000). This pattern was noted by Shore and Wright (1999) who report a comment from a HEFCE official at a 1993 Conference of the Society for Research in Higher Education.

> A HEFCE official admitted that performance indicators should only have a shelf life of about two years because 'after that people get wise to them'. The undeclared policy, therefore, is to keep systems volatile, slippery and opaque.

A lecturer in Spanish cites the problem of constant change:

> Part of the resistance comes from the system keeps being changed and with, I think, increased work load; they are increasingly fed up with doing these things and four years later the system has completely changed and they have to redo it. Redo it all again as it were and I think it's a climate of constant, almost constant change . . .

A further strategy of domination in the assessment of teaching quality is the introduction of arbitrary performance indicators internally and externally, at any point of the proceedings. This is justified in terms of the open-endedness of continuous improvement. This can resonate with academic training, making academics feel as if they will never achieve closure. A philosophy lecturer describes how demoralizing this practice can be:

> . . . a couple of days before the team arrived I was instructed by our teacher quality unit that my statutory documentation of student progress and achievement wasn't up to scratch because I hadn't traced what had happened to students who had dropped out. I hadn't tracked them to their new university, and found out what degree they'd got . . . I mean they're looking for three years, you've got three cohorts that you're tracing, and in those cohorts they were saying to me, coldly, and without

any clerical support that I had to go away and trace these students. You know, like phone up the universities and say 'What did X get in 1996?' At that point I thought that's the end.

... I think why that stuck in my mind was that it was a judgement that no matter how much you do there is always something else that you should have done. And I think academics are a bit prone to this as well, the sort of feeling that you should be delivering, you know that it's not quite good enough ... the need to please or the need to perform. It was at that point I recognized that it was just this endless set of demands.

Turbulence is manufactured in order to avoid any suggestion of stagnation. Higher education is attempting to emulate the change-driven cultures of many profit-motivated corporations (Birnbaum, 2000). An assistant registrar in an old university reports how their preparations for one system of QA were soon date-expired as a new system was introduced:

We spent a great deal of time last year working up our support arrangements for the new system for quality assurance, only to have it blown out of the water by the changes that happened over the summer, and subsequently through the HEFCE consultation.

The emphasis is on the ability to adapt to turbulent markets rather than to stabilize and as numerous theorists of public service organizations have noted, we have to live with ambiguity, uncertainty and constant change (Hassard and Parker, 1993; Reed and Hughes, 1992). While organizations invest large sums in uncertainty avoidance, responsiveness to change is itself a performance indicator.

Never mind the quality, feel the cost!

The cost of quality assurance is difficult to estimate. The official figure is 0.1 per cent of the Higher Education Funding Council's teaching budget dedicated to subject review (Yorke, 1999). *The Times Higher Education Supplement* (30 March, 2001) estimated that teaching quality assessment cost every department in each university in Britain between £20,000 and £200,000 in paperwork and staff time. A report for HEFCE found that the bureaucracy of subject review cost universities £250 million a year (THES, 4 August, 2000: 1). This figure excluded the costs incurred by institutions and the substantial opportunity costs of staff allocated to extensive preparations. Floud (2001) estimates that the £250 million annual cost currently being spent on quality assessment is the equivalent of fees for 250,000 students; the cost of 5 universities; the pay of 10,000 lecturers.

In Britain, approximately 10,000 people – most of them academics – have been involved in inspecting universities and higher education colleges over the past seven years. More than 2000 individual institutions underwent subject review. Only six courses were found to be failing and four of those were franchised. The image of the sledgehammer to crack a nut is prominent in discussions on the economics of quality assurance (Yorke, 1999). A reader in social policy notes:

> I think it costs a fortune. I mean when we did our teaching quality assessment we actually employed a body to put it all together for six months . . . I remember our head of department saying you know the amount of extra photocopying and equipment that we'd brought would probably run into the thousands. . . . It seems to me it's a sledgehammer to crack a nut.

A head of a quality unit argues that while the costs are excessive, some benefits to students have resulted:

> I do think that, I mean it's a very heavy sledgehammer to crack a relatively small nut. But despite that I do think that it does result in improvements for students, if, if the recommendations that come out of all of it are acted upon, in a sort of sustained fashion.

A sociology lecturer finds the cost of quality assurance unacceptable at a time when controversy over tuition fees, earning-to-learn, lack of resources and student debt (see Callender and Kemp, 2000) rages:

> . . . practically all of our full-time students work, often they have full-time jobs as well. Increasingly we don't get mature students now because mature students just can't afford to come to university. You know, so with things like the introduction of fees, the removal of grants . . . every single course committee I go to the students say 'There aren't enough books in the library'.

Universities appear to be increasingly responding to the needs of auditors and funders, rather than users. A lecturer in Spanish expresses her concern about the wastage and inappropriateness of the expenditure:

> . . . the money was poured into the mechanisms rather than improving the provision of the teaching itself.

This process involves a kind of double think. Staff are repeatedly told to make efficiency gains, while witnessing the wastage involved in foyerization and impression management. A senior lecturer in education describes how this makes her feel:

> It felt to me like a complete paperchase, it felt like a waste of time and a waste of money, and a waste of my life. . . . We don't have enough computers for our students, we could do with more books in the library, we're not providing the sorts of online facilities the students would really like. If we had that money to really spend on things, like we need more transcribing machines, we need better resources for our PhD students, if we had that money to spend on students then I would say great. But I have to say, to my mind, it's a sin . . . to spend all of that

money, all of that money on such a trivial gain, when there isn't enough money we're told.

A similar view was expressed by a principal lecturer in a new university, who comments on the parsimony elsewhere in the academy compared to the profligacy of quality assurance:

I think the amount of money that it's costing just can't be justified, when we're economizing on photocopying and paper, and holding posts and not paying decent salaries, and yet we're investing all this money in quality assurance systems, I think it's got to change.

A justification for the introduction of new managerial processes in the public services was to challenge profligacy and waste, yet ironically, it seems to have increased it. An assistant registrar in an old university comments on cost-effectiveness:

There is no way of calculating this meaningfully. . . . The report for HEFCE last year, which came up with the figure of 250 million a year for accountability exercises. I don't know I believe it, but I do believe the figure that they used as an average for a QAA visit, of around a £150,000. I'll go along with that . . . that's too high . . . for the benefit that's gained out of it. . . . My view on the QAA exercise was that it lost sight of it's own cost effectiveness.

An assistant registrar in an old university, who gained an overview from having been institutional facilitator for all the subject reviews in her organization argues that the methodology of auditing subject, rather than institutional provision involves significant repetition and wastage:

They have a tendency to go over a lot of aspects of quality assurance many times. In a sense that there are a lot of areas like elements of the student support systems particularly those concerned with pastoral support and things like support for disabled students which are the same in the university irrespective of subject. And, certain facilities in the library are in the same kind of category, so you tend to find that those are being gone over several times by subject review teams. I think that it is actually also very hard to assess in a proper way the quality management enhancement aspect of provision at the subject level because it really needs to be seen in the context of the overall institutional requirements for quality management. You don't get a reasonable sample if you are only looking at one subject.

A dominant theme in critical texts is the disproportionate relationship between input and outcome. A professor of French in an old university comments on what a poor investment subject review was:

When you think about it the nature of the process, the amount of time of man [*sic*] hours . . . there can't be, then, justification for the amount of money which has been spent on this process. . . . It's been a very laborious, time consuming and expensive procedure, and the results really haven't changed the landscape very much.

A pro-vice chancellor in an old university attempts to calculate the costs, again, commenting on the lack of return or value for the investment:

We're talking about 300,000, for every subject review I would think, from inside the university.

In a politically significant article in the *Guardian* newspaper, academics in the economics department at Warwick estimated that subject review cost their department between £150,000 and £200,000 in staff time alone (*Guardian*, 30 January 2001). This provoked questions to be asked in parliament and was seen as contributing to the abolition of subject review. However, John Randall, the former chief executive of the Quality Assurance Agency, responded to the article. He argued that academic time should be spent on monitoring standards and ensuring fitness for purpose anyway, not just for the purposes of subject review (Randall, 2001). The director of academic affairs in a new university also believed that quality costs get inflated:

I think heads of institutions, mostly, well mostly ones which have got loads of money anyway, make too much of it, and they inflate the costs, of course it's possible to waste money on these things, but I actually think it's not a big issue.

Costs could have been inflated as a consequence of competition. For example, elaborate badging and presentation of documentation. The costs of quality assurance also reinforce power relations in so far as well-endowed organizations have been able to invest significant sums in the preparations. In this regard, they could be accused of 'upping the stakes', as they have created their own benchmarks.

James (2000: 44) describes how, in Australian universities, vast amounts of data are now collected, tabulated, circulated and scrutinized in costly evaluative activity. He adds that there is little to show for all this effort. Angelo (2000) relates a similar situation in the USA:

Since the beginnings of the current higher education reform movement in the mid-1980s, thousands of American academic developers, administrators, and academic staff leaders have promoted change under banners of assessment, continuous quality improvement, active learning, strategic planning, distance education, and other related movements. Much has changed as a result of their efforts and much has improved, of course. Nonetheless, there are still surprisingly few well-documented examples of significant, lasting gains in student learning. . . .

The insatiability of the quality industry has produced a range of metaphors. Newton (2000) describes quality audits as 'feeding the beast', with ritualistic practices by academics seeking to meet accountability requirements. The implication is that by feeding the beast one will stop it from eating you! But the feeding process seems to be getting out of control. A registrar in an old university describes the direct and indirect costs:

> The sheer volume of work that's involved and the sheer volume of paper that has to be put into it if you're going to do it properly.... And it has all sorts of spin-off costs for us because there are numerous things that come up which simply have to be dealt with under quality assurance – student problems, invoking our procedures to address a particular issue, which we didn't do before. And, I mean, we don't quantify in money terms what it costs in staff time but it's enormous, it's enormous.

An assistant registrar in an old university feels that the sector has become obsessed with the creation of costly committees. These function more as reception mechanisms that comment on the presentation of policy, rather than act as decision-making fora:

> I think it's a costly business, and I also think that sometimes universities beat themselves up too much about it, and set in place systems which are overly bureaucratic, and don't actually meet a direct need. So I think we're all too inclined to set up committees, to address a particular issue, when somebody coming along and talking to people might actually do the trick, or even managing things more straightforwardly.

There is a panoptic, just-in-case aspect to quality assurance. Human resources, plant and documentation have to be prepared in case assessors seek a viewing. A principal lecturer comments on the demoralization caused by preparing documentation that is never actually consulted:

> I mean taking back the boxes.... It is obvious that a very high percentage of them just haven't been looked at.... These beautifully prepared boxes, exactly as we left them, in the room, and there are an odd one or two that you can see they've been through, that the corners are turned, and they're not in the wallets. But I would say that a fifth of the evidence has been gone through, if that. And that's just so soul destroying really.

Demoralization is rife in quality assurance. Informants talked about material, opportunity and human costs. A head of economics in a new university noted how subject review is supported by the unpaid labour of a minority. This disguises the budgetary implications, but has human consequences:

> I mean people have worked extra hard, so there's been no extra cost on the faculty . . . I think the burden has actually fallen on a group of about six to eight people. They've done it without extra cost, without extra reward. There's been cost on their lives. . . . So in a way we've sort of managed within the existing budget, we haven't created a huge amount of cost I don't think. Certainly not a financial cost; there might have been a human cost.

A philosophy lecturer also discusses the human costs:

> We had a meeting at the beginning of one semester, where our head of department said that we needed now to completely concentrate on the subject provision review. And that was in the September, and the review was in the February, and that was all we did. We taught, we managed to fit in the teaching hours, but we went from meeting to meeting, we wrote documents in lunchtime . . . we spent our time finding numbers and tracing students, and becoming quite highly skilled administrators and it was a very intense period of work. So we were working quite extreme hours and having to do six-day weeks merely to do the teaching and the marking, and the preparation for the SPR. So that lasted, in terms of workloads . . . a good seven months, and probably more.

It appears that quality assessment of teaching and learning requires significant amounts of self-sacrifice. This is evocative of Handy's (1993) notion of the psychological contract between employees and their organization. Professional commitment and loyalty are exploited to underwrite the costs. Indeed, employers are even told that the excessive demands of quality assessment is good for them in terms of their development. The director of academic affairs in a new university believes:

> If it's (quality assessment) done properly there's a lot of good professional development value in it.

It could also be argued that quality assessment is a new job creation scheme. A faculty manager in an old university comments on how a new cadre of manager academics is being developed:

> The appointment, relatively recently, of deputy heads for quality has been a concern to those people who have been put in that position. It never is easy for an academic to relinquish time for research, and shoulder what is a pretty big administrative burden, and so that, in 23 departments or whatever, we've probably got 23 pressed persons, but they're getting used to the role and it's quite key to get the right sort of person in there.

Entire management systems are being designed for audit. A professor in a new university outlines the organizational structure for managing quality, with information about new tiers, posts and committees:

> We have a pro-vice chancellor whose title is quality assurance, or some such. The pro-vice chancellor chairs a committee which is called the academic quality committee, that consists of a number of individuals but particularly of the associate deans of academic quality in each of the faculties. And each of the faculties has an academic quality committee, which the associate dean presides over. So if we go about it the other way round, the faculties have quality committees chaired by an

associate dean, that associate dean is a member of the university's academic quality committee, chaired by a PVC.

While the evidence for the cost of quality assessment of teaching and learning is fairly uneven, so too is the evidence of the benefits. In a policy context of best value and evidence-based research, what value do assessments of teaching and learning and research productivity add?

4

The Psychic Economy
of Quality

Identity: the professional is political

There is a psychic economy involved in quality assurance. Quality assessment, accountability and the auditing of academic work have had a profound impact on reconstructing academic conditions of work and academic identities. The academic *habitus* has been challenged. Academics have to be simultaneously self-managing and manageable workers who are able to make themselves auditable within prescribed taxonomies of effectiveness. There is a new cultural logic governing academic professionalism (Walker, 2001). These cultural and political changes demand additional temporal and material investments. They also involve significant emotional labour. Anxieties, aspirations and fears invade people's interior spaces, as every individual working in academia is made aware that their performance, productivity and professional conduct is constantly under scrutiny within non-negotiable frameworks.

Issues of quality and standards take on a particularly emotive tone (Case *et al.*, 2000). The academy has long represented the life of the mind. In line with the Cartesian dualism, emotions and embodiment have been largely understated in the quest for abstract knowledge. Traditional myths, symbols and rituals of universities have centred on carefully choreographed ceremonies, control and constraint. The detached, cold and emotionally inept academic has become a professional stereotype. Indeed, in traditional, positivistic academic culture, impersonality was presented as the hallmark of quality and reliability. Emotion was a signifier of bias and unreliable knowledge. In the 'pop' psychology text Goleman (1996) cites academics as exemplars of a professional group with low emotional intelligence. However, recent accounts of life in the academy suggest that strong emotions are surfacing. There have been reports on occupational stress, the long hours' culture and the requirement for academics to provide emotional support for an ever-increasing number of diverse students (Fisher, 1994; AUT, 1998; Malina and Maslin-Prothero, 1998).

Professional identity is essentially socially mediated. There is a strong relationship between public discourse and social and professional identities. There is an element of intersubjectivity in the constitution of identity. Hence, public 'discourses of derision' (Ball, 1990b: 31) can be internalized and believed at some level. Traditionally, universities have been able to assign individuals with a ready-made identity embedded in notions of social hierarchy. Now professional identities are constantly in flux. It is not enough simply to reproduce the skills and knowledges for which one was originally appointed. There is an imperative to be entrepreneurial, innovative and to add value to one's organization. Multiskilling creates anxieties about maintaining expertise. Jarvis (2000: 45) observed that no matter how hard academics argue for their independence, they will be forced to respond to the infrastructural social pressures that shape the world as a whole. McWilliam *et al.* (1999: 62) observe that there is the emergence of an instrumental workplace culture that is centred on 'galvanising the economic potential of knowledge'. Academics are being asked to reinvent themselves, their courses, their cultural capital, and their research as marketable commodities.

For some, quality assurance can represent an area of danger in the academy (Douglas, 1966; Acker and Webber, 2000). Danger in so far as the purity of disciplinary divisions is being contaminated with bureaucracy. But also danger in the sense of witch-hunts and blame culture. For example, Ramsden (1998) suggests that individuals who resist quality management of their performance should be identified in order to maximize the performance of their organization. Danger also exists in the form of a threat to professional autonomy, for example, the sense of invasion and powerlessness to control one's time, priorities and objectives. Quality assurance is presented as a consensual discourse yet it produces system-induced identity threats. A senior lecturer describes how she experienced identity change, responsibilization, domination and sense of menace. Something sinister is lurking just beneath the surface of inspections:

> I didn't feel like an academic, I felt like, I felt like the prey to the QAA, that whatever they wanted they must have, whatever they wanted I must produce a document, and I must get all the documents and put them all in boxes for them. And I felt that that was my job, and everything else came second, and I had to do their bidding, and do it as well as possible, because otherwise, I don't know what the otherwise would be. There is . . . in a sense there is a silence on the other side of what will happen, both to you as an individual and to your institution. And there is that threat, the unspoken threat. And that's the other side of the accountability and the audit society, the unspoken threat that . . . you can be a failing university. And you know, again if you're in a more prestigious position you can lose that prestigious position.

As this observation illustrates, preparation for quality assessment has social and affective consequences. Time, resources and workers are locked into the practicalities, as well as the fear, morality and consequences of the process (Strathern, 2000a). Pirsig (1974: 233) states that 'quality is not a *thing*. It is *an event*'. Henkel (2000: 96) found that for her academic informants the audit of teaching and learning quality was 'a dramatic intervention in their working lives, dominating the semester or term in which it occurred, and the whole academic year for those with responsibility for organizing it. Arrangements for quality assessments are making academics and administrators increasingly mutually dependent. Academics and administrators are forced to provide more documentary evidence as proof of their professionalism and competence. There are internal and external audiences resulting in multiple accountancy pressures and high visibility and vulnerability.

Quality assurance involves making distinctions – classifying, segregating, drawing boundaries – dividing people and organizations into categories simultaneously united and separated by similarity and difference (Bauman, 2001a). A resignifying process takes place. Some people are authorized to speak authoritatively because others are silenced. A question remains as to whether the culturally constructed subject can rewrite the script when all resistance is perceived as defensive action.

Trust me, I'm a doctor!

Accountability, audit and the relentless pursuit of evidence of professional competence are challenges to relationships of trust. Douglas (1992) argues that checking only becomes necessary in situations of mistrust. Hence, it carries sinister overtones. Power (1994) notes the paradox. Audit is introduced largely when trust has broken down, yet 'the spread of audit actually creates the very distrust that it is meant to address'. For Shore and Wright (2000) trust has been replaced by measurement. Untrustworthy behaviour in the professions is perceived as costly, dangerous and wasteful. As suggested by Sitkin and Roth (1993), escalating cycles of distrust are frequently misunderstood as being rooted in details associated with reliability and competence. Trust, accountability and competence have been discursively linked. Predictability offers some indemnity against risk. Scores in the RAE and the subject review operate as performative utterances signifying a ritualistic movement from one state to another, similar to sentencing in the judicial service. The scoring has both cognitive and emotional power, reassuring consumers of safety and classifying areas of 'strength' and 'weakness'. However, a further irony is how we are invited to place total trust in the agencies and auditors, many of whom are drawn from the profession on trial in the first place.

The compilers and executors of taxonomies of effectiveness are left unquestioned. They are trusted, but the audited are not. A senior lecturer comments on the delicate balance between accountability and trust:

> Well I actually think that there is a little issue, which is called overkill . . . I actually think that accountability is a two-way process and there

is also a very old-fashioned word called trust. And I think that you have to have, if you like, a synthesis between accountability and trust, and without a balance between those you run the risk of . . . this utter focus on performativity, at the expense of what's really going on at a ground level.

When there is a mismatch between the tasks that workers have to perform and the management systems that they have to accommodate, distrust can proliferate (Kramer and Tyler, 1996). The emphasis on performance and performativity paradoxically reduces trust, as nothing can be construed as authentic.

Performativity and the power of discourse

Performativity involves a damaging process of ventriloquism and impersonation as academics and managers attempt to represent themselves in a language that quality assessors will understand and value. Producing the right kind of optimistic and promotional self-description in mission statements, vision statements and self-assessment documents incorporates self-subversion and ritualistic recitation and reproduction. It implies a lack of ideological control over the task. Womack (1999) observes that the language of authority works not only by what it says to us, but also by what it induces us to say. The text-producers in quality assurance, according to Cameron (2001) are not just passive recipients of other people's propaganda, but have been induced to create their own. Oswald (2001: 15) reminisces that 'When I was a young lecturer, universities were the one place in the country where you could not bluster your way through life. Hype was useless; content was everything'.

The (hyped) text is complicit in the reproduction of quality norms. The slow subjection of individuals involved in quality assurance takes place via language and the authoritative power of text. Organizations are compelled to repeat the norms of quality assurance in all its documentation. Failure to reinstate the norm in the right way opens up the possibility of sanctions. Hence considerable effort is invested in the preparation of documentation, codes of practice and textual representation as a principal lecturer in a university college explains:

> So everything from the codes of practice impacting on the revision or the validation, or re-validation of programmes, through to the way we work with collaborative partners, through to the way we work at distance or overseas, the way we organize placements, the way we accredit and train staff. I mean those codes of practice seem to have spread tentacle like into all sorts of areas of work. What they've meant operationally has been a proliferation of paper, confusion, more paper, a bit of clarification, maybe yet more paper. But it's led to a sub-industry, I suspect, in most institutions, where the institutional people are trying

to clarify what they mean, and then tried to clarify with others what they mean. So it's led to an enormous amount of people pondering and working out what it means for the institution. And then an awful lot of work with people at kind of ground level, trying to put that into operation.

Codification of practices have increased workloads for administrative and academic staff as a registrar indicates:

The first thing to say, I suppose, is what anyone who's been in higher education for a while would say that ten/twelve years ago, there really was none of the work and procedures and scrutiny in the area of quality assurance which we now have with us. So, from that point of view, for a large number of people both non-academic and academics, there's been a whole new area opened up. And it's not only been opened up; it's also brought work with it . . . it has been helpful because it's enabled us to codify, formalize, get down on paper, document a large number of procedures which hitherto operated sometimes formally sometimes a lot less than formally and really did need formalization. And although there is an argument that says that some of that has gone too far.

Academics have to operate without and within the quality discourse (Henkel, 2000). Being watched makes them watchful. This liminal position, according to Butler (1994: 38) should be where resistance and recuperation happen'. Yet this does not always occur in relation to quality. Continuous improvement is linked to what Pels (2000: 136) describes as a liberal constitution of the self. This is 'a schizoid modern self that is both the object of improvement and the subject that does the improving'. Academics have to move between the objectified and the objectifier. Womack (1999: 5) argues that being the assessed and the assessor at the same time means that 'we assert our self but also act out the role of the other; we speak as the child seeking approval but imitate the booming voice of the father who may bestow or withold it. In short, our prose keeps stumbling because it is schizophrenic'. Gewirtz *et al.* (1995) names the process of educationalists negotiating two or more sets of values and cultures as 'bilingualism'. Different linguistic codes are invoked in appropriate contexts to represent different values and priorities. However, performance and ventriloquism can create cognitive dissonance and alienation.

Giddens (1990: 6) recognizes that modern institutions 'hold out the possibility of emancipation but at the same time create mechanisms of suppression, rather than actualization, of self'. The proliferation of critical literature on quality from across the globe suggests that some spaces have been opened up for a certain type of democratic contestation. However, the protests remain largely at the level of text, for example angry letters and articles in the public press and memoranda to the QAA. Direct action to resist the quality industry carries too many financial penalties. Current funding arrangements operate to suppress critical engagement. Cameron (2001: 103) points out how the system of representing one's organization in glowing terms in self-assessment documents for example, is a convenient one for the government which underfunds Britain's public institutions. She argues that institutions can be relied on 'to produce, apparently of their own free will and in their own words, an endless flow of discourse in which their services are represented as excellent and constantly improving; where problems are trivial (and always already in the process of being solved), and where catastrophic failures are non-existent'. Academics are being forced to create their own propaganda to promote the practices that many of them criticize.

Performativity is linked to discourse. Fraser (1997) suggests that the conception of discourse can illuminate how the cultural hegemony of dominant groups in society is secured and contested. Hegemony is the discursive face of power. Fraser also argues (1997: 160) that discourses are 'historically specific, socially situated, signifying practices'. She sees them as 'communicative frames in which speakers interact by exchanging speech acts'. Discourse frames practice and the way in which practice is discussed and conceptualized. Dominelli and Hoogvelt (1996: 84) suggest that it is through discourse and practice that 'the individual and the group gradually become drawn into a new world of lived experience that gradually detaches them from their own critical consciousness, ideology or value commitments'. The quality discourse is engulfing professional consciousness and dominating organizational priorities. Butler (2000: 108) claims that 'If the power of discourse to produce that which it names is linked with the question of performativity, then the performative is one domain in which power acts as discourse'.

Lyotard (1984) argued that universities are structured around bounded discourses including disciplines, faculties, and professorial authority. New managerialism has reinforced performance discourses. Staff have performance reviews, individuals and departments are required to have performance targets, there is talk of introducing performance-related pay in universities, as in the schools sector (Shore and Selwyn, 1998). Lyotard (cited in Dhillon and Standish, 2000) points out that one of the dangers of performativity is that any new moves that are made, anything that looks like becoming critical, can be encompassed and assimilated. As with any powerful metanarrative asserting 'truths', other 'truths' are silenced and excluded from the quality discourse. A faculty manager describes this process in action:

> . . . a university would have to be composed of fools to expose a known problem to that quality assurance process. You know you can always send your bad boy [*sic*] on holiday for a week,

The imperative to perform and conform is antithetical to the expansionist culture of the 1960s higher education system in Britain. Between 1963 and 1973, there was an increase in full-time tenured academic staff from 16,881 to 26,429. Dominelli and Hoogvelt (1996: 72) argue that the expansion 'provided a home for intellectuals critical of society looking for alternative visions'. They identify two categories of intellectuals:

> . . . the professional bureaucratic/technocratic intellectuals or 'hegemonic' organic intellectuals who serviced the welfare state and endorsed the Establishment in its activities; and the critical thinkers or 'counter-hegemonic' organic intellectuals who organized around welfare issues and demanded changes in welfare state structures, including the delivery of personal social services, as well as more radical changes in the allocation of power and distribution of resources in society.

New managerialism has demanded that all academics display characteristics of the 'hegemonic' rather than counter-hegemonic intellectuals. Any analysis of power and power relations has to be suspended while performing technocracy. When the ratio of inner beliefs to public presentation changes dramatically, this can produce feelings of being duplicitous and inauthentic.

Performativity is not fun, as in playfulness. It is not a way to find expression, but to repress it. Ball (2000) sees performativity as a technology, a culture and a mode of regulation through which power operates. Performances act as measures of productivity or displays of quality. In the context of quality assurance, performativity is the reverse of carnival. The subversive value of representation is questionable. It is the period of dis-licence in which every utterance must be carefully censored. My informants told me how they were warned that careless talk costs lives and that in the panoptic ethos of quality assessment, there is no such thing as an off-the-cuff remark. Referring to teaching quality assessment, Shore and Selwyn (1998: 162) observe:

> . . . we find ourselves in educational spaces which have become theatres: where classrooms become 'stages', teachers and students 'actors' (performing to a script imposed upon them by government), and where inspectors, journalists and 'market forces' act as audience and critics.

An assistant registrar in an old university argues that the emphasis on stage management only has temporary benefits:

> . . . it creates a kind of hot house atmosphere in which everybody is on the same side, but I think it is a fairly short lived sort of fact. It concentrates peoples' minds for a short period, but you don't always get permanent benefits from the kind of work people do for subject review. Because, it tends to be creating a kind of stage-managed situation.

Goffman's theory of dramaturgical compliance (for example, 1972) suggests that the theatricality involved in performance can serve to protect and distance actors from the corrosive effects of alien bureaucratic requirements. They employ role distance in order to reintroduce a sense of personal autonomy (Case *et al.*, 2000). In his study of quality procedures in New Zealand's higher education sector, Barrow (1999: 34) notes how staff aim to present themselves in a positive light in ways appropriate to the particular role and setting. A question arises as to whether there is a fundamental injustice involved in requiring professionals to represent themselves in terms and roles that are alien. However, this can also be seen as academia's coming of age. An assistant registrar in an old university describes performativity as a type of loss of innocence, as students and teachers are interpellated in quality discourses that are scrutinized by third parties:

> But I do think there's a negative long-term implication, which is that the activity of quality assurance, particularly at departmental level will no longer be innocent . . . I mean that people will not treat it in its own terms as an interaction between themselves as teachers and their students. There will always be external third parties lurking in the background. . . . The performative ritual will change.

A philosophy lecturer describes how performativity imposes compulsory disciplinary regimes:

> . . . in a department of seven we managed to have something like four separate sub-committees. And on the students as well, so for example now we have to take registers at lectures and seminars, and we have to follow those up. And then you get to the end of the process, and while you're doing it, you're doing it with an eye to the SPR, you know we have to do this because if we don't do it then we'll lose a mark. So we introduce all sorts of regimes on ourselves, get to the end of it, get our full marks, and in fact recognize that all we've done is introduce regimes that we don't agree with, and have killed ourselves to do, and to what end, it hasn't, and we knew it wouldn't. I mean we knew it wouldn't increase the quality of, enhance the quality of teaching.

A professor and director of staff development in a new university says that performativity involves internal imitation of external procedures:

> . . . we've almost generated a mirror image, internally, of some external procedures, just because there is felt to be some virtue in imitating the external procedures, apart from anything else, so that we are practised when the QAA arrive.

Ludic imagery was highly visible in my study. An assistant registrar at an old university notes:

> In terms of subject review . . . we felt people were simply playing a game, and there was a degree of artificiality about it which was unhelpful.

A senior lecturer comments on the precariousness of the game:

> The QAA' s quality assurance is a matter of playing the game. . . . And if you don't quite know the rules of the game you then make

mistakes. . . . In terms of teaching, only in the last two or three years have they actually woken up to how to play the game . . . and sometimes you're lucky with the game so you get a weak referee, sometimes you get a nasty referee and you get sent off.

Another noticeable feature of my empirical and textual research was how often literary metaphors, allegories, symbols and genres are used to describe the affective impact of quality assurance regimes: the theatre of the absurd, Greek mythology, surrealism, farce, Orwellian dystopia, Kafkaesque trials, comedies of manners, were recurring images. This could be a display of cultural capital, or a sense that quality processes are fictive. The recourse to 'culture' can be a resistance to the discourse of utilitarianism. It is also as if a code is needed that is drawn from a recognizable cultural form. This can both symbolize and provide some degree of emotional distance. Lawson (1998) compares academics to Odysseus strapped to the mast forced to listen to the song of the Sirens. Intellectual desires are suppressed and frustrated by the entrapment of bureaucracy. The trend to use literature to capture and summarize feelings is reflected in the title of an edited collection about the impact of inspection on teachers using the title of J.B. Priestley's play *An Inspector Calls* (Priestley, 1965; Cullingford, 1999). Often, Eastern European literature famous for its exposition of totalitarianism and mindless bureaucracy is cited. Johnson (1994: 379) invokes Kafka:

> It no longer really matters how well an academic teaches and whether or not he or she sometimes inspires their pupils; it is far more important that they have produced plans for their courses, bibliographies, outlines of this, that and the other, in short all the paraphernalia of futile bureaucratization required for assessors who come from on high like emissaries from Kafka's castle.

The message being that there is menace, authoritarianism and the imperative to follow rules that are constantly in flux. A senior lecturer also evokes Kafka to communicate mystification and the necessity of conforming to arbitrary rules and regulations:

> I mean I felt, all during the process, like it was a Kafkaesque experience. . . . Well I mean you're sort of in this new language, you're caught up in a new discourse . . . and I can't remember all of the different acronyms. I've probably blanked it out, tried to jettison it from my subconscious. But we all spoke the language, and we all did the dance, and we all jerked the jerks.

Oswald (2001: 15) also jokes that as a result of the totalization of QA in higher education 'Joseph Stalin must be dancing a jig – if in a pleasingly confined space'. Performativity involves presenting a vision of purity, with a connection between signs and meanings. However, there are questions about the location of the unrepresentable, such as the affective domain and the hidden curriculum.

Job satisfaction:
alienation and 'counterfeit' reflexivity

The audit culture can appear to promote discursive space for reflection on practice, but when it is so highly performative, this can produce a 'counterfeit reflection' (Clegg, 1999: 177). It is questionable whether there is any ontologically intact reflexivity; any reflexivity that is not itself culturally constructed (Fraser, 1997). Reflexivity can also be a type of 'self-beratement' (Butler, 1997a: 67) or 'benign introspection' (Woolgar, 1988). For quality assurance, reflexivity is prescribed and circumscribed by external agents. It allows very little theoretical departure or development. It can be another example of capillary power, with academics policing themselves and others in the service of quality assurance. This can result in an alienation that leads to disaffection. De Groot (1997: 134) characterized academic work in the 1990s in terms of three themes: 'alienation, anxiety and accountability'. By alienation she means 'the growing sense of separation between work and personal identity experienced by many academics and to the experience of loss of control or even influence over many aspects of teaching, learning and research' (De Groot, 1997: 134).

Ball (2000) argues that alienation is a result of inauthentic practices and relationships. Caught between the state, employers, the market, industry, student/consumers and the wider economic concepts of globalization, employability, international competitiveness, universities and academics in Britain are struggling with a hybrid identity that can be demoralizing and confusing. Hatcher (1998: i) notes how self-regulation is now the dominant mode of authority in the production of managers. She argues that responsibilization techniques become 'both a leverage for change as well as a closure on what it is possible to become' (1998: 382). A faculty manager in an old university describes reflective practice, as 'navel gazing', that is unproductive introspection. He attributes this to lack of clarity from the auditors, rather than to a process of development and innovation:

> My perception then, of my university is that we were concerned about the preparations for subject review as was. I think that I perceived that there was very much a lack of clarity, definition, at national level, of the expectations of that process. . . . There was a lot of thrashing around and debate in the university, as to the meaning, the purpose of the subject review. And we did an awful lot of naval gazing.

This comment suggests that a lot of time is consumed decoding and that there is limited opportunity to interpret. One explanation can be that there is only ever a partial explanation of the organizing principles of quality assurance. Another view, argued by McWilliam *et al.* (1999: 61) is that the precise means of acquiring the identity of effective academic or academic manager is 'not an open question, but is framed within the dominant rationality for constituting best practice'. The combination of being constrained and partially informed has an impact on morale and job satisfaction.

Job satisfaction is one of the single most extensively researched topics in the field of organizational psychology (Oshagbemi, 1996). An early application of Herzberg *et al.*'s (1959) theory of job satisfaction and motivation to the academic profession (Hill, 1986) found that principal contributors to job dissatisfaction related to factors extrinsic to the actual job. Reports have shifted their emphasis over the years as policies and priorities have changed. However, as far back as 1983, morale was reported to be low (Williams and Blackstone, 1983: 68). Job satisfaction can be socially constructed via performance indicators or what is valued and rewarded in the academy. For example, later studies, such as Henkel (2000), note how important research is to academic job satisfaction and self-image. The 1992 Carnegie study revealed that while academics felt that their field was creative, their profession's respect was declining and its influence insubstantial (Fulton, 1996; Baron, 2000). A report in the THES (1999) indicated that only 275 academic staff are earning over £100,000 a year. Only 12 universities had 10 or more staff earning over £100,000.

Increasingly, job dissatisfaction relates to lower-order preoccupations including fear of job loss and rates of pay. Lacy and Sheehan's study (1997) found that the two central causes of job dissatisfaction in eight different countries related to opportunities for promotion and the way in which the institution was managed. They also discovered that male academics tended to be more satisfied than females with most aspects of their job. Oshagbemi's studies (1988, 1996) found that administrative responsibilities contributed to job dissatisfaction as they were not seen as primary functions or core obligations and that competence in administration and management contributes little to promotion prospects. The notion that quality assessment decreases enjoyment and job satisfaction was corroborated by a senior lecturer in an old university:

> Subject review has taken up an enormous amount of my time. . . . It's changed the nature of my job and well, to how much I enjoy it . . . I worked for a hundred-and-twenty hours in the week before subject review.

A survey carried out with 2322 academics in Britain in 1969 (Williams and Blackstone, 1974) found that while most staff were critical of the low salaries in university teaching, they felt compensated by the opportunities to organize their working methods. However, this was a period following expansion and prosperity in Britain. These findings are in stark contrast with more recent research in which 'morale is widely agreed to be low' (Fulton, 1996: 393). Features contributing to the fall in morale tend to be pay, job security, employment conditions, increased workload and bureaucratization and loss of autonomy. Kemp *et al.* (1996: 64) note that 'probably no other "professional" group . . . in either the public or private sectors, has fallen faster or further in terms of pay and social status than have academics in the past fifteen years'.

The Sheehan and Walsh survey (1996) also noted dissatisfaction with government interference in academic policies, with Korea at the top, followed by Australia. Academics in Germany, the UK and Hong Kong also cited poor information flows in their organizations and they felt that they possessed little knowledge or influence in their organizations. McInnis (2000) reports how a 1999 survey of 2609 academics from 15 Australian universities reported the overall satisfaction with the job dropped from 67 per cent to 51 per cent since 1993. Fifty-five per cent believed that their hours had substantially increased over the last five years. A senior lecturer attributes this to the shift in importance of teaching:

> Like most academics I became an academic out of interest, in my sub-
> ject rather than really an interest in teaching, and I know very few aca-
> demics who really became an academic because they were interested
> in teaching.

Scott (2000: 5) notes how universities themselves 'can be regarded as classic "Fordist" institutions still preoccupied with the large-scale produc-tion of public service, professional and business elites. Despite three dec-ades or more of massification', quality procedures, with the imperative for academics to act managerially, enforce a form of multiskilling and flexibility more associated with post-Fordist employment regimes. Hence a major ten-sion is created, as quality discourses focus on universities purely as educa-tional institutions and ignore the fact that they are workplaces too.

Unhealthy organizations and occupational stress

Concerns about stress have begun to enter the academic profession (Fisher, 1994). An AUT (1998) survey reported that two-thirds of respondents found their work stressful, and one-quarter had recently taken stress-related sick leave. The discourse of occupational stress can serve to expose the human costs of new employment regimes. It can also medicalize or personalize complex political and organizational pressures. To inscribe oneself in the narrative of occupational stress can sometimes result in the acquisition of a spoiled identity (Goffman, 1968). Hence, there is additional pressure to disguise the effects of pressure. Fast capitalism is requiring more of people and creating an unhealthy imbalance between work and life (Knight and Trowler, 2000). Negotiating new identities, coping with multiskilling and changing employment regimes are having an impact throughout the public services in Britain. The quality discourse is not being applied to employ-ment conditions. Professionals are expected to mine their resources to be increasingly creative, supportive and managerial. Using a different meta-phor to discuss the findings of her Australian study, Adams (2000: 69) suggests that 'the gap between resources and responsibilities gives a mess-age to academics that they are being used as "human putty" to plug the holes of the unravelling university system . . .'. These holes often get exposed in quality assessments and this is when the 'human putty' can be most damaged. Shore and Wright (2000) go further and assert that stress is not a byproduct, but an intended outcome and that quality assessment is meant to be stressful.

The mind, body and emotions are punished by the regulatory processes, rather than by direct violence. Rituals of conformity carry a cost. Informants in my study frequently commented on the disabling effects of the stress induced by quality assessments. Stress was referred to in relation to increased workload and bureaucratization, fear, panic and a range of emotions connected with assessment and the negotiation of competing demands. Lack of opportunities to de-brief and articulate the feelings were also cited as constituent factors. Stress was perceived to affect personal and professional relationships, physical and emotional health, creativity, identity and productivity.

Quality assessment should become a health and safety issue in the workplace. Basic human resource management approaches do not seem to have been applied to quality assurance. Employees are not being adequately protected and employers' duties of care are being overridden by the demands of quality assessments. The failure to factor in the costs of stress on academic providers is a major managerial and policy oversight. New managerialism is supposed to be concerned with cost-effectiveness, yet occupational stress is not cost effective. In Britain, the Health and Safety Executive (1998: 13) noted that 'stress, depression or anxiety' is the second highest cause of reported illness (after musculoskeletal disorders). In the UK, it is estimated that 270,000 people are absent from work with stress each working day (Troman, 2000). The annual cost of stress to the Education Service in Britain in 1998 was estimated at £230 million (Brown and Ralph, 1998). Whereas stress has become a pervasive feature of contemporary life, there seems to be some correlation between high stress levels and high levels of regulation. There is also a distorted belief that increasing workload leads to enhanced efficiency. More quality procedures are seen to equate with increased quality of services. For example, Lafferty and Fleming (2000) reported that, in the Australian Workplace Industrial Relations Survey, 35 per cent of educational professionals reported high work intensification and stress, compared to 28 per cent for all workplaces.

Research into schoolteacher stress in Britain is linking teacher stress with the wholesale restructuring of national education systems that began in the 1980s. The impact of inspections on the school sector is well-documented (Wilcox and Gray, 1994; Dean, 1995; Brimblecombe *et al.*, 1996; Travers and Cooper, 1996; Case *et al.*, 2000; Troman, 2000). Nias (1996) discovered that stress could be exacerbated when teachers are asked to compromise their values. Travers and Cooper (1996) identified ten main factors contributing to teacher stress and these included performance monitoring and lack of participation in decision making. Case *et al.* (2000: 617) note the irony that 'The fatigue produced by preparing for inspection actually reduces teaching effectiveness for a significant period following the inspection visit'. The school sector in Britain has been subjected to highly structured quality assurance interventions for a little longer than universities. Hence, it might be possible to learn something from the current teacher recruitment and retention crisis in Britain's schools.

An assistant registrar in an old university felt that the failure to acknow-ledge the extent and impact of stress was irresponsible and insensitive on the part of the Quality Assurance Agency. Academics are framed as servants whose views and needs do not need to be taken into account. The construc-tion of academics as mere factors of production and the punitive approach to audit overlooked the fact that those being punished and disabled are the same group that has to deliver a quality service:

> I do think that the issue of occupational stress, the levels of anxiety that have been induced, has been absolutely enormous. I don't think the QAA has taken this properly on board . . . I think the stress falls critically upon certain key officers, within an institution, within a department, and by officers. . . . This is a kind of opening up that most academic staff have not been exposed to, have found themselves threatened by it, whether rightly, or wrongly, and I think the QAA has actually been irresponsible, I think I will go that far, in not seeking to take account of this. . . . And I don't think the QAA has been sufficiently sensitized to the impact its work has within institutions. I'd actually take this a stage further. [The former head of the QAA] positively had a belief that institutions were there to be done to, almost adversarialist. . . . It's very striking, he never regarded them as stakeholders in higher education, they were providers.

Audit is constructed as some sort of virility test, with unhealthy practices embedded in the process. An assistant registrar cited an example from subject review:

> One of the most outrageous nights we had in a review last year, was the review chair saying at the start of the visit, 'Our team will be working sixteen hour days and we expect you to do so too.' Now that is an absolutely outrageous thing for an external to do also.

In her study of stress in academic life, Fisher (1994) found that stress was related to loss of personal professional control and the feeling that de-mands outweigh capacity. Fear of non-coping coupled with the impossibility of coping leads to frustration, shame and a sense of utter powerlessness. Stress operates at all stages of quality assessment – before, during and after. All my informants mentioned stress to varying degrees. For example, one lecturer used the word 15 times in a half-hour interview. A professor in an old university reports how the stress involved in the preparations wore people down before the actual stress of the visit. Furthermore, it was impos-sible to predict just how stressful the visit would be:

> I mean it's not just the week, it's the build up to it . . . I mean I thought the week would be bad, but the week was far worse than I ever ima-gined, and an experience I would not like to live through again.

Fear relates to the panoptic and prolonged nature of quality assessment in which nobody ever seems to know what might be demanded, or whose teaching will be observed:

> The real pressure, I think, was the feeling of being in an exam situation, which extended, seemingly, forever, with no sense of the content of the exam, and no real way to revise for it. And academics are rather prone to over-preparation anyway, otherwise we wouldn't be here. So there was . . . it was like doing your finals but for nine months.

This observation captures Bourdieu's (1998) view that precariousness is everywhere today. There is a political economy of uncertainty as everyone is potentially replaceable and every education provision has a limited shelf life. This is supposed to foster productivity and innovation, as adrenaline-charged academics fight for their survival via new programmes, contracts, services and modes of delivery. The quality assessment process itself is precarious as nobody can predict how it will unravel. Informants had various reports of the actual subject review. A principal lecturer outlines the damaging effects of preparing for quality assessments:

> I mean every group that's prepared for a QAA review here has suffered. The quality of their teaching will have suffered, the quality of the research . . . if you have people here doing things at all hours, and at weekends, and at evenings. Then they're not seeing the kids, and they're not seeing their families, and they're not going out and playing golf, or whatever it is they do. I mean people, you see people losing weight, you see people getting whiter.

A philosophy lecturer in an old university noted the deleterious effects of stress on support systems and relationships outside the academy in the build up to audit:

> This is in the build up to it, this is the sort of four, five, six weeks build up, when you're writing lists all the time of things that you haven't done and things that you've got to do. And relationships suffer. You know there is no way of keeping or maintaining any sort of family life while that's going on, because you don't have anything to give anyone.

An academic registrar in a new university comments that the allocation of scores and points was a major factor in stress induction:

> But of course I mean they (the academics) themselves are getting desperately stressed about the situation and building up for this review. And, of course, academics take the whole thing incredibly seriously. I mean, you know, they're very into what points they get and all of that.

This observation seems to imply that it is academic competitiveness and dispositions rather than external demands that create pressure. This view is also held by Floud (2001) who believes that academic stress is self-induced as academics compete for league table points. Floud's explanation is victim blaming and does not take into account the complex interrelationships between self and society, and the extent to which emotions, attitudes and dispositions can be socially and politically constructed and manipulated. For example, Giddens (1990, 1991) explored the dialectical relationship between the individual and the globalization of capital, information and human relationships. He sees recursive links between changes in society and individual dispositions. In the structures/agency framework, anxiety and dread can be byproducts of a high-risk, low trust society (Case *et al.*, 2000).

The head of the academic standards and support unit in an old university offers a practical explanation. She comments that one of the reasons why the preparations for subject review were so stressful was that they were in addition to everyday responsibilities:

> Well I mean preparing for subject review and any form of external audit is always painful for people, because it's not like the rest of their work stops while they're supposed to be doing this. So you do see people looking dreadfully tired, and being completely stressed out, especially in the couple of weeks beforehand. That is very stressful.

Some of my informants seemed to feel guilty about feeling the stress. This left them feeling isolated and panic-stricken. If they prioritized preparations for quality assessment, they felt a sense of failure in their other responsibilities. A senior lecturer describes the pressures of split focusing before subject review:

> I got incredibly stressed through it. I found that I couldn't sleep. I found that I was panicking because we were told that we really couldn't afford to do badly, that it was critical for us that we were going to be 21 or above, and I knew that we had a lot of gaps. We had incredible gaps. Some of my colleagues had no paperwork for courses they were teaching. And it uncovered a lot of holes . . . I didn't do any research. I just didn't do any . . . the pressure grew and I have to say that I was drinking too much, you know as a strategy to cope. I would sort of go home and think 'Oh God I can't handle it' and drink a bottle of wine, and feel very ill the next morning, but still have to talk to staff. I did no research . . . I got so behind . . . I feel ashamed saying that I was drinking a lot in that week and the weeks before . . . I mean I might have over-reacted but you felt caught up in a dreadful, dreadful experience, and it eats at you, it eats at you.

This exemplifies how the responsibilization process works and the myriad feelings that are activated in the service of quality, for example panic and fear. This informant attempted to alleviate the stress by drinking which instead of numbing feelings produced additional feelings of guilt and shame. Shame is particularly disempowering as it internalizes rather than externalizes the anger (Acker, 1996). The informant also uses the image of being 'eaten'. This is reminiscent of Newton's (2000) metaphor of quality as a 'hungry beast' that consumes and devours in an insatiable desire for documentation, information etc. In this case, the informant felt that she herself was being 'eaten at'. R.D. Laing used this image long ago (Laing, 1965) when he theorized that ontological threats could be categorized in terms of three processes – engulfment, penetration or petrification. Colloquially speaking this means being smothered or eaten, cut or invaded or frozen into immobility. Informants in my study cited all three types of threat. For example, the language that many of my informants used was evocative of narratives of violence. Terms such as 'abusive', 'violation'; 'bullying' were frequently invoked to describe the sense of invasion. Invasion is used to describe the entry of outsiders into the workplace, and also in the sense of disruption. A professor comments:

> I mean the trouble is it's, you know, it's so invasive in a sense, that activity stops you know four weeks before hand, as the paperwork is put together.

The recent QAA consultation document on its new methodology of institutional audit contains power-laden imagery (QAA, 2001). For example, the penetrative geological metaphor of 'drilling down' is repeatedly used to describe the audit process. The Quality Assurance Agency also uses the terms 'light touch' and 'heavy touch', implying an invasion of body space to a greater or lesser degree. Perhaps the academy needs a 'Just Say No' campaign to reinstate boundaries!

A director of academic affairs at a new university believes that the stress was induced by the urgency and speed required for responses to information requests from subject review teams during the visit:

> I think the stressful nature is that the whole period is compressed into three or four days. There's a lot of emphasis on producing written evidence, and finding bits of written evidence . . . everybody's trying to do a job in a very short period of time, and the result is that people, you know. . . . It's a bit like an outward-bound management course. You know everything is done at a 150 miles an hour, and that simply creates a sort of pressure that people get when they get tired.

This observation about who determines the pace of events is evocative of Bauman's observation (2001a: 35) that the 'new hierarchy of power is marked at the top by the ability to move fast and at short notice, and at the bottom by the inability to slow down these moves'.

The director of academic affairs at a new university notes that existing management styles in the institution also played an important role in inducing or relieving stress:

> Of course in some institutions where the senior management have a punitive view to what they will do if people get low scores, it puts pressure on senior members of departments, which has caused, you know, people to be seriously stressed, and you know in some cases in extreme ways.

The extreme ways in which stress is experienced are often concealed from the assessors. A head of a quality assurance unit in a new university comments on how the performance appears polished, while considerable human misery is unfolding behind the scenes:

> Now to me the major disadvantage is the load that it puts upon people, in terms of stress. I mean I've seen people have breakdowns. I've seen people collapse into tears, I've seen people walk out – blah-de-blah. Not during a review, I understand, because everything is always all right for a review, it's all the fall out either side.

The industrialization of higher education means that the product, the production plant and its workers must exhibit near-zero defect properties. Stress is a defect that has to be concealed for quality audits. However, the 'fall-out' was something that preoccupied several informants. An assistant registrar comments on the physical and professional aftermath. It was almost as if people were in shock after an accident or some other form of trauma, even when the result had been favourable:

> A department . . . which did unexpectedly well . . . the fall out damage – for a period of about four weeks afterwards they felt like they . . . had some sort of serious illness, and they weren't providing a proper level of service to their students, and they were conscious of this, but they were just too exhausted.

Some informants commented on the fact that quality assessment represented a type of personal and organizational trauma. However, there were limited opportunities for closure and debriefing. Individuals were left to find their own support mechanisms to carry them through the period immediately after the inspection. While there were often ritualistic celebrations, and congratulations, these were often felt to be inauthentic as they were performed on top of a lot of pain, anger, exhaustion and disappointment. A philosophy lecturer explains that the exhaustion and demotivation following subject review related to the feeling that it had all been a useless exercise, performed solely for extrinsic reasons:

> De-motivation, straight after it. We got a 24 out of 24, and the next day all of us felt as though we'd been cheated. . . . Even if you come out with top score, at that point you recognize it has nothing to do with you, and you've been thoroughly exploited, and the impact of that, in terms of how you once viewed your sort of autonomous working conditions is almost irretrievable . . . we performed to our absolute optimum, and achieved, we achieved nothing for ourselves, and really nothing for the department, you end up recognizing that the score is really meaningless, that you've knocked yourself out for nine months, possibly longer, and to what end. And then at the point you ask 'to what end?' then you loose faith in all the management processes. . . . Well I think people don't get enough opportunity to talk about how it does

impact on them, a lot of them, they talk about the task rather than how it feels being made to do it.

The emphasis in the academy is business as usual. Hence a conspiracy of silence follows, with limited opportunities for individuals and groups to share experiences. A senior lecturer in education comments:

> It's a bit like you've had constipation for three weeks and Dynorod's come round and cleared you out, that's how it feels, sorry to be so crude but that's what it's like. It's a massive relief that it's all over and we've survived to tell the tale. And then it was like it had never happened, because for a lot of people it hadn't, and it was like 'Right, back on with it', you know, on with the teaching and end of term and that's it . . . you know we sort of almost needed to be de-briefed, and there was nothing happening, it had gone.

Here quality audit is decribed as an excremental function! But the evacuation process leaves academics and administrators so drained that they cannot mobilize in the form of caucusing, de-briefing or campaigning against it. A principal lecturer describes the aftermath of subject review:

> Well first of all it's made me absolutely shattered . . . it made me feel very drained. I'm still feeling drained now, and a lot of colleagues have said how tired they felt the week after, and it's very difficult to actually get re-motivated once, and prepare decent lessons once it was over. You know this was sort of the pinnacle that we'd been working towards for so long, and after it was over you felt very flat. . . . But it was, in some respects, quite difficult to feign energy into the lessons the week after, although we all tried.

Work intensification based on uninspiring activities can lead to professional burnout. Power (1994: 42) notes that anxiety and insecurity can destroy professional commitment and loyalty 'to such an extent that this may undermine performance'. Many informants commented how this piece of research itself was the first time that anybody had asked them about their feelings and views on the experience of quality audits. A senior lecturer describes how resistance is stifled by exhaustion and patriarchal power relations:

> Because what happens is it gets done to you, you get surveyed, the gaze is on you, and when it's passed, it's a bit like an evil warlord, and it is masculine, and the evil warlord's gaze – it's only one directional, and it spots on you and then it moves off, and you're just so grateful it's not there any more, and you've been drained of energy so the capacity to band together and fight is very, very difficult.

Many of these accounts discursively locate quality audits as a form of bullying, or a force that presses on the subject from the outside. However, power can form the subject as well. Weakened by the effects of externally imposed power, individuals can internalize or accept its terms (Butler, 1997a). Regimes of power can be identified by their effects on bodies. The body is a political field. Corporeal vulnerability such as illness, insomnia, exhaustion were frequently mentioned in this study. A pro-vice chancellor outlines how a professor in her university had to ignore the state of her body in order to complete preparations for subject review:

> She'd just come back from America on a research trip that she had there . . . she came back to the country and went to the doctor because she'd picked up something . . . and the doctor said '. . . you've got bronchitis. You need two week's rest and I'm prescribing that for you.' She came back in to the institution on the Monday, or whatever, to the boxes that she had to complete, and she had not been able to take that time out because she knows that if she does the bits of the boxes that she's responsible for, these are of course these aspects and module boxes, she will not be able to complete it in time, and that's letting her colleagues in the department down. So she is in at the moment, despite doctor's orders . . . it's her health that she's putting on the line.

Disavowal of the body and self-mortification are required because the demands are non-negotiable. They invade every aspect of one's life, as a reader in social policy in an old university notes:

> Well in terms of what it's done to me, I mean I'm certainly not sleeping very well, sort of waking up in the early hours of the morning with a notepad next to my bed, and writing down all the things that I've forgotten to do that day, or haven't done, or thought 'Oh did I do that or not?' It's sort of a case of, I know the work is always with you anyway but, but now it's all, it seems to be more so.

A philosophy lecturer in an old university also observes the impact of stress on the emotions:

> Well, one of my colleagues was finding that she was going into the supermarket and just sort of crying, she didn't therefore want to go out.

A professor and head of department of economics in an old university comments on what he perceived as the connection between the stress and increased illness:

> I mean there are the mental costs and the stress. I mean we had one guy who was rushed to hospital on the Wednesday night, and everybody thought he'd had a heart attack . . . I'm sure the actual stress of the week didn't help.

A lecturer in Spanish also comments on the negative impact on health:

> The thing that particularly stands out in my mind . . . was the head of school having a suspected heart attack during the period of audit, and another senior member of staff having one shortly after. And casting

my mind back for more than six years now, what stands out in my mind is the negative impact on the health of members of staff.

A director of quality and learning support in a college of higher education believes that the human costs of inspection and audit need to be given more attention:

> I don't think anybody looks forward to subject review . . . there is a human cost to all this of course, you know the personal anxieties that people suffer going through these scrutinies, it's not inconsiderable I think. The same actually applies to RAE, the pressures on staff to produce publications is quite considerable, and there are personal problems that can result from that process. . . . It's just the excessive amount of work associated with it all that gets people down I think.

However, some organizational members are better able to protect themselves against stress than others. Quality assessment appears to have reproduced divisions of labour in so far as those who are conscientious are more susceptible to increased stress, as an assistant registrar observes:

> There is a view that the stress is caused by people being galvanized into action who were previously dysfunctional – it's a good form of motivation. Whereas in fact, for many cases, it is extra pressure on those who are already galvanized . . . and some can stay inert, if that is the right chemical metaphor.

It appears that there is a basic conflict between the needs of the organization and state system and those of the individual and collective workers. The latter tend to lose out to the former.

Naming and shaming: post-modern torture

Quality assurance is a form of assessment and it has long been argued that there is a powerful affective impact of assessment in so far as it influences confidence, self-esteem and identity (Broadfoot, 1998). Assessment also translates dominant discourses into broad social understandings and specific practices (Bernstein, 1996). New organizational regimes demand considerable temporal investment and emotional labour. Emotions are becoming increasingly important in the quest for excellence and best practice. Quality procedures require the activation and exploitation of a range of feelings such as guilt, loyalty, desire, greed, pride, anxiety, shame and responsibilization, in the service of effectiveness and point-scoring (Ozga and Walker, 1999). These feelings are easily activated and manipulated in today's fear-laden academic culture. The desire to survive is an exploitable desire. 'The one who holds out the promise of continued existence plays to the desire to survive' (Butler, 1997a: 7). Top–down bureaucratic requirements seem to be serving disciplinary functions. One explanation for the lack of resistance to change and the culture of compliance is the idea expressed by Trow

(1996) that academics experienced a 'vague sense of guilt' about the short-comings of the old system. Bad conscience is cultivated in order to legitim-ate the punitive impact of regulation. Insecurities, according to Prichard (2000) underwrite receptiveness to new regimes.

The quality machinery is labelling organizations and individuals by asso-ciation. There are profound ontological issues at stake in the scoring of organizations. The culture of scrutiny implies deficiency and incompetence. It impacts on interpersonal relationships, self-esteem, and organizational cultures. Ostensibly, the scoring purports to offer value-added information. However, a low score is a badge of degradation. Within a performance culture, to gain a low score is to be addressed and labelled injuriously.

Naming is a significant aspect in the constitution of identity. Butler (1997b: 2) observed that: 'to be called a name is one of the first forms of injury that one learns'. Althusser's (1971) theory of interpellation suggests that a sub-ject is constituted by being hailed, addressed, named. Naming can bring affirmation or insult. The labelling of universities iterates and inscribes the discourses in a complex chain of signification. Audit and the ensuing certi-fication and grading means those private inhouse matters are now in the public domain. The results of audit provide a reified reading, which becomes a truth. There is a strong relationship between identity and reputation. For universities at the bottom of the league tables, identity is a form of negative equity. The damage to reputation becomes an attack on the competence of every organizational member. For those at the top, there is an artificial halo effect, which invites the projection of a range of positive attributes on to their services. These identities have cash value in the marketplace, as they purport to speak directly to newly empowered student consumers.

Naming and shaming can simply highlight latent organizational risks as an academic registrar at a new university indicates:

> And I suppose on the other side, the disadvantage for a head of sup-port department is that if there's too much criticism of your depart-ment then you can be vulnerable institutionally, you know, to merger or whatever.

Success in audit can also stimulate pride and a sense of achievement as a head of department in a new university says:

> And personally, I'll look back on this as being a sort of milestone in my career I think . . . how we responded to the queries that were raised by the assessors, how we managed to sort of lead a whole team of 20 people until 10.30 on Wednesday night. You know beavering away, writing seven different reports and stuff . . . it looks very well for the school as a whole, and, you know, the head of school; I think it has impacted personally as well.

The director of academic affairs in a new university records the qualit-ative aspects of a subject review in hospitality and tourism as a pleasurable experience and how critical feedback was felt as positive validation:

They got 22 out of 24, which was fine, and fair, I think, probably, but the feedback was extremely positive about a number of things to do with student experience. . . . And I think people really valued the qualitative aspect of that, it wasn't just the numbers . . . I have strong memories of . . . the pleasure in those good things.

A lecturer in sociology in a new university describes the feeling of success as 'empowering':

You know we felt very nervous. Obviously we were a new university, and the fact that we'd known a couple of other universities that had been done, kind of in our sort of area that hadn't done very well, and we did very good, we did very well, and we did very well on things that we think that we're good at. We did very well on student support and those kind of issues. And so all in all it was quite an empowering experience.

The head of academic standards in an old university describes how success in audits can boost morale:

We had put in train a system for preparing for subject review, and really sort of making sure that people were confident to speak out about the good things and so on. And the first time that really took effect was about two years ago when we got our first 'excellent'. And I can't tell you, as an institution that had never got one before, how positive, and how completely delighted people were in the departments concerned. They were over the moon. . . . It did raise people's morale, and it was nice to see us going up the league tables for a change, which started to really change then, and go up.

Whereas emotion and embodiment were once seen as oppositional to the intellectual life of the academy (Dyhouse, 1995), now modern management literature attempts to integrate them. The rationality/emotion binary is currently produced as complementary, with emotional responses being subsumed and harnessed to a rational framework (McWilliam *et al.*, 1999). The activation of emotions provides a new source of energy and motivation. In this dyad, the economic imperatives of the organization become linked to the personal objectives, aspirations and goals of the individual. McWilliam *et al.* (1999: 66) argue that 'The emotions themselves are connected to entrepreneuralism'. The activation of desire, for example, the wanting and craving of high scores in league tables, suggests that there is a libidinal economy involved in quality assurance too.

Quality assessment can produce a powerful blame culture. A senior lecturer describes how, while she felt that subject review was a worthless exercise, her integrity and identity were at stake:

And so I started to personally panic, and you know I had a couple of really bad weekends when I just thought 'Oh God it's all going to be terrible, and it's all going to be my fault, so I'll get blamed.' So I felt, personally, terribly caught up in it, I felt personally that my integrity was at stake, and I felt that my integrity was divided. Because at one level you do your best to get your institution through these things, to just sort of survive to fight another day. On the other hand I knew that my integrity was compromised because I knew that what I was doing was completely worthless, a complete waste of time.

An academic development officer (quality enhancement) in an old university felt that academics were complaining inappropriately about the effects of quality assessment – particularly as academic professional judgements had long played a role in the naming and shaming of students:

I think there's been a lot of whinging about the quality assurance. If you turned it, you know, about negative effects upon institutions, a poor review, you know marked for life, all that sort of thing, the subjectivity of these judgements and so on. All I would say is just turn that spotlight round, and say what about all the judgements that are made upon students, you know, and happily classified into, you know, firsts, 2is, 2iis, thirds passes and so on. I don't think most staff think that much about it, or they're absolutely damn sure they're right. And students can go away with, you know, a pass degree, and in that sense they're no less marked, in fact they're probably far more so, than a department that comes out with 18, or has come out with 18 on a QA subject review.

I will conclude this chapter by quoting a senior lecturer who describes quality assessment as a sado-masochistic ritual:

And it's just the whole thing is so unutterably awful . . . it's like a postmodern form of torture. It's like, you know, beat yourself up before they come to beat you up, and then you will get beaten up again. It's the most awful, awful process!

5

Changing Employment Regimes

De- or re-professionalization? Scholars or knowledge workers?

Quality assurance procedures can both re- and de-professionalize academics. In the academy identity is no longer linked solely to disciplines. Quality assurance regimes mean that identity, status and reputation can also be linked to league table scores. It becomes a spoken and unspoken economy in organizations, like dress and linguistic codes. In the new universities and vocational courses in the old universities, identity has been more often linked to membership of professions. However, professional knowledge itself is being weakened as new managerialism continues to dominate the public services. Quality assurance involves a degree of multiskilling, as academics also have to operate managerially. The rise of the corporate campus and new competitions for the production and delivery of knowledges mean that a key element in academic identity formation is that idea that 'every professional person should understand themselves to be a leader' (McWilliam *et al.*, 1999: 60). Herein resides a paradox. While public service professionals are increasingly expected to operate managerially (re-professionalization), they are also expected to consent to being led (de-professionalization).

Studies on the de-professionalization of educationalists tend to cite two salient features: (i) the removal of discretionary power in the area of pedagogy, and (ii) constraints imposed on teaching practice by having to meet bureaucratic criteria imposed by quality assurance agencies such as the QAA in Britain (Bottery and Wright, 1997). There are those who believe that externality enhances quality and professionalism. Hart (1997: 305) suggests that 'everyone needs a voice of contradiction somewhere, which may also be a voice of conscience, to keep them up to the mark'. The hegemonic implications of knowing the precise configuration of 'the mark' are frequently left untheorized. A question is whether the external voices displace professional judgement, with quality assurance perceived as the authoritative construction of norms. There is an array of identificatory sites in academia, but quality assurance assumes the dominance of norms. Foucault (1979b: 182–3) describes the process of normalization:

> (T)he regime of disciplinary power . . . brings quite distinct operations into play; it refers individual actions to a whole that is once a field of comparison, a space of differentiation and the principle rule to be followed. It differentiates individuals from one another. . . . It measures in quantitative terms and hierarchizes in terms of value the abilities, the level, and the 'nature' of individuals. It introduces, through this 'value-giving' measure, the constraint of a conformity that must be achieved. Lastly, it traces the limit that will define difference in relation to all other differences, the external frontier of the abnormal. . . . In short, it *normalizes*.

There are limited opportunities for individuals to question the legitimacy of the norms and move beyond conventional justified beliefs and values. Bauman (1987) believes that university teachers no longer legislate for what is correct knowledge. In the knowledge society, they are more like interpreters of the workplace or consultants to knowledge workers such as teachers, managers, journalists etc. Academics could be perceived more as knowledge workers too. Rifkin (1995: 174) describes knowledge workers as 'the creators, manipulators, and purveyors of the stream of information that makes up the post-industrial, post-service global economy'.

The imperative to make universities more responsive to the demands and fluctuations of the market means that employment conditions have changed. Economic rationalism and the re-assessment of the economic benefits of educational spending have created increased pressure for organizations and individuals. Flexibility produces winners and losers. For example, academic tenure is rapidly disappearing in the UK, Sweden and the Netherlands. Hence, academics are easier to exploit as existence as subordination is preferable to not existing at all (Butler, 1997a).

Higher education has been positioned simultaneously as a contributor to national wealth production and as a consumer of national resources. Shore and Wright (1999: 559) argue that professionals have been re-invented as units of resource whose performance and productivity must constantly be audited and measured so that it can be enhanced. The emphasis on resource consumption increasingly justifies state intervention. In the context of the global fiscal crisis, parsimony has become increasingly attractive. Universities are now seen as recipients of welfare. Recipients of state welfare have been traditionally constructed as profligate, insatiable and deficient. Chomsky (1998) argued that universities are parasitic institutions in so far as they depend upon public and private funds. The administrative harassment, surveillance and stigmatization of universities could be seen as similar to the way in which all recipients of welfare are treated (Fraser, 1997).

Bauman's (1998b) metaphor of vagabonds and tourists can be applied to the genesis of the quality movement. Public service workers in general, were discursively constructed as 'vagabonds' as they were perceived as living off society, rather than contributing to a consumer-oriented, wealth-producing society (tourists). There is an increasing trend to force people receiving any public service funding, either in the form of wages or welfare, to account for their time, much of which must be spent in activities that satisfy the regulations of these policies.

Increasing workloads and the long hours' culture

The audit society has contributed to the long hours' culture in Britain. Greedy institutions have been given the right to become even greedier, with sacrifices demanded for the sake of a greater good. The Association of University Teachers (AUT) undertook a survey in 1994 of 2670 academics, and found that the length of the working week in British universities, averaged across term time and vacations, was 53.5 hours, with administration consuming an average of 18 hours a week (Court, 1996). This survey was conducted before the audit culture set in! There is a myth that increasing workload enhances productivity and effectiveness. The 'full diary' syndrome is thought to be a signifier of productivity. My informants frequently noted the long hours' culture. A registrar observes how hard work has always been part of academic life, but that it is increasing, with boundaries becoming more difficult to negotiate:

> And I would say I've worked hard for as long as I've been here, which is nearly 20 years. But in common with many colleagues, the workload is not decreasing, it's increasing and for me and numbers of staff it's not stopping at what I would call perhaps a reasonable boundary. I and numbers of staff work weekends – not the whole weekend – but a substantial part of the weekend. Many of us work in the evenings as well on top of working what is a fairly long day. Now, of course, in the end you could say, 'Well it's up to you, you draw the line where you think the line should be drawn.' But I think there are dangers . . . I do worry about the amount of work that some of my colleagues are doing. I have one colleague who, when he was dealing with the research assessment exercise this year, towards the end of that exercise was working 80 hours a week, which is too much. And I mean he knew that but it was a particular peak but a lot of it is almost beyond our control in that something like that is imposed from the outside. We've got to do this and if you want to do it properly you've got to work hard at it . . . I do sometimes perhaps resent the fact that at the weekends I feel guilty if I'm not doing (university) work.

The internalized imperative to overwork is a good example of the psychic life of power. There is a psychic operation of a regulatory norm. The workload has increased while the political and psychic strength to resist it has decreased. The feeling of guilt is an example of how the 'master' who first appears as an external to the slave re-emerges as the slave's own conscience (Butler, 1997a). One way in which to alleviate the guilt is to do yet more work.

For several of my informants, there was concern not just over the increase in volume, but also over the low level of the activities. The sense of being on trial and needing documentary evidence was pervasive. The task of representing practices textually was proving labour intensive and highly irritating to many. A professor comments:

> . . . ever since I arrived it (QA) has been a major part of my working life really, because everything you do has to be geared up to that. But in particular, over the last 12 to 18 months, it has just sort of dominated my life as head of department . . . in terms of ensuring that everything that we do is well documented and follows everything through. I mean producing useless pieces of paper really, it's only writing down good practice that has been going on for many years. But there's a feeling that we have to now document absolutely everything to ensure that the systems can be followed through. . . . For example, the minutes of our departmental teaching and learning committee went from sort of two pages when I arrived, to sort of, three or four, five pages with actual minutes with then wads of appendices to go with it, just so everything is there for the review team to see.

There is a defensiveness embedded in academic services now. The 'just-in-case' production of documentation is a questionable use of academic time, as a deputy vice chancellor observes:

> . . . I've only been through two quality assurance processes, personally. But they have dominated the horizon. They have taken an enormous amount of time, and a great number of people within the university have been quite severely distracted, I think, by the process, and by the requirement to produce reams and reams of paperwork, for example, which the panels don't always look at. . . . It's very hard to get time to do very much other than keep up with the work that's generated by the university . . . I was hoping to get a day free a week, from administration, to concentrate on research. But in practice that hasn't happened.

A registrar argues that the increased bureaucracy is linked to the newness of the process and excessive workloads will be normalized:

> At the moment much of it is still relatively new and upsets people by its newness and the fact that it's a change and it's not the way things used to be. When – we keep saying to people, 'You've got to accept we're not going to go back to the way it was. This has got to become part of our culture. We may want to change it or reduce the workload but it's going to be with us for good now.' And maybe then it won't seem so excessive in the workload.

A reader in social policy notes the sense of relentless pressure and powerlessness in the face of excessive bureaucratic demands:

Well I definitely think it's increased pressure of work. And workload in fact. And it seems like a constant treadmill now, which I was just saying to a colleague this morning basically, that there seems to be one thing coming after the other, you never have a chance to stop and catch up . . . I think it's having to do all the paper work. You know having to fill out lots of forms, in terms of keeping a check on things, having to photocopy handouts to put in boxes for when the inspectors come, and having to do that three times because you have to produce it for the three different departments who might be being done. And I think it's just increased the stress, because I think, I personally feel more individually pressurized. I think it's all been quite individualized, and I just think it's all stressful. Less time with the students really.

The image of the treadmill suggests slavery and a dehumanizing lack of opportunity to prioritize how professional time is allocated. A deputy vice chancellor comments on increased workloads as a consequence of preparation for quality audits:

So you know we're starting at 8.30 in the morning, and finishing at 8.30 at night. It's ridiculous!

The long hours' culture has gender implications. A principal lecturer describes the complex domestic arrangements women staff had to make for subject review weeks:

I made my husband have the week off. So that he was actually at home . . . I did all the dinners at the weekend . . . I just knew that if there was a problem he was at home. And he worked from home that week . . . and he picked up my son from school, and did all the things, did the shopping, and did those sorts of things. But I actually had another colleague stay with me that week, because she lives in Bath, and it would just have been impossible for her to have gone home . . . I know it had very major impact on her little girl. She has a younger child and the husband was supposed to be picking up the child for two evenings, and the train was delayed from London, and she's recently adopted the child, and it caused great stress. . . . And I know that colleagues were having sort of children delivered here, and then keeping them here in offices while their husbands came home and picked them up, and things like that. So there were quite major spin-offs, and particularly for the women.

Quality production and reproduction seem to be in oppositional relationship. Several informants commented on the deleterious effects of increased workloads on their family lives:

Your family have to be very tolerant. I mean it's quite clear that it's not a job for a young person, you know, because it would be very hard to cope if you had a young family, you just wouldn't see them for weeks on end. So most people involved in the university are sort of in their fifties, so their children have grown up or are not dependent in quite the same way any more. I think that what tends to happen is that it becomes a kind of frenetic activity, where everything else gets displaced for two or three weeks.

A curriculum leader in a new university supports this view and outlines how quality assessments take priority over new babies, relationships etc., and yet give little back in return:

I'd only had my first baby sort of a few weeks before . . . so I'll never forget that period of time. So I was sort of working extremely long hours and sort of leaving my wife at home with the baby all day, which strained things a little bit. . . . But again it does bring home the question of how much work can people be expected to do really? A bit of an issue for me following it was, I mean I never really felt I got a sort of pay-off for it if you see what I mean. . . . The people who took the lead in the QAA were often given sabbatical leave the following term, or some kind of relief from teaching, and that hasn't really happened for me, related to a situation at the university here with financial constraints and things I'm sure. But that was a bit of a sore point with me, I felt I'd put an awful lot of work in, and although we got a good result I'd like to have got something else out of it.

A director of quality and learning support comments on how his family has become habituated to his long hours:

I mean the main impact on my family will be that I'll be home rather late, because of the meetings late on in the day, and during the evenings . . . it will sort of be quite late before I get home. So it'll be that and I'll be generally tensed up, no doubt, as one is with these things. But beyond that we're getting quite used to them now.

A professor describes how his family used humour to diffuse the pressure:

Well I think my family would have said it dominated my life . . . if I ever said TQA at home it was 'Oh no not again'. . . . My eldest daughter sings the TQA to the YMCA song, you know whenever I mentioned it, it got to a stage when they just didn't want to hear about it you know. . . . The little ones used to keep saying 'What is this TQA?' and the 16-year-old would just take the Mickey out of it. And it was a way of just lightening the process. And they were all glad when it was over, definitely, especially my wife and 16-year-old, pleased it was over. . . . I was gradually working longer and longer hours, and near the end doing a couple of weekends as well, which . . . I try not to work weekends with a family, but just had to.

Those who are childfree are still affected by increased workloads. As well as the psychic economy, there is a libidinous economy, as sexual and social energy get used up in the excessive work that is involved. A passionate attachment to quality is nurtured and exploited. Like athletes economizing their sexual energy for desired victory, quality workers in the academy have to measure embodied passionate relationships. A head of a quality assurance unit relates how subject review impacted on her:

> My significant other – he's very good, if a subject review is on, he just does everything, he doesn't bat an eyelid at whatever happens, whatever time I turn up, whether I've eaten and whether I haven't eaten, he's absolutely brilliant. . . . He's really subject review trained now . . . think he rather enjoys it in a strange sort of way . . . not having sex for a while. Ha, ha.

Quality assurance as a new type of monastic order! There is a notion that the increased workload and transcending social and sexual needs was good for professional development. The purifying rituals involving humiliation, hard work and a wide spectrum of emotional responses were tests of strength of character. Denial of pleasure and a social life is essential preparation for quality audits, as the head of a quality assurance unit explains:

> You can't really go out and have meals and things . . . I certainly wouldn't go wildly socializing, or going out to you know, a theatre, or concert or anything like that. I just wouldn't have the energy, you're very focused those three or four days, on that, and that's all you can do really. So, yes it does affect your life. And it is very stressful just sort of worrying about it beforehand, especially the weekend before.

A lecturer in Spanish expresses her anger at the social isolation that overwork can produce:

> I was living on my own at the time, working until 11 o'clock every night for a couple of months, extremely antisocial . . . I often had to take work of this nature home on the weekend which impacted on my social life.

Quality takes over lives, organizations and consciousness. Quality assurance is a job creation scheme. As my research repeatedly demonstrates, quality assurance can offer new opportunities for visibility and career progression for those who subscribe or at least perform its central requirements. The ratio of observers to observed is growing. New posts and descriptors are proliferating, as an assistant registrar notes:

> I think this has a very interesting impact on the role of the quality assurance administrator. This job didn't exist in British Universities ten years ago. And now in some universities, particularly the larger civic universities, they are positively cadres of these people . . . and that's fair enough, you know, they need it to cope with something like 20, 25 subject review visits a year. What, of course, those people aren't in a position to do, is to be the kind of seat of authoritative judgement within the institution. They can churn out the data, they can get it into

position for external review, but they rarely take the kind of evaluative stance, positive, or negative, and they rarely act as the kind of link into quality enhancement.

The new cadre represent a major vector for quality assurance as it comprises boundary-spanning individuals whose job it is to operationalize procedures and ensure compliance. An assistant registrar in an old university describes how the quality workload had moved from being fractional to total:

> In 1993/94, quality led issues I'd say took up about three-quarters of my workload . . . by about 1996/97, two thirds of our output was directly related to quality. . . . And now . . . my job is full-time academic quality.

The head of academic standards in an old university describes how quality business has begun to absorb the agenda for her academic policy committee:

> And last year, because of the huge, huge weight of stuff that the QA were bringing in, the quality assurance framework, all these codes of practice and so on, I would say 70 per cent of what we did in APC was just purely a response to the QAA's framework.

Quality management has increased at local as well as at central management level, as a faculty manager indicates:

> I think the aspect of my job that is involved in ensuring that the quality processes operate at the faculty level is quite a substantial job. And I think over the last few years I've certainly seen that aspect of the job growing in size, in terms of the time it takes to carry out that satisfactorily. Really because the quality processes in the university have become more specific and defined, so much so that I know as of the last few weeks I've employed a faculty officer, brackets, quality, who reports to me and actually handles the detail of that part of my job on my behalf.

The director of quality in a Scottish university, like many other informants, comments on the increased bureaucracy:

> I mean being director of quality assurance is, well, theoretically 40 per cent of my job, actually probably more like 60 per cent and wouldn't have existed without such things . . . I mean somebody who wanted to be – since it's regarded as a mildly pejorative expression – mildly pejorative about me would say almost all I did was administrative now. . . . I mean the quality – the external quality assurance industry can be viewed as entirely bureaucracy. I wouldn't go that far but it's certainly increased the bureaucracy a great deal, yes.

A director of planning felt that the bureaucracy was stifling innovation and risk-taking, or leading to 'planning blights'

> . . . there's been an enormous increase in the bureaucracy required, I mean a huge amount of form filling . . . it's led to a degree of planning

blights in some areas and a desire to avoid innovation for fear that the assessors won't like it . . . it's the bureaucracy that's been the really big thing. And in an institution like my own, most of my colleagues would regard the whole thing as a complete waste of time. I mean I think they're wrong to regard it as a complete waste of time but that would certainly be the general view.

It appears from much of my empirical data that academics and administrators often feel a sense of personal investment in the outcomes of quality assessment. This can produce profound contradictions and discomforts. The bureaucracy involved in quality procedures sometimes meant that they have the reverse effect on quality of teaching and learning. Low levels of job satisfaction and low morale are highly undesirable for organizations dedicated to intellectual growth and creativity! A head of department in a new university outlines how compliance is in opposition with creativity and innovation and how the outcomes approach closes down exploration:

> I think it introduces compliance into a culture that ought to be much more innovative and experimental. I mean for example if you're trying to create knowledge professionals for the twenty-first century, and you're trying to do it on a compliance model then it seems to me to be completely out of line. Because basically we don't know what the skills required are going to be, if you want to encourage creative thinking you don't do that by, by setting up a very rigid set of parameters where students have got to demonstrate very limited successes.

In Britain, one constituent of the increasing workload relates to massification. Between 1987 and 1993 alone, student numbers rose by 50 per cent to more than one million full-time equivalents, while academic staff numbers increased by only 10 per cent to 72,000. The unit of resource was reduced by more than 20 per cent in the same period. The AUT (1993) calculated that while student numbers increased from 547,000 to 1,220,000, recurrent spending per student declined in real terms from £6090 to £4537. This was euphemistically classified as 'efficiency gains'. A philosophy lecturer observes that the quality movement is preparation for mass delivery:

> Because they [the Government] have ideas about what higher education ought to be, and their arguments for open access, for all the 50 per cent of school leavers into higher education, and the lifelong learning, and the skills agenda, are a definite shift in terms of what universities used to deliver and what they, what the government seems to want them to deliver. And taking the university system head on would have been very difficult I think. I think what the government has done is to push most of us into this position of a sort of mass delivery, and will leave a few research-based institutes to get on and do interesting research.

The academy is being restratified while academics are being multiskilled.

Split focusing

Academics, like many other professional groups, have become split subjects, simultaneously interpellated in different ways and caught in damaging
oscillations. The university is sometimes referred to as a 'bundle' institution
(Habermas, 1992; Delanty, 2001) in so far as it combines a range of functions including the research process, general education, the training of
future professionals and the formation of public opinion. The professional
self has been fragmented into 'researcher', 'administrator', 'teacher' and
more recently 'entrepreneur'. According to Habermas (1992) this reflects
the complex position of the university, which he sees as being located
between social and cultural structures on one hand, and the system of
money and power on the other. In relation to quality assessment, academics
have to negotiate a range of roles in order to perform in the various categories that mark out the inspection of their work. There has been a division of
labour in the academy between the task-defining and task-executing work.

McInnis (2000: 150) reports that the policy imperative to improve quality
teaching at the same time as demanding more research output is placing
academics under 'enormous pressure'. Academics have to spend more time
supporting students with a wide range of abilities, more time on pastoral
care and far greater engagement with new technologies for teaching. Delanty
(2001: 87) argues that the four current academic roles are 'professional
researchers, professional trainers, teachers, and intellectuals – and the danger is that the latter two will be overshadowed by the first two'.

The issue of split focusing is vexing many academics. This is experienced
as the lack of opportunity to focus on one area effectively. This was related
to multiskilling – the concept that employees must be flexible and adaptable, rather than over-specialized. Talking of academics, Oshagbemi (1996:
390) notes that 'Hardly any other group of workers performs such a dispar-
ate array of functions'. Many of the demands that appear to be exceeding
the capacity of academic labour relate to quality assurance procedures.
Terms like 'diversion' and 'distraction' were frequently used in relation to
the effects of quality audits on academic time and energy. A discourse of
loss is often evident in studies of higher education today. The coming of
quality represents a type of death of the previous academic *modus operandi*.
The nostalgia can sometimes constelate around a normatively construed
former age. This is accompanied by a type of grief, mourning or sense of
dispossession in the transformation process. Some losses are ungrievable,
for example loss of precariousness, the hidden curriculum and under-
performance, while others are grievable, for example loss of control over
use of time.

A theme running through many of my interviews for this study was the
oppositional and complementary relationship of teaching and research
(Robertson and Bond, 2001). Informants commented on how conditions of
labour and production were often at odds with each other. Fuller (1999:
587) describes how the two activities used to complement each other:

. . . teaching curbed the esoteric tendencies of research, while research disrupted the routinising tendencies of teaching. . . . However, this delicate balance between the two functions is in danger of being lost. On the one hand, teaching is being reduced to the dispensation of credentials; on the other, research is being privatised as intellectual property: the one driven by the employment market, the other by the futures market.

Senior management in universities will often focus resources on preparation for the research assessment exercise, rather than for teaching quality assessment as the former has cash implications. A senior lecturer notes:

> The head of the school . . . believed that we didn't have to worry about the QAA, it was something that we could handle very quickly, we didn't need to prepare, and that all of our energies should be going into the RAE which was the big piece of administrative work that we had to be involved in.

However, in practice, this meant that she was left to take responsibility for the subject review, while senior men focused on the RAE. A philosophy lecturer believes that the differing conditions of labour and mindsets for research and for administration placed them in an oppositional relationship:

> I don't think anybody wrote during probably a six- or seven-month period, and many of us have had trouble starting again actually . . . to say demotivation, that's probably too simplistic, it's a sort of dislocation I think, and, and . . . it's administration really eats into the spaces in your mind and it's those spaces that you need to be quiet and to concentrate and to reflect, and I think the SPR makes us too frantic, sort of vibrating with administrative energy, and that makes it very difficult to concentrate . . . I think some of us will end up going 'Oh I'll just do administration now'. Because that's how you are, you're vibrating on that frequency, it's so difficult to stop that and to go in to the quiet space and complete absorption that you need to be productive.

A head of department in a new university comments on the impact of quality procedures on research and scholarship:

> I can't remember the last time I went down to the library to look at a journal. I can't, but you see I took over as head of school about two years ago, so just over two years ago, and since then we've re-validated all our programmes, with significant changes . . . it's just being head of school I think is extremely demanding time-wise. And it's meant that my research is, I've managed to do one little project with the environment agency, which I've written up into a paper . . . but that is, but that's the only thing I've managed to get done in two and a bit years. . . . SPR has been on the horizon . . . so I think you can tie most of it into SPR.

A deputy vice chancellor uses the metaphor of drowning to describe the demands of management and organizational restructuring:

> We're going through a quite extensive self-analysis in the university, to look at how we are going to be structured in the future. . . . But I found it very hard, I was hoping to get a day free a week, from administration, to concentrate on research. But in practice that hasn't happened . . . I just about keep my head above the water with the commitments that I have already undertaken, but it's going to be very hard.

Quality assurance has produced a whole range of meetings, committees and working parties that cut across the teaching curriculum. Many of the meetings are crisis driven and cannot be planned. A professor who became a deputy vice chancellor explains how this wreaks havoc with teaching commitments:

> I've also been sharing some teaching with the post-graduates whom I supervise, but that's actually been very, very hard to manage, because meetings come along, and they come along at times when they can't always be planned . . . quality assurance aspects . . . it's taken three deans from their normal activities, their full activities that involve talking to students, understanding appeals, going in to the details and so on, and other aspects of our curriculum.

Seniority in one area seems to imply specialization and the imperative to de-emphasize the other two main areas of academic life. A director of quality in a university college explains:

> I'm part of the senior management team. The executive group here . . . so I really don't have time to publish any longer, I did do years ago, but I've kind of left that behind. For the simple reason that I haven't got the time . . . I have this longing to sort of pick up research again, and then I think about it for a while and then realize I haven't the time. It would be nice, it would be nice ideally but there just isn't the time really.

An irony permeating this study was that actual activities being audited were frequently displaced, eclipsed or maimed by processes involved in their quality assessment. A professor in an old university comments that this can reach crisis point when both accounting systems come at once:

> As head of department, as I say, it's dominated my life. It [subject review] also came at the same time as the RAE for us, which doesn't happen to everybody, but we had to prepare the RAE for submission for April of this year. The same time we actually had to prepare our self-assessment document for the quality assurance visit. So the combination of those meant that for one's actual research, for me personally, went out the window, and for six or seven key players within the department, course directors, examinations officers, and things like that.

Research just went out the window completely. In fact it completely dominated our lives in that sense. And I think the one thing teaching quality assurance, as it used to be called, or whatever TQA used to be called, the one thing that suffers is actually the quality of the teaching.

A vice provost notes similar difficulties when asked what impact quality assurance has had on his research and publications:

Oh, enormous! I don't do either of those things anymore ... but I keep up with the literature a bit and so on but I'm not active in research anymore ...

He had a similar response in relation to the impact on his teaching:

I do less teaching than I used to, considerably. ... The main problem with teaching isn't so much time, as availability of particular time slots. In other words, I have more things – I have some things now which take priority even over giving a lecture, whereas in the past giving a lecture would have always taken priority over almost everything. ... We have regular meetings ... we have meetings of so-called research intensive universities. The QAA occasionally has meetings in Gloucester, that kind of thing would probably take priority over teaching.

In the 2002 Reith lectures on 'A Question of Trust' Onora O'Neill suggests that 'plants don't flourish when we keep pulling them up to check how their roots are growing. Equally, political institutional and professional life does not thrive when we constantly uproot them to demonstrate that everything is transparent and trustworthy'. This sentiment is also expressed by a director of learning in a university college:

Both my colleagues and myself are becoming more aware of the need for having adequate QA procedures in place ... in some respects it's taking the place of teaching, to some extent, and we're finding ourselves with less and less time to concentrate on the teaching aspects, and to worry more about the quality enhancement procedures ... it's getting the documentation in place really, and I suspect that probably the central feature is demonstrating feedback loops, and the amount of time taken in ensuring that those loops are transparent is really eating into the teaching time I think.

A reader in social policy argues that it all seems to be about processes, rather than the actual product:

Well I mean there is less time to take up with teaching I think, and in that sense, because of the pressure to publish more, because of the research assessment. And it just seems to be all about processes. You know we're keeping lots of forms on the type of teaching we do, but that leaves us less time to actually improve our teaching techniques.

The sense of the virtual or textual university is expressed by a lecturer in sociology in a new university:

You actually spend so much time doing kind of admin. around improving teaching that you have less time to actually improve your practice . . . the academic world, it's just seen to be kind of increasingly paper driven. And you know quality assurance and RAE and all the rest of it just kind of adds to that kind of paper drivenness of it. It just seems to take away from the kind of research and teaching which is in theory why we're all here. . . .

Repeated references to the paper-driven nature of quality assessments suggest that it is not the activity that must be witnessed but that the signs that denote effectiveness must be scrutinized.

6

The Micropolitics of Quality

The everyday life of power

Quality assurance procedures can introduce and expose organizational fissures and cracks in the quotidian life of higher education institutions. Quality assessment demands consensus and continuity in relation to organization goals and priorities. Yet, the theory of micropolitics suggests that organizations are riven with conflicts and competing interests. However, for purposes of representation, these have to be sanitized. Performance indicators can be social as well as technical. They have the potential to disrupt and enhance the social relations of academic work. Micropolitics focuses on the ways in which power is relayed in everyday practices. It discloses the subterranean conflicts, competitions and minutiae of social relations. It describes how power is relayed through seemingly trivial incidents and transactions. As such, it can provide an analytical corrective to traditional notions of disembodied objectivity and meritocracy. The conceptual framework of micropolitics can help to reveal the increasingly subtle and sophisticated ways in which dominance is achieved in academic organizations. A micropolitical perspective allows one to see how power is exercised and experienced in organizations, rather than simply possessed.

Theoretically, micropolitics is linked to feminist and post-structuralist conceptions of power. Power is seen as capillary. For decades, feminist scholarship has reminded us that the personal is political (Morley, 1999). Macro-systems of dominance are rehearsed and internalized at the micro level, thus ensuring conformity and minimizing resistance. Micropolitics has been read as a subtext of organizational life in which conflicts, tensions, resentments, competing interests and power imbalances influence everyday transactions in institutions. Micropolitics is about influence, networks, co-alitions, political and personal strategies to effect or resist change. It involves rumour, gossip, sarcasm, humour, denial, 'throwaway remarks', and alliance building. Blase (1991: 1) defined micropolitics as being:

. . . about power and how people use it to influence others and to protect themselves. It is about conflict and how people compete with each other to get what they want. It is about co-operation and how people build support among themselves to achieve their ends.

The exercising of power in organizations can be overt and identifiable but also subtle, complex and confusing. The examination of quotidian practices, relationships and emotions in organizations can reveal 'power operating in structures of thinking and behaviour that previously seemed devoid of power relations' (White, 1986: 421). Micropolitical awareness renders competition and domination more visible; revealing processes of stalling, sabotage, manipulation, power bargaining, bullying, harassment and spite.

The identification of power in organizations is an intensely political project. Ball (1994: 27) reminded us that according to Foucault:

. . . the real political task is to criticise the working of institutions which appear to be both neutral and independent, and to criticise them in such a manner that the political violence which has always exercised itself obscurely through them will be unmasked so that we can fight them.

Power imbalances in the academy are both structural and played out in micropolitical struggles. Like many aspects of racial and gender oppression, bullying and sexual harassment at work, micropolitics can also be subtle, elusive, volatile, difficult to capture, leaving individuals unsure of the validity of their readings of a situation. What appears trivial in a single instance acquires new significance when located within a wider analysis of power relations. The attribution of meaning and decoding of transactions, locations and language is an important component of micropolitics. Micropolitics privileges processes, rather than structures. Like feminism, it can label unnamed feelings, experiences, practices and transactions, as the language in which oppressed groups express these phenomena is often politically and socially subjugated and rendered irrelevant or illegitimate by dominant discourses.

Micropolitical activity is engaged in from both ends of the organizational hierarchy. It is about relationships rather than structures, knowledge rather than information, skills rather than positions, talk rather than paper. For example, the politics of non-decision making argue that issues and demands can be suffocated, maimed or destroyed before they gain access to the relevant decision-making arena (Lukes, 1974: 18/19). In the academy, processes of power are complicated by the autonomy and authority that accrue as a result of expert power. It can mean that those beyond the boundary of knowledge cannot question a professional judgement. This is particularly pertinent in the case of quality assurance where judgements of worth can be nebulous and arbitrary. Hence the quality movement, with its emphasis on externality and transparency, has had some support from stakeholders who have been traditionally beyond the boundary. The boundary has been maintained, to some extent, by a type of professional collectivism, or collegiality that is itself another regime of power.

Collegiality

There is a powerful discourse of nostalgia, loss and golden ageism running through contemporary higher education literature. One lament is that current arrangements for quality assurance are in opposition to traditional collegiate practices for managing the academy. Collegiality can reinforce hegemonies, by assuming common values, professional and academic ethics, goals and lifestyles. Nixon *et al.* (1998: 283) suggest that collegiality 'is one of those words . . . that often masks complex power relations and the manipulative practices to which these can give rise'. Some theorists have deconstructed collegiality and exposed it as a gendered form of social relations, whereby men are seen as more equal colleagues than women (Bensimon, 1995; Deem and Ozga, 2000). However, it is common for social structures and diversity relating to race, class, sexuality and disability not to enter into the debate on 'peerness'. Collegiality is seen as professional self-regulation (Dill, 1995). Some of my informants felt that collegiality in the academy was a myth. A senior lecturer in education felt that the term disguised naked self-interest:

> I don't think higher education is noted for its collegiality. What it values is the autonomous individual, the privileging of the individual. And one of the problems, as we all know in the academy, is that it often means that certain individuals construct their lives at the expense of others, and that is what happens in labour production in the academy, and I think that the QAA is one more formation which encourages that. It encourages people to dump on others, it encourages people to escape, and I can understand the escaping, and the getting out of it, and the leaving it to others, but when you actually are one of the others that it's left to, and eventually, as inevitably it is left to some others, who carry more of the weight than the others.

Her observation suggests that current arrangements for quality assessment reproduce divisions of labour. Power operates in so far as there are those who are able to escape the regulation of teaching quality and there are those who are not. This is related to hierarchical positions, the teaching/research opposition and to gender.

Several informants cited enhanced collegiality as a major biproduct, or unintended consequence of quality audits. A philosophy lecturer felt that preparation for quality assessment promoted collegiality as the process felt like a war effort. However, she believes that it also exposes internal cracks and fissures:

> I mean we ended up with added collegiality I think, because it was a sort of a bit of a war zone. We pulled together, but that's because we're

a small department. I know other departments where it has completely fragmented any working relationships that were there. . . . Because when you have members of staff who opt out of the process, and when it's left with a few, people get very angry. I mean the emotions that are driving this thing towards the end of it are really heightened. I mean most of us weren't sleeping, most of us had broken nights, at least three or four of us were waking up at sort of four in the morning and sort of getting up and doing the ironing.

The emphasis on war effort raises questions for me about whether there is a role for pacifists or conscientious objectors in quality assurance. What would happen to the system if academics refused to collude? Is the opting out that so many informants resented based on a political objection to quality, or on power relations that leave some colleagues to do the unattractive domestic labour? Should there be equality in misery? Yet enhanced social relations is a dominant theme in this study. Post-modern management principles value teamwork, devolution, and lateral decision making (Luke, 2001). A professor and head of department in an old university cites the opportunity for team building that preparation for subject review provides:

But there are some benefits, you know, I mean the other benefit, which I'm not sure is the sort of benefit you're looking for, but the other benefit is that the actual visit itself acts as a wonderful team building exercise . . . the team together, for a week, when you're all fighting the common enemy as it were, which is nice actually.

Again, he uses the imagery of war and bonding in the face of a common enemy. Audit becomes the academic equivalent of an outward bound course, where strength of character, leadership and endurance are tested. He also remarks that the event exposed those who were trustworthy in a crisis:

I think, again in terms of head of department I know the strengths and weaknesses of my staff a lot better than I did before, definitely, and you know who are those you can rely on in a crisis as well.

The totality of quality assurance can confront the segmentalism of universities. It sweeps across departmental boundaries and can create new coalitions. The head of the quality assurance unit in a new university felt that preparation for quality assessments enhances information flow in the organization, as it cuts across traditional boundaries:

So if you look at it as a sort of long-term project, actually getting a department together to write a self-assessment document, for example, or if it's a split review, sort of across faculties involving people who'd never spoken to each other in their lives before. To get that kind of thing working for a couple of years beforehand I think is incredibly useful. Because people get to talk to each other perhaps in a way they're not used to, or not had the time to before.

The director of quality and vice provost of the faculty group of medicine and veterinary medicine, in an old university describes how his role as a quality manager has enabled him to form working relationships with a wide pool of colleagues:

> The reason why I find this an interesting job is because I now know colleagues absolutely throughout the university in a way I never did before. I'm one of the rather few people, one of the very few people on the academic side actually who really knows quite well what's going on in all the faculties and so on. I spend quite a lot of time trying to enforce – not exactly enforcing – trying to bring in changes imposed from outside with which I don't necessarily, entirely agree myself.

Collegiality is nurtured in order to ensure compliance. His observations raise issues about authenticity and alienation, as quality managers have to perform quality management with colleagues in a way that is not always contingent with their belief systems. There is a watched, watching and scornful self at play. Collegiality can be intensely performative and instrumental.

The registrar of an old university also cites the problem of being perceived as a 'policeman' by colleagues. He describes how he challenges this perception by entering into supportive dialogue with them:

> I mean there is the potential, I suppose, for this scrutiny role if you like, being a policeman as it were, it could make you seem like really the enemy to academics and someone who gets in the way of them getting on with their business which they just want to do without us telling them, 'Well you've got to do it this way, rather than that way.' I don't think it's caused too much damage. We still are able to liaise with our academic colleagues and bring up difficulties and get them round a table and try and sort them out, I think. . . . It's probably brought me into contact with a wider range of academics in some ways because we've had to make sure that everybody's aware of our procedures.

Collegiality here is interpreted as enhancing information flow and also facilitating compliance. The head of the academic standards and support unit at an old university also felt that team building was enhanced. Yet this was under-, or un-resourced as an activity:

> I think it's helped to, it has helped to join us together as a team, and we tend to have teams working together, with central people from my area, under the central areas working with departments and members of academic staff. And I think it's tended to create a feeling where we're actually saying 'Yeah, we are all working together' rather than you know the centre sort of beavering away thinking up terrible things to do to the departments and so on. That's been good. On the other hand the down side I guess would be it's just more pressure, more things to do with less resource.

Team bonding can be perceived as supernumery and enforced. An assistant registrar in an old university felt that preparation for quality assessments facilitated the development of new networks. However, some of these were experienced as coercive:

> There's the wider populous who have far too much to do as it is, and find the whole thing very, very burdensome, and I think that's particularly apparent in areas where you've got quite distinct areas of activity, which don't necessarily come together, but areas forced to come together for things like subject review, for example.

A principal lecturer in a new university believes that preparation for subject review allowed opportunities for two newly-merged organizations to bond:

> The whole process has created a team feeling amongst two disparate groups of people. Disparate groups who had worked on separate systems in the past, because we were two institutions that had just merged. An unintended spin off was actually bringing us together in that respect, and creating stronger teams of people. So that was, you know, with a clearly identified joint goal of trying to get a good grade.

The head of economics in a new university also comments on the bonding potential:

> But nonetheless, you know, even before we got the result last Thursday evening. I think many of the benefits of having gone through the review were quite evident . . . our dean has now called it virtual bonding, you know that people have been sending around e-mails, patting each other on the back, you know even before we knew the result, just because of the way everybody pulled together.

A lecturer in sociology comments on the bonding, but also points out that the relationship building is between people who tend to be easily responsibilized:

> It felt like quite a bonding experience . . . I've actually made kind of stronger relationships with some of my colleagues, because you know we're preparing things together, and we're writing documents together, and we're kind of sharing things together. But, having said that . . . there are always people that do, that do a lot of work, and always people that seem to not do very much.

The divisions that quality assessments expose can work against collegiality. A reader in social policy in an old university felt that the quality assessment of research and publication is decreasing collegiality:

> Well I think it's much less collegiate now, people seem to keep ideas to themselves . . . and you get much more . . . pressure to do things in order to get papers, the pressure to do everything in your name, or your name goes first. And I think that that's had a damaging effect on the place.

While many of my informants saw enhanced collegiality an unintended micropolitical consequence of quality assurance, a central question is team building for what? Coalitions are formed for safety and defence, with creativity displaced into protection, rather than innovation. It was noticeable in my research that some of the most vociferous critics of current arrangements for quality assessment did not cite collegiality as a benefit.

Peer review: outsiders within or insiders without?

Peer review is a political act. My study produced mixed responses to the concept and practice of peer review in quality assurance. Many applauded the concept, but had had negative experiences of the process. Some perceived peer review as developmental and consultative. Others saw it as an abusive relay of power. Academics have been co-opted into the policy process. The debate is whether this has helped to steer policy or to implement unacceptable policies. The involvement of academics in quality audits can be seen as a strategy to ensure that external stakeholders do not monopolize the structures and processes. It can also be seen as a form of capillary power in which professions are seduced into policing themselves. Peer review and external examining is based largely on social capital, that is social networks and horizontal communications. Hence it is open to inclusions and exclusions that can reinforce or challenge academic power relations. The inclusions and exclusions can relate to the personnel, but also to concepts and practices. An argument in favour of peer review is that it keeps quality matters firmly in the grasp of the academic community itself. However, the term 'community' can often be used to disguise the boundaries and barriers that operate within a professional group. Iris Marion Young (1990) notes that 'the ideal of community . . . expresses a desire for the fusion of subjects with one another which in practice operates to exclude those with whom the group chooses not to identify'. An army of peers has been created to enforce professional identification with predetermined norms.

In Britain, the assessment of quality in teaching and learning and in research excellence purport to be more collegial as they are executed by peers. Brennan *et al.* (1994) believe that there is a difference, however, between the 'moral' authority of peers in contrast to the bureaucratic authority of quality bodies. Peer review involves a complex combination of insider and outsider status. In the tradition of academic endeavour, externality is seen to represent objectivity (Reay, 2000). With peer review there is both a blurring and marking out of boundaries. Strathern (2000b: 316) notes that there is an interdependence between the performer and the spectator. The relationship relies on each consenting to review or be reviewed. It is a comedy of manners (Morley, 2002).

Quality assurance, as a political technology, also produces new categories of experts. Shore and Wright (1999: 560) maintain that these specialists fulfil four main roles:

First, they developed the new expert knowledge that provided the classifications for the new normative grid. Second, they advised on the design of institutional procedures. Third, they staffed and presided over the new regulatory mechanisms and systems, and judged adherence to or deviance from them. Fourth, they had a redemptive role in so far as they made their expert knowledge available to individuals who wished to engage in the process of self-improvement in order to modify their conduct according to the desired norms.

Hence peer review appears benign and collegial, but is underpinned with a set of values and hegemonies that are highly problematic. Peer review mediates government policy. While the situation described by Shore and Wright (1999) appears clinically efficient, my research suggests that the process is chaotic and amateurish. There is little evidence to suggest that quality assessment is a stable, coherent and unified project. My study revealed many stories of abusive power relations and bad professional practice sanctioned by peer review. It also revealed several acts of resistance and challenge. A recurring issue was that subject reviewers/assessors frequently came with their own prejudices and agendas, which they sought to impose or substantiate in the organizations they were reviewing. These represent a major form of micropolitical interference. An assistant registrar in an old university, who had experienced quality assessments in three old universities, concluded that 'The danger of peer review is that it becomes amateur review'. He comments on the problems of prior agendas:

> I've seen a case . . . which reached the stage where on the Thursday, the last day of the visit, the departmental team, refused to have anything more to do with the QAA team . . . because of sheer bad professional practice on the part of one reviewer in particular . . . he had an agenda of his own, particularly about the level of resourcing appropriate to the subject.

A director of quality and vice provost in an old university comments on the lack of objectivity and the existence of authority and certainty among peer reviewers about what constitutes best practice:

> Among many things that concerned us is the reviewers have gone on fishing expeditions and have expressed their own opinions a great deal. For example, they have in all cases gone on and on and on about our lack of a laid down teaching programme and departmental strategy and so forth. We've never done that kind of thing and we're not persuaded that doing it would necessarily improve our teaching and they've produced no evidence that it hasn't.

A similar view was expressed by a lecturer in Spanish:

> We had external visitors during TQA and it became very obvious that there were quite different ideas based on the pedagogy of teaching of languages between their university and staff here and it was felt by one

of the parties within my school that the visitors hadn't necessarily been entirely objective and fair in their assessment.

Quality audits are hierarchies of interests, involving value-judgements about the relative importance of different organizational goals. There is a certainty present that could be said to lack humility or reflexivity. The pervasive clichés of 'best/good practice' and 'excellence' imply discursive orthodoxy, normalization techniques and common goals. The position of the observer, or compiler of the *aide memoires* for inspection, is not subjected to the same critical analysis as that of the organization or individual under scrutiny. The role of values is skirted and there is an emphasis on what is seen to be effective rather than whose interests are being served.

In addition to the problem of peers projecting their priorities on to the reviewed, the issue of what constitutes peerness frequently surfaced in my research. Elite organizations prefer to select their own peers. They resent having peers thrust upon them. The vice provost in an old university comments on the institutional diversity in higher education:

> I think peer review has been reasonably successful. The problem with it, of course, is that what constitutes a peer is open to discussion and while I'm not sure this is my view, most of my colleagues would not really regard someone from, I don't know, the University of X since we're speaking confidentially, as being a peer. I mean they just aren't interested in their opinions – wrongly in many cases I'd be the first to concede. But in our own internal process where we send select reviewers, external reviewers from other universities that we regard as comparable, these people have a lot more in common with most of my colleagues.

There is often considerable hostility to colleagues who elect to be quality assessors. Shore and Wright (1999: 567/8) argue that the quality industry has produced a range of 'parasitical new professions' who are 'agents for subjecting staff to a new normative gaze and instilling its rationality into their working life'. Thompson (1998: 290) uses the concept of kakistrocracy – that is government by the least able – to describe how mediocre colleagues ascend new managerialist hierarchies and form a critical mass to block resistance. In my study, the role of quality assessor was sometimes seen as providing a type of psychodrama for some colleagues to act out their hostilities, frustrations, disappointments and lust for power. The power relations of quality assessment enacts particular types of subjectivities. Quality assessment provides new professional identities. It exposes tensions and competitions in the academic community. There is an issue of fitness for purpose of the review teams themselves. The two accounting systems are played off against each other. Colleagues who invest their time in quality assessments are often perceived as lacking a research focus or track record. They were constructed as fraudulent academics or imposters. Hence, they are not considered as peers by the prestigious research institutions.

Colleagues from low RAE scoring institutions were seen as inappropriate judges of teaching quality in high scoring RAE institutions. An assistant registrar explains:

> ...a critical problem within this whole exercise, within the subject review, as it has been done, exercise ... is the choice of teams, the appropriateness of people. We had, let me give you another example, we had a review ... this year ... the QAA first nominated a team of four people, and when we did a check, we found that the departments they came from, none had scored more than four in the RAE, and none had more than ten-per cent post-graduate provision.... And these people were supposed to be coming to X as academic peers, for a provision which is almost totally five star.... And we could not see how this team was in a position to judge teaching and learning happening in a research-led environment.... We complained. So the QAA added a fifth reviewer, from B University. And when we did our research on that we found that precisely the same problems applied. OK the QAA is to some extent hamstrung by those who put themselves forward, and to some extent there's a kind of impasse here, where institutions like ours will complain about the reviewers, but certainly not put staff forward to be reviewers, because of the disruption that it causes.

A senior lecturer in an old university attributes the low calibre of assessors to the accounting systems themselves. That is, serious academics focus on their research and publications, not the assessment of teaching and learning:

> ...the type of person who becomes a subject reviewer is probably doing it because in some sense he [*sic*] is not a fully-fledged academic or has stopped a research career. I just find it odd, how departments can accept somebody leaving their department for a week to do a subject review somewhere else, and just not do their teaching. They are in some senses expendable, or retired.

Prejudices seem to work in all directions. Reviewers from non-research oriented new universities think that elite research universities know nothing about teaching and learning or student support. High status research-led universities can feel that members of new universities cannot tell them how to teach if they lack credibility in the disciplines as researchers and writers. It appears that different constituencies use a range of micropolitical strategies to protect and promote their own interests, life histories and career trajectories.

Challenging the calibre of the peers can be seen as a way of reversing the gaze and resisting domination. It can also be seen as the refusal of powerful high-status organizations to make themselves accountable unless they control the terms of engagement. A head of department in a non-elite new university expressed similar misgivings about the calibre of assessors in subject review:

Working in culturally diverse societies you almost need a kind of multi-literacy, to be able to recognize the dynamics of a definition of quality that lies outside your own, but it has an internal validity, that it can be sustained, that it's legitimate. And that failure to achieve, the multi-literacy of quality, I think is a very sad reflection on the way in which the QAA operates. So what you got was time servers, apparatchiks, bean-counters, box-tickers, you get the, I hesitate to say it, the account-ancy model, where you count it, weigh it, measure it, and it's the price of everything and the value of nothing.

These observations suggest that quality assurance represents a closure of the intellect and that the people drawn to quality assessments are those untroubled by relativism and the uncertainties of critical knowledge. Instead they espouse a modernist certainty that is sometimes at odds with the beliefs systems of those they are auditing. Assessors are represented as mono-vocal, with a limited repertoire of responses and interpretative frameworks. The cultural clash between 'experts' and intellectuals raises questions about shared values in the so-called academic community. The quality 'experts' demand conformity, while the intellectuals should attempt to subvert dominant orders of discourse. Said (1994: 8) fears that intel-lectuals are under threat of the mundane:

There is a danger that the figure of the intellectual might disappear in a mass of details and that the intellectual might become only another professional, or a figure in a social trend.

The mass of bureaucratic details involved in quality procedures threatens to submerge critical thinking. Ryan (2001: 16) believes that the QAA shares 'Stalin's view that variety is the first step to treason'. A head of an education department who became an assessor for subject review describes his discom-fort with the role:

Well, basically you had to learn to write what was called QUAAHILI – QAA prose . . . it was basically inducting people into a set of behaviours which were acceptable within the sort of defined norms of QAA. And then getting you to write a suitably selective account around the main headings within a very tight time-scale, because that's the way in which they implement the exercise. So it wasn't a big debate about the model, and whether it was possible in this fleeting snapshot to engage with the real quality of the programmes or whatever. I mean it wasn't a philo-sophical discussion about quality, it was a 'This is what it is, and this is how you do it' factor of compliance.

There are growing tensions within the academic profession between those who promote and those who resist or critique the quality movement. The product champions are seen as cultural dopes ventriloquizing government policy. An assistant registrar describes a particularly negative experience of subject review:

Our worst visit this year, or last academic year actually, was in October, a year ago to the day in fact. And this team turned up, only one of whom, one of the five, who had done a review previously. And we were large and complex; we'd stuck together thirteen filing cabinets of material. And they saw this stuff and their jaw dropped. Very understandably. They were out of their depth. . . .

Lack of sensitivity about boundaries and institutional cultures and procedures are noted by an assistant registrar in an old university:

We did have one review chair who we thought was very unsatisfactory, who we complained to the QAA about. We never got any response, but we haven't been given that person again. . . . This person tended to have a rather overbearing approach to how the visit was being managed and wouldn't let the university make its own arrangements for the administration of the visit and interfered in the relationship, the detailed relationships between the institutional facilitator and the department in what was a really quite bizarre way and was extremely overbearing about the time scale in which documentation should be produced, which showed very unrealistic expectations and incidentally a lack of understanding of the way things operate in her own institution, which is, to my knowledge quite similar.

While the quality movement aspires to zero defect and standardization, there is considerable product variety in the quality of the peers reviewing the quality of higher education. A principal lecturer notes that the QAA does not adequately quality assure its reviewers. The absence of checks and balances empowers the mediocre:

We've had experiences of, in one instance, a QAA reviewer being appealed against, not just by us, but by their fellow reviewers. The chair obviously complained about that reviewer. We've had reviewers who seemed, in running aspect meetings, unable to run meetings, clearly struggling, intellectually struggling with what they were meant to be doing. . . . But what the QAA allows people to do is to ask stupid questions, questions that they may well not even want asked of themselves, but they feel free, and able, and at liberty to ask those on reviews. . . .

A professor in an old university relates how peer review is supposed to be developmental and interactive, but the formal externally driven exercises deteriorate into an inspection of documentation:

You know if you say 'We're being visited for teaching quality' then most people would assume, naturally, that some professional people were coming to the classes and to see how people teach. But it's not that, it's the paperwork which is inspected. . . . The problem now is that you have to have an inordinate amount of paperwork saying that the review has taken place, and giving, you know, sort of details about what has happened, when it happened, how it happened, the outcomes, the follow up and so on. . . . There has to be an 'audit trail' to prove that it's happened . . . and you're actually creating paper on the day of the visit, you know, it's just a nonsense.

In addition to significant concerns about prejudice, bias, intellectual and professional limitations and lack of preparation, some informants chose to comment on what they perceived as lack of interpersonal skills, emotional literacy and sensitivity. For many, peer review is experienced as a corrosive form of power mongering, as a professor in an old university relates:

> There was a couple of members in the panel . . . who were obnoxious . . . one of them, when we had an aspect meeting, would start every sentence with 'We have a problem with this' or 'We've found a problem with this'. And it just wound the whole team up, and we got aggressive back, and that's not the way . . . maybe it's the system, maybe it's the personalities, it's probably a combination of the two, but I just don't feel they were up to the job really.

This case seems to suggest that the reviewers were playing the 'We're OK, You're not OK' game which can elicit defensive and unhelpful responses, as it replicates critical parent and disciplined child dynamics. The director of academic affairs also notes the lack of quality performance by assessors in a new university:

> If you, as we have had, on one occasion, in the early days of the process a lead reviewer on whom I had to make a formal complaint, only to be told he'd already been sacked by the quality assessment committee, this happens to be somebody who keeps appearing in the national press as an expert on quality, but that's another matter . . . then, you know, clearly everybody gets a bit upset. . . . And of course you always get one or two assessors who are a bit odd . . . I mean you get people who fall asleep, and people whose judgement one finds a bit problematic. . . .

Lack of reflective practice about prior agendas, prejudices and subjectivity on the part of reviewers caused considerable concern in many organizations. Peers are seen by some as agents who have gained the power to superimpose their conceptualizations of quality on to others. This can be experienced as a form of symbolic violence. An academic development officer in an old university explains how he supports peer review as a concept, but had had some negative experiences in practice:

> We had one subject review . . . and this guy had produced a list of positive features, a list of negative features, and then put a score, and he was doing two aspects and he already had a score there. You know he'd not even been in the department. . . .

Some prejudices relate to geographical location! An assistant registrar relates:

> We had a case . . . where a reviewer came along, and more or less said, on the first day, that he didn't approve of the students doing

degrees in London . . . and at that point the credibility of the team just disappeared.

The head of the academic standards and support unit at an old university observes a clash between the access and quality agendas:

> We had, several years ago now, a particular subject review where they appeared to be criticizing us because we took students with a low level of intake score. . . . You know what we were actually doing was a widening participation agenda, taking students in, adding a lot of value, and making sure that they were employable at the end, with really good degree results. But we were criticized for that, and we believe we lost a point for it, because they came thinking, evidently, you know you should have a certain standard of entry. . . .

Espousing an access agenda involves taking risks that can be penalized in quality assessments. This raises questions about the lack of intertextuality between different government policies. On the one hand, organizations are being instructed to take more students – particularly from working class backgrounds. On the other hand organizations, rather than socioeconomic factors such as poverty, lack of student finance, are blamed if the students drop out. A curriculum leader also notes this inconsistency in a new university:

> One of the fears that maybe comparing different universities is not always comparing like for like, is, well, one of the things we lost a point on was progression statistics. The fact that, you know, students were dropping out, or taking a long time to get their degrees and that. Again it was a point we tried to argue, it was about, you know, our whole university is built on the ethos of widening access to students, and so, you know, taking on non-conventional kind of students. And we kind of, you know, built in to that, of course, is you will tend to have greater drop out figures. And we argue that sort of case strongly, but we kind of came away with a feeling that we were inevitably going to lose a mark on that simply because, you know, students drop out here.

Complaints about the lack or limited rights of appeal against judgements perceived as unfair was a motif in this research. The silencing of appeals was experienced as a form of domination. Domination, as Bauman (2001a: 34) observes, is 'achieved by removing the rules constraining one's own freedom of choice'. Several informants reported a sense of injustice about the results and process of their subject reviews. A belief was that the QAA makes the rules and the assessors can ignore them but the assessed cannot. The process is supposed to be evidence-based, with triangulation of data, and yet it is often impressionistic. The head of an education department in a new university expresses his anger and frustration at the calibre of the assessors and the precariousness of procedures:

> I was very angry about it. I don't believe that the team that was fielded really got to grips with the issues. I think the judgements that they

arrived at were not supported by evidence. I've got areas in which they have docked us a point, or made a criticism where in fact the evidence from students and external examiners directly contradicts it. And my staff were very angry at the end of the process. It was hugely costly. I mean it cost us I guess the equivalent of a senior lecturer, in that year, in the amount of time that went in to it. It costs us an absolute fortune in administrative time, and creating the base room, it was intensely bureaucratic. And it eroded my faith in peer review I have to say.

He attributed his sense of lack of fair play to the closure and false totalization of the grading system with its potential for misrecognition:

Now maybe that's got more to do with the grading processes than it has to do with the dialogue, yeah? And I think I'm still in favour of provocative, constructive, professional dialogue, you know, which is challenging, gets you to re-examine your paradigms, and has sufficient authority, and experience to propose alternatives, you know, to develop your thinking. That I regard as a very constructive kind of quality-oriented encounter. What I don't regard as constructive is being assessed by people that I consider to be less well equipped to make judgements than my course team are.

Administrators with an overview of different departments and with experience of several subject reviews often commented on the lack of continuity of judgements across different review teams. Quality is not moderated nationally or across disciplinary boundaries in organizations. The head of the academic standards in an old university observes:

A lot does depend on the team you get and the extent to which they understand and identify with the situation that you're in. You do sometimes see things where one area is criticized for something that another area is not, or vice versa, and you think well 'Where's the comparability there?'

An argument in favour of peer review is that it allows the profession to self-manage and self-regulate. Peer review is often discursively positioned as the alternative to state inspections. Administrative staff can sometimes construct it as the scrutiny of documentation, as an academic registrar from a new university observes:

Peer review has to be very substantially about following audit trails and listening to everybody's voices rather than just having a discussion . . . . But I mean I used to be on CNAA boards and things and I mean I prefer it as an approach to an inspectorial approach; it's positive in that respect.

A fear in Britain is that higher education will be subjected to similar inspection practices that exist for schools, as an academic development officer in an old university describes:

> I'm not sure I see an alternative. You know when you compare the sort
> of situation in schools, with things like OfSTED . . . I think peer review
> is probably about the best way of doing things.

The TINA effect (there is no alternative) is a potent relay of power. It
diminishes expectations as people internalize feelings of powerlessness and
constraint. However, peer review can also be a management tool. An assistant registrar in a new university felt that peer review allowed the unsayable
to be said. Using the image of palatability, she felt that academics would
swallow more from other academics than from administrators:

> I think my role as an administrator involved in quality assurance is to
> facilitate and get together that sort of sharing. I think if it were some-
> body like myself and saying 'Well your personal tutoring support is
> rubbish' and I would be given short shrift and sent on my merry way.
> There are some areas, I think, where only an academic can talk to an
> academic . . . you can get sociologists coming in to talk to sociologists
> about how they might translate some of these concepts into their own
> discipline. . . . It's much more palatable isn't it, in the context of some-
> body that you respect as part of your academic community?

Again, this raises questions of whose interests peers represent and whether
peer review is a form of ontological complicity (Bourdieu, 1981). Peers act
as intermediary bodies, mediating state policy. Neave (1998: 279) asks if the
intermediary bodies are 'emanations of central authority reaching out and
down or are they extensions of the university world groping up and back?'
    The miserable performance of peers has left some academics feeling
cheated or defrauded. They thought that they would be able to control the
process, but the peers have changed allegiance. A philosophy lecturer in an
old university believes that peer review is a mechanism that academics have
supported in order to be self-managing, but it is fraught with problems of
transparency and the arbitrary nature of decision making.

> I mean the problem with peer review is we assert its value because we
> wish to be self-managing. So it's a sort of best worst possible scenario
> cases. However, there are endemic problems with peer review to do
> with transparency – the assumption of neutrality. The fact that what
> appears to be a neutral and above the board process, thoroughly trans-
> parent process, in fact can turn out to incorporate judgements based
> on prejudice. . . . So if we're going to assert the value of peer review I
> think we need to do quite a lot of work on our picking what those
> presuppositions are. . . .

It appears that some academics place their trust in disciplinary power –
divesting it of any ideological underpinnings. The head of economics in a
new university felt that peer review allowed people with shared expertise
and disciplinary knowledge to enter into a dialogue:

I certainly can't imagine being reviewed by anybody but peers . . . because much of what they're after is, you know one of the aspects is curriculum design, content organization. It has to be an economist, and it has to be somebody we could respect.

There is also the element of pastoral power and moral technology. Confessing and disclosing can be a purification ritual or period of atonement. The director of academic affairs in a new university saw peer review as an opportunity for professional reflection:

I think good quality peers come to your institution and give you what in effect is, well it's not free consultancy, but it's good quality consultancy about what you do, and good advice, and a bit of reflection, is a good thing. . . . The QAA is something that we do to ourselves, it's people like us who do it. It couldn't work unless the academics agreed to be the reviewers.

The quasi-religious elements of quality assessment mean that it can function as a corrective. A director of teaching and learning in a university college describes the success of a confessional approach:

You know we took the decision, I think quite rightly, as most other institutions would take, in that we would try to hide nothing, because it doesn't work. We held our hands up when we felt we were weak in certain areas, and I think the inspection team appreciated that.

Peer review can be a form of domination packaged as equality. There is evidence, from this study, that trust has been tested and in some cases, betrayed. Some individuals have acted inappropriately, while others have inherited a 'horns' effect, as the system that they represent is so mistrusted. It is questionable whether academics should act as peer reviewers in quality assessments. On the one hand, it is seen as highly preferable to state inspections, but there is a major question about whose interests reviewers serve – those of the evaluative state, the academic 'community', or their own, sometimes fractured identities? This reflects the age-old debate about change from within or without. By accepting to act as assessors are academics colluding in an oppressive technology, or protecting their colleagues from a worse fate? Dominelli and Hoogvelt (1996: 83/4) suggest that the system of peer review means that 'professional scholars also have been co-opted into creating the conditions for their own disempowerment'. From my research, it seems that peer review offers opportunities and threats. While it purports to be developmental, it is profoundly judgemental. The micropolitics of peer review suggest that some peer reviewers are reflective and power sensitive, there are those who use the role to rehearse myriad frustrations, prejudices and certainties. For some, being a peer reviewer seemed to provide an ideal opportunity to enact resentment and revenge on a system that had undervalued them. Peer review can be seen as a form of accountability and validation. It can also be seen as a form of contamination and interference by amateurs. Can there be collegiality and peerness in a competitive, market-driven higher education economy? In a market economy, organizations are placed in competition for students, research funding and links with industry. For some, peer review is a benign way of sharing expertise. An academic registrar in a new university marvels at the co-operation in spite of the competition in higher education:

> I think the higher education sector is remarkable, in that it's, you know, because it's very competitive, you know every student I get another university is not getting, and that costs us a lot of money, it can cost the sector a lot of money. And I think it's remarkable that the sector has remained as collaborative as it has. So I do a lot of QA work, you know I do a lot of audit work for QAA, I do institutional review and that sort of thing, and the way in which people are willing to share practice across the sector is, I think, remarkable.

Within organizations, the different accounting systems and drive for entrepreneurialism mean that individuals are often in competition. Yet, peers are expected to enter organizations altruistically and with no prior agendas, expectations or prejudices. In a much-publicized event in 2001, the London School of Economics voted 70 to 2 to reform, transform or terminate the QAA. One of their many concerns also related to the quality and prior agendas of the assessors:

> Our colleagues have been perturbed by the nature of review teams, and great variations in their calibre – in their preparation and professionalism; academic competence and reputation; dispositions towards both the departments visited and towards the LSE; and their intentions to impose their own pedagogical agenda (draft resolution to LSE Academic Board, 14 March, 2001).

This is open to multiple readings. Is this resistance to the domination of the QAA, or the refusal of an elite organization to make itself accountable to a wider constituency? The invulnerable have begun to be vulnerable to the influence of an 'other' that was previously occluded. A head of department in a new university expresses his discomfort with the elite being in the vanguard of resistance:

> My problem with that resistance is this, is that it's really come from the elite. It's come from the elite because the elite still has the cultural power to deny the accountability, and I'm not sure that that's the most healthy form of, if you like, re-appropriation of the quality of debate. So I've got very, very deep reservations about that.

The refusal to acknowledge colleagues from lower status organizations as peers could be seen as an example of the covert binary divide and also as evidence of the competition and hierarchy reinforced by the market culture. It is also an example of the elite, 'first world' organizations asserting sovereignty.

Gulliver and the Lilliputs: reinforcing the binary divide

The issue of elitism and the binary divide in UK higher education recurred throughout my research. Macro issues of status and power are enacted via micropolitical practices of inspection. There are different higher educations. Elite, 'first world' organizations have been invaded and sometimes overtaken by the 'third world'. The proximity of the dissimilar 'other' provokes a type of discomfort not unlike the current hysteria over asylum seekers. Boundaries are being transgressed. Some of the elite organizations see themselves as Gulliver-type entities, with Lilliputians crawling all over them. There is a strong sense of contamination fear or purity and danger permeating accounts (Douglas, 1966). Arrangements for quality assurance seems to have exposed fundamental differences between old and new universities. New universities were more centrally managed under the Council for National Academic Awards (CNAA). The head of an education department in a new university outlines the cultural differences between old and new universities:

> I'm talking about the old polytechnics, when they subsequently became the new universities, that pattern was quite well established, so you had a corporate management of quality in the institution, which was really quite different to the culture in the old universities, where it was much more relaxed. . . . Those of us who had been in the CNAA sector were quite used to sharing with colleagues a much more, you know, professionally-based overview of how one would integrate one's various contributions to the totality of the student experience.

In the post-1992 or new universities in Britain, formal mechanisms of QA have existed since their establishment from 1969 to 1972. They were subjected to visits from Her Majesty's Inspectorate and offered awards validated and overseen by the CNAA. Hence the external gaze, with its associated power relations, was embedded in the culture of new universities. An assistant registrar in an old university describes how colleagues who have worked in new universities have influenced the process of assessing teaching and learning. Hence there is an in-built tension, as he argues that it was conceived to 'catch out' the research-led organizations. There appears to be a punitive or revengeful edge to the process:

> And I think that the QAA has largely been staffed by people from an ex-polytechnic background . . . I think it's a difference whereby, very crudely speaking . . . polytechnics tended to be more centrally directive, from the director's office, where the collegial model, the collegial expectation, the institution as a sum of its parts is still a model which many old universities think they're working to, particularly in the area of teaching and learning. . . . When subject review started, in the old universities we all thought this was going to be the CNAA's revenge.

The idea of familiarity with quality in new universities as opposed to shock waves and resistance in old universities is corroborated by the director of academic affairs in a new university:

> I don't think it's changed it that much actually, because I think institutions like this used to work under the CNAA. We have a tremendous amount of our courses accredited by professional statutory bodies. So we're very used to the idea of working with external people and being accountable. . . .

A reader in social policy in an old university observes that changing relations between academics and administrators is a new form of power. This represents a signifier of difference between new and old universities. The interface between management and professionalism was the mark of a new managerialist university:

> I'm tempted to say it's made it more like a new university rather than an old one. And I think that's got advantages and disadvantages. In terms of like, as I said, it does make us more structured in filling in forms, that you do sometimes think that what's being measured is a process, so you get a sense more that administrators are more in control, have more power over what you're doing.

Some new universities did better in subject review than elite institutions (Beckett, 2001). This provided further evidence of Philistinism and justification for the abolition of both the QAA and subject review. A professor at Warwick quips 'According to the QAA, the quality of physics teaching is higher at Sheffield Hallam University than at Cambridge University. You remember Cambridge, that flat place with all those Nobel prizewinners' (Oswald, 2001: 15). However, the head of quality assurance in a new university describes how high scores for new universities provide an accolade and vote of confidence in their academic procedures. Their student-centred efforts gain recognition and reward:

> X got its first 24 last year . . . and you know for new universities that is a major achievement. And they were absolutely delighted about that. . . . The other thing I thought was really interesting coming here, is that you'd get people saying 'Ah well that review team, they've all come from, they're all from old universities, they won't understand us.'

Survival in the academy is maintained on terms that demand subjection. The head of quality in a university college explains how the transition from the status of university college to new university is dependent on scores received in quality audits:

> In terms of the priority of the institution, getting quality right is absolutely central I would think. I mean our priority as an institution is to become a full university . . . and our strategic objective is to achieve full university status within the next whatever, you know, few years. And

obviously we want to achieve that ensuring we have appropriate quality assurance systems, and that our curriculum reaches appropriate levels of quality, is central to it all. So the outcomes of subject reviews, and RAE exercises are important. Any problems there and it would jeopardize the strategic direction of the institution.

Split-site or newly merged organizations can use scores as important intelligence about previously unknown areas. Areas undervalued internally gain new status when they are credentialized by external agents. A principal lecturer in a new university explains:

It's given us credibility in the university as well. . . . The old, two separate institutions, certainly the old school of education at X wasn't thought very highly of, within the university, and there was expectation, I think, from senior management, that we would get quite a low grade. But colleagues have noted that when we go to central university (we are on a different site), now, at meetings the message seems to have got through that we did quite well, and people seem to be commenting on that, and seem to be taking the institute, the newly formed institute more seriously. So the external sort of confirmation of what we do has had benefits.

The struggle for recognition has long been associated with power and status. A principal lecturer in a university college explains how they comply as they want external approval:

Here, where you've got an institution that's, you know, evolved out of a teacher training college into a university college . . . it's going through the hoops now of trying to get research degree awarding powers. Traditionally, I guess, it's always been more compliant, because it's had to play more by those rules.

A lecturer in sociology argues that elite organizations can afford to invest more resources and hence skew the scores:

We don't have the resources of our nearest university, which is an old university with a huge reputation and lots of money. I think that's bound to affect the way, you know the time we can give the students, the amount of books that we've got in the library, you know the computing resources we've got, and all of those things count in terms of quality.

The binary divide condenses cultural constructions of the mental/manual or abstract/applied knowledge polarizations. A vice provost in an old university notes a culture clash between applied and disciplinary approaches to knowledge in new and old universities:

We've had a real culture clash in one particular area where people from other sorts of universities said, 'How do you manage to persuade prospective employers that your students have acquired the core and transferable skills that employees need?' And we have really quite strong evidence that our employers are not actually interested in the core and transferable skills. They actually want our students traditionally trained in the relevant science. Which I would argue actually involves acquiring the core and transferable skills but it's a different issue.

Sometimes, the clash is confronted. On other occasions, it is disguised and a comedy of manners ensues, as a senior lecturer in education describes:

I work in an old university, and the people who did our QAA were from new universities, and I don't want to be elitist, and I do think there are people in old universities who probably are far lacking in the experience, the expertise of some of our colleagues in new universities, but generally speaking . . . we were visited by people with very little expertise in our areas of expertise, and those who did have expertise didn't have it to the level that we have. So for example, Professor X was visited by somebody who hasn't even got a PhD in teaching. Someone who'd just come in from schools a couple of years ago . . . so we actually felt we were being polite to people who didn't have a lot of expertise in our area, who we didn't see as our equals. Now that sounds elitist, and I'm aware of that.

Quality assessment exposes prejudices, suspicions and mistrust that are deeply embedded in the academy. The methodology of quality assessment is wide open to micropolitical interference. Observations about the precariousness and unreliability of peer review imply that audit is methodologically flawed. It is the illogical quest for the logic of practice.

The methodology of quality assurance in higher education: modernization or a return to modernism?

Quality assurance is located within the systematic discourse of modernism. There are elements of positivism with reviewers claiming to be able to unearth a 'truth' about the complexities of organizational life, simply by consulting the 'right' documents and asking the 'right' people. The readings become 'truths', encoded in league tables and reified for several years. This is in direct opposition to post-modern and feminist research paradigms that suggest multiple readings, situated interpretations and discontinuities. Strathern (2000b: 313) notes that 'There is an assumption that a university is first and foremost an organization whose performance can be observed'.

The crisis of representation and the plurality of texts are not considered in quality assessment. There are limited opportunities for interpretative pluralism. The imperative to represent one's organization textually imposes a modernist rationality and a set of certainties that cannot always exist in complex organizations. For example, organizations are regularly required to provide audit trails documenting how issues/student concerns etc. move through the committee cycle to a satisfactory resolution. This implies a linear rationality which completely overlooks micropolitics, creative non-implementation, and the politics of non-decision making (Lukes, 1974).

Elsewhere, the methodology has also been criticized for being too 'soft' and open to distortion. In a major form of recuperation of power, economists at Warwick wrote (*Guardian*, 2001) that:

> The method is not scientific. We supplied the hypothesis, the evidence and the witnesses. We chose the students and employers, the samples of student work, and the internal documentation to be seen by the panel.

While subject review is supposed to espouse an evidence-based methodology, there are questions about what constitutes evidence and how this is constructed and evaluated. A professor in an old university comments on a breach of procedure, that is a point was deducted without prior warning or opportunities for redemption:

> I mean one problem we had is that they, the quality management and enhancement aspect meeting, they did not mention at all the factor that was used to deduct a point at the end of the process . . . I found that very upsetting. They did mention something on the Wednesday night, but as I said we produced a document including comments from external examiners over the last seven or eight years, and e-mails from our current examiners saying there is not a problem in this particular area, and they just ignored all that, and still said there's a problem. And I just think that, you know, this chair kept saying it's evidence-based, but to us they didn't have the evidence to draw the conclusion that they actually drew.

Scores in subject review were not absolute, as they related to how providers met their own aims and objectives. Paradoxically, higher standards and aspirations could mean a lower score. An assistant registrar in an old university comments on the subjective indicators of worth meant that the same department received different scores for the same aspect in two subject reviews:

> The particular negative experience with subject review that sticks out in my mind, was one where we got a 3 for quality management and enhancement in the department which I considered to be one of our best departments from that point of view. It was a situation in which this particular individual had got his own view of the way in which quality assurance should be managed, which was extremely bureaucratic. And he had detailed expectations at the level of exactly how minutes should be written for departmental committees which we actually thought was bizarre and was not underpinned by any published

QAA requirement or our experience of the QAA's expectations. . . . That was born out by the fact that it was in a two-discipline department. So it had two subject reviews and then the other subject review, which was very shortly afterwards, because it was of the same department it had exactly the same quality assurance procedures, but it got a 4, but the difference was that it was a different subject reviewer doing quality management and enhancement.

Assessment is a major relay of power and expertise in the academy. It was also one of the six aspects scrutinized in subject review. However, there was little evidence of expertise in assessment in the methodology of subject review itself. A faculty manager in an old university comments on what he saw as flaws in the marking system for subject review:

But it's this very strange marking system isn't it, right at one end the goal post doesn't shift right to one end of the scale. In the parlance you don't use the full range of marks available when you're judging a department, no one gets 1s. So it's really pointless saying it's out of 24. . . . What I thought was particularly daft was a whole sector that perfectly well understands marking and assessment choosing such a feeble one for exam judgements.

An assistant registrar in an old university felt that the extensive preparation suggested a systematic approach, but the reviewers are unable to engage significantly in the documentation in such a limited time.

There's a general sense that it's an awful lot of work and an awful lot of energy, and a lot of paper driven activity, and actually the reviewers, when they actually arrive, aren't necessarily confident to digest, assimilate and reach judgements in the short time that they've got. So I think it's as much as anything the methodology, the big bang approach. . . . The extent to which they are able to test out the evidence effectively, and can reach judgements which are evidence-based. There are concerns about that I think.

Whatever the ideological hue, there are widespread beliefs that the methodology of quality assessment is characterized by ad hocery, instability and unreliability. It is also wide open to micropolitical distortions.

7

Reconstructing Students as Consumers

Delighting the customer!

The customer-care revolution and an outcomes-based approach, with the emphasis on product specification, entitlements and consumer rights has changed social and pedagogical relations in the academy. In a market economy, students are no longer constructed as recipients of welfare, but purchasers of an expensive product. They too have been transformed from vagabonds into tourists (Bauman, 1998b). The introduction of tuition fees in Britain has nominally raised the influence of students and their families as stakeholders. There is a promotion of market approaches to higher education choice and services. Democracy has turned into consumption practices As Apple remarks: 'Rather than democracy being a *political* concept, it is transformed into a wholly *economic* concept. The message of such policies is that of what might best be called "arithmetical particularism", in which the unattached individual – as consumer – is deraced, declassed, and degendered' (Apple, 2000: 60). Modern consumption involves the manipulation of signs (Baudrillard, 1998). Signs of quality have been introduced to reassure consumers that their interests are being met. There has been the introduction of an array of mechanisms including learning contracts, guidelines, assessment criteria, learning outcomes, core skills – all of which in various ways attempt to systematize and codify student–teacher interactions. A principle of TQM is customer delight and planned satisfaction. Happiness has to be measurable. There are fears that this process is eclipsing traditional identifications with academic disciplines and that presentation and contract are gaining hegemonic power over content. This is part of a significant realignment of the university away from epistemological foundations of the knowledge base and towards a more technocratic instrumental view of knowledge (Brooks, 2001).

Image and efficiency underpin the representation of quality services. McWilliam *et al.* (1999) note how criteria for best practice are no longer being driven by the dictates of the intellectual field, but by the degree of client satisfaction. A professor in a new university notes:

I think presentational matters have been quite dramatically changed. . . . QAA seems to have focused attention a great deal on procedures related to teaching rather than the actual quality of the teaching.

Shore and Selwyn's (1998: 161) analysis of a Scottish university document prepared to help students evaluate courses revealed nearly twice as many columns devoted to the lecturer's 'style' and 'communication skills' than to the content of the course. The form of teaching, in their view, has assumed dominance over the content. Meadmore (1998) argues that what is being taught or researched has become less important than it should be done 'excellently'. Excellence is represented as value free and the student is a disembodied sign. However, the focus on peripheral details paradoxically means that excellence can produce mediocrity.

Quality assurance, while appropriating and rearticulating concepts such as student empowerment, is viewed by some as a profoundly conservative construct. Conservative, because it is about disembodied standardization. For example, Bensimon (1995: 608) believes that quality or TQM in particular, is a 'natural ally of those who believe it is more important to defend traditional values than to reconstruct the academy to make it more responsive to diversity'. It comes as a surprise then, that the radical student body in Britain – the National Union of Students (NUS) – supports quality assessment. Their rationale is that it is a form of student empowerment as it encodes rights and entitlements, it gives students a voice and privileges the student experience. Furthermore, it is assumed to inform consumer choice. The NUS vigorously opposed political moves to lighten the touch of quality audits in 2001, with the then president, Owain James, saying 'NUS is in favour of universities undergoing Teaching Quality Assessments because they give students clear and consistent external information on which to base their decisions when researching courses and colleges or universities' (Major, 2001: 9).

In a mass system, students are no longer constructed as scholars to be handcrafted, but rather as entities in an industrial process. Access policies have created a moral panic over standards and 'dumbing down'. There are contamination fears expressed in the idea that massification and the entry of 'non-traditional' learners presents a threat to academic standards. This sentiment was expressed by the Conservative Secretary of State for Education in 1993, John Pattern, who discursively positioned access in opposition to quality and excellence in higher education and dismissed equity as a form of political correctness (Pattern, 1993):

Opening the doors to all and sundry is one way of growing a higher education sector. It is, however, not a good one if universities are to remain the pinnacles of excellence. . . . The day we sacrifice these essential principles on the ever-growing altar of political correctness will mark the beginning of the self-destruction of one of the nation's greatest assets.

One way of heading off the contamination of academia by the masses is to sculpt boundaries, barriers and a minimum sense of entitlements. Codification can offer some solutions to the chaos of expansion. It marks out the relationship between purchasers and providers.

From change agents to consumers?

The construction of students has shifted over the decades. Whereas in the 1960s students were seen as radicals and transgressives, their identity at the beginning of the twenty-first century is described in the language of the market. The Dearing Committee (Dearing, 1997: 64, 4.59) made reference to the development of a consumer consciousness:

> There is now greater emphasis on recognition of the individual as customer or consumer. People's expectations of publicly funded services have arisen and they no longer accept unquestioningly what is offered.

It is debatable whether students have ever unquestioningly accepted what they were offered. The history of university students internationally is riven with protests, uprisings and challenges to the establishment.

The student uprisings in Europe in May 1968 were perceived as marking changing relations between universities and society. The uprisings of the 1960s stimulated considerable social and political comment. Students were constructed as revolutionaries, transgressives, social commentators and change agents – demonstrating against the forces of reaction and authoritarian practices – inside and beyond the university. The university became a political site. For Habermas (1971), the university was not defined by either organized or liberal modernity. In his view the task of the university was to provide a political education by shaping a political consciousness among its students. Marcuse (1969) believed that a major challenge to power resided in the student body and that the university was potentially a site of social revolution. Touraine (1971) theorized that the students' movement was developing in response to universities' failure to respond to a changing society and that the university existed somewhere between knowledge and politics. For Riesman (1998) the central consequence of the student protests of the 1960s was the curbing of the power of academics. Delanty (2001: 63) describes how, in 1970 at Warwick University, students, protesting about lack of accountability in the university, occupied the administration and gained access to controversial information about what E.P. Thompson (1970) later called the 'industrial–intellectual oligarchy'. One explanation for the current student support in Britain for quality assessment is that it is a new device to curb the power of academics and challenge the intellectual oligarchy. Yet the intellectuality of the higher education contract seems to have been eclipsed by attention to service level agreements.

Words, words, words: writing risk reduction

Service level agreements are part of the low trust/high-risk society. Quality assurance is often grammartocentric and reliant on textual representation. Documentation is proliferating in the academy. Every transaction has to be specified and formalized. The emphasis on product specifications is supposed to demarcate expectations, rights and responsibilities. A noticeable feature of my research is that no informant actually cited improved teaching or enhanced disciplinary knowledge as outcomes of quality assessment. They all tended to focus on procedures, structures and documentation.

In response to my direct question about whether quality assurance has impacted upon his actual teaching, the director of quality in a new university states:

> Well I mean only in as far as it's made me more aware I suppose, of quality mechanisms, and how important it is to get student feedback for example, and to do something about that feedback. But I think I always realized that, you know, even before I moved into this post, but it heightened my perception about that I suppose.

A professor in an old university argues that enhanced documentation might have resulted in more reflexivity about process, but he has doubts as to whether it has enhanced professional practice:

> There have been advantages in the sense that it's made all of us think more carefully about how we proceed, and the amount of documentation that students, rightfully, can expect. I think that's the advantage, and I don't think it's actually made us any better teachers.

Another professor in an old university also notes the procedure versus practice binary:

> But there are some benefits. I mean I do think that it may, it does make you think about your procedures, and it does make you therefore, make changes to your procedures.

The director of academic affairs in a new university observes how he has become a more reflexive teacher as a consequence of quality requirements:

> I think it makes me more conscious of the need to think about why I teach, why I teach the way I do, and what I'm trying to achieve. And what the students are going to get out of it, rather than A just giving them a good time, and B getting through it.

A reader also comments on enhanced reflexivity:

> I suppose it does make you think about the structure of lectures, perhaps, you know the educational achievements you're trying to achieve. I think we all had that sort of somewhere in the backs of our minds, and, you know, ideas about it. But I think now you have to put aims

and objectives, and we now have to give handouts that have a standard pro-forma, which have aims, objectives, learning outcomes etc., etc.

There are still questions about whether enhanced reflexivity automatically leads to improved practice, especially when reflexivity is within prescribed taxonomies of effectiveness. Some informants report a 'tightening up' rather than a significant change. Feedback to students is one way in which the product can be specified. Impressionistic, subjective judgements of value are no longer acceptable in a quality culture. A principal lecturer in a new university describes how external requirements have impacted on her self-management:

> In relation to my teaching I suppose it's tightened up. I mean I think we did have good practice in place, but it's certainly made us tighten up more on the quality of feedback that goes to students, ensuring that we were clear in our module handbooks, so it actually subtly led to improvements in quality to a certain extent.

A theme running through my research was the irony that while quality assessment of teaching and learning was supposed to focus on 'student experience', it actually serves to impoverish it as the labour intensity reduced time available for students. A principal lecturer in a new university described how quality assurance procedures in general and subject review in particular, actively took her time away from students:

> I think that that was one of the things that we said, students must come first. Although I must admit that, having a student wanting a tutorial that week [subject review week] was a bit difficult, and I did still see the student, but I did feel a certain amount of resentment that they should really have understood what we were going through.

The QAA is thought to damage what it claims to improve. Ryan (2001: 16) berates the wasted time, stating that 'Anyone accumulating a room full of paper for no more useful purpose than to ensure it is present if the inspectors want to see it is not improving tutorial services, is not organizing departmental mentoring, is not fostering the essay-writing skills of under-equipped students . . . A director of learning and teaching also notes:

> What I have noticed is that I, again this is a personal observation, I've got less and less time to see the students as often as I'd like to . . . I certainly don't see them as often as I used to.

Students are being perceived as a site of danger. Whereas fears of litigation are well established in higher education in the USA, they have now entered the UK academy. This has resulted in a performed solicitousness, with numerous tests of the new forced 'unconditional love'. Interpersonal skills are instrumentalized to pacify the customer. Several of my informants noted that it was becoming increasingly dangerous to set aside time for writing and research, as the dominant culture now is to be permanently accessible to students for fear of grievance procedures and negative student evaluations. Presenteeism is facilitated by new technologies and multiple modes of communication are now possible between students and academics (Blackmore and Sachs, 2001). A philosophy lecturer in an old university observes how there has been some cultural reversal as providers and 'customers' enter new forms of relationships. Academics now have to be acquiescent and accountable to students. Her observation raises questions about the discourse of demands, the parameters of professionalism and the climate of anxiety:

> . . . you are in a position where you can't refuse the students anything, you know you really can't, if they knock at the door at any time of day you have to say 'Please come in, you know, what would you like me to do for you?' Just in case one of the SPR team stops them and says 'What's your experience?' And they could be the one that says 'Well they're never in', or even 'They don't help very much'.

The issue of boundaries is evocative of Shaw's (1995) theory that teaching is often elided with mothering. Part of the traditional construct of mothering is to have no boundaries, needs, and limits. Allowing oneself to be used up is a prerequisite of maternal care. In this context, consumption is about devouring. Academics have to mediate between their own depletion and increasing student demands. The corporatization of universities is being achieved with a cottage industry labour infrastructure. Becher and Trowler (2001) claim that the total expenditure per student over the 20-year period between 1976–96 was reduced by 40 per cent. Performativity is demanded without the resources to ensure a polished performance. In exasperation, Skeggs (1995: 482) exclaims:

> we are dissatisfied, the students are dissatisfied. We all want more, we all want it to be better. We don't want to be the physical embodiment of un-met student demands. . . .

Care is being commodified. Higher education is becoming more like the hospitality industry. In the quality context, student services can be more linked to market exchange relations, rather than humanitarian commitment. When completion rates are key performance indicators in quality audits, student support and welfare are linked to keeping students on track for their economic value to the organization. This is humanitarianism in the service of the market. In the market culture, all student services can be read as manipulative. Student support is also open to performativity, underpinned with intellectual and emotional labour.

A new 'contractualism' has emerged (Yeatman, 1995). Caring has to be encoded. Education has to be delivered defensively. The rights of one group become the duties and responsibilities of another. A registrar describes how procedures are documented and formalized now in anticipation of student complaints:

> Students – well perhaps in some ways it's the formalization of procedures and in particular putting in place grievance procedures which

we've had for quite a time, and a complaints procedures has chimed in with the increasing litigiousness of students anyway. Students are given to complaining more and they will complain and say, 'Well I wasn't taught properly'. Or 'I wasn't examined properly'. Or 'I wasn't supervised properly'.

Significations of quality are cyclical. Student complaints are perceived as permanently in flux, and should be viewed as one data set, rather than the definitive truth, as an assistant registrar records:

> Students are articulate, students will complain. There is always the issue of course, that what students complain about one year, they will be perfectly happy with the next year, and vice versa. There is a danger in where we're heading at the moment, that the notion of consumerism will lead to student opinions being over-rated in importance. They are important, but they are important as a clue rather than as a solution in themselves.

The mass system means that there are fewer opportunities to engage face-to-face with students. Furthermore, the decrease of trust means that the spoken word no longer has validity. Hence documentation is a form of communication and contract. A senior lecturer relates the cultural shift:

> There are too many students for us to carry on with that sort of closed personal sort of environment. So we had to start documenting things. . . . We're having to really, really move very dramatically from a culture where there was very little paper, everything was word of mouth, to everything being documented. I'd say that a greater proportion of the students are getting a better deal than they were before, actually, because we didn't used to have module handbooks. We didn't used to evaluate courses systematically really. It was all a bit random. Reading lists varied very much from tutor to tutor. There's a better baseline I think in terms of what the students get from us, and the transparency to them . . . we've had to move from a very old-worldy sort of culture to a very sort of paper culture very quickly, and I think it's to the good.

There are implications that improving the quality of documentation leads to improved quality of the service. A director of quality in an old university approves of the increased information to students as a consequence of quality assurance, especially in research-led organizations:

> Well, I mean subject review, or what used to be called TQA, has meant I think very often that students get rather better information about the courses that they're taking, for example. The quality of course books has probably improved. . . . It was all done a bit *ad hoc* in the past without a doubt. I also think that if we had had the RAE without the quality assurance on the student side then in institutions like mine, or indeed also come to that, yours, one might have found teaching suffered even worse relative to research than it has in those such institutions.

A curriculum leader in a new university also notes the benefits:

> And of course it's also good for students, getting back to this issue of
> students becoming more like customers. I think it's good that they can
> refer to a QAA score as a point of reference. I know, I mean I'm
> slightly biased because we got a better than we expected score.

Segal Quince Wicksteed's (1999) survey discovered that only 12 per cent
of respondents considered QAA reports to be the single most important
source of information about quality. Yet, a common belief in my study was
that student decision making was influenced by codified information. It is
questionable whether it is the existence of scores or the internet itself that
has influenced the ways in which students search for colleges and universities. However, a professor in a new university believes that enhanced
consumer information and the introduction of tuition fees has led to
more discriminating and informed decision making and higher aspirations
of the service and product for all students and their parents:

> Students are increasingly sophisticated and their parents are, in look-
> ing at league tables, QAA scores and so forth so I think that's one issue.
> I think students are more aware now of their position as quote cus-
> tomers unquote, than they were heretofore. . . . Part of it is external
> quality procedures and so forth. But also part of it has been the chang-
> ing nature of funding. So if you're paying for something overtly out
> of your own pocket, it changes your disposition a bit. So I think, yes, I
> think it's probably made students more clearly aware of, if you like,
> their rights and what they should reasonably expect.

In this analysis there is an equation of information with enhanced choice
and informed decision making. Information is seen as part of the democratization process. Blackmore (2000: 144) identifies how human capital theory
is premised upon 'the self-maximizing, autonomous, individual chooser and
upon national productivity measures'. However, the market economy tends
to overlook the influence of *habitus*, and how choice is invariably structured
by gender, social class and ethnicity (Ball *et al.*, 2000). Findings in Britain
and the USA suggest that students from middle class backgrounds, with
university-educated parents are more likely to find rankings important and
to devote time to strategic decision making (McDonough *et al.*, 1997; Ball
et al., 2002). Pugsley (1998: 85) observes that 'there are class inequalities
involved in making decisions about higher education which have persisted
for the 40 years since Jackson and Marsden's 1962 study'. Reay *et al.* (2001)
discovered that conceptions of the 'good university' are both racialized and
classed. Working class students in their study were more concerned with
feeling comfortable, safe and happy, that is not othered, than with league
tables.

    If information is aimed at attracting consumers, the introduction of fees
can act as a deterrent. Research released by the *Guardian* of sixth-form perceptions suggests that over half of the sample had been put off attending

higher education by the cost (*Guardian*/UCAS, 1998: 11). Burke's (2002: 35) study also records how 'mature students from poorer socioeconomic backgrounds must calculate the risk of debt and negotiate complex funding systems before accessing education'. The rhetoric of the student experience homogenizes and ignores diversity. It is an exercise in norm making. It also disguises the regulation of academics. A philosophy lecturer discusses the hidden curriculum of quality audits:

> I'm not at all clear whether the education, the learning that takes place, I'm really not at all clear whether that's more effective now, than it was prior, because the QAA is based on assessing really our performance, although it's couched in the language of student experience. That's not really what it's doing, and it can't be doing that because student experience is made up of such a multi-faceted thing, which includes resources, and grants and working and all sorts of things. Although it was talked about as though they were interested in the student experience, in fact what they audited was our management, our knowledge of the students, and our teaching performance.

In this analysis, it would appear that the emphasis on customer care is simply a regulatory device, with considerable moral potency.

Educatainment and student evaluation

Within the context of the learning organization, students, as customers and consumers, are also perceived to be a source of knowledge production. Critique is a democratic value, with student evaluation seen as the yielding or redistribution of academic power in order to apprehend the demands and views of others. Ramsden (1998) argues that feedback from the client, the customer, the consumer, the student, the lifelong learner is the one measure of performance that should count in any organization. This tends to assume that the 'voice' of the consumer is stable, pure, concrete and is the authentic indicator of democracy. This view suggests that there is a culturally untainted place from which students speak and theorize. It homogenizes student voices and overlooks power relations within the student body. Furthermore, it suggests an algorithmic relationship between input (student evaluation) and output (organizational change). Marginson (1997: 5) critiques the idea of an 'imagined line of causation from competition to consumer sovereignty to better efficiency and quality'.

Lecky and Neill's (2001) survey discovered the following types of feedback mechanisms in use:

- unit/module evaluation questionnaires (the most commonly used);
- course/programme evaluation questionnaires;
- student assessment of course and teaching questionnaires;
- teaching performance questionnaires;

- 'stage' questionnaires (which seek student body opinion on the year just completed);
- graduate/leaver questionnaires of student satisfaction with all aspects of student experience.

Student evaluation can be methodologically unreliable because it is driven by provider assumptions and concerns (Clouder, 1998). Rowley (1995) believes that student evaluation questionnaires are flawed because they tend to be retrospective and summative. Thus, whilst the findings may result in the enhancement of a particular course of study, or improvement in teaching performance, the students from whom feedback has been obtained are not normally the beneficiaries of any subsequent improvements. This approach was described as an 'autopsy' model by a head of department:

> As far as I'm concerned the autopsy model of quality, where you inspect the patient to see what they died of, and then think what you might do to the next patient is really not very helpful.

The autopsy model leads to slowness of change and is dependent on the commitment of students to the good of the collective. However, student evaluations can provide the opportunity for a quasi-therapeutic catharsis, revenge and anonymized attacks. Furthermore, they can reproduce gender inequalities. Luke (2001: 59) reminds us that 'Teaching performance indicators, such as those commonly culled from student evaluations, do not always account for students' (skeptical and often negative) perceptions of women in positions of intellectual authority'. This poses questions about the reliability of the evidence, as a lecturer in a new university observes:

> I don't think that the really good systems of student feedback that are part of quality assurance always help. They encourage students to be critical; rather than encourage students to develop a healthy critique . . . I don't see that as much kind of evidence.

It appears that academic staff are increasingly being subordinated to unaccountable and anonymized student criticism. A lecturer in Spanish also remarks on the increasing tendency of students to complain:

> Well, it is partially to do with the quality assurance procedures and partially to do with new funding arrangements and payments of fees with students seeing themselves more in a way as almost clients with the right to reply and a right to complain.

A further question is whether the client or consumer is the ultimate authority. Like surgery and legal advice, it is difficult for purchasers to evaluate at the point of delivery. Evaluation is often more related to the quality of service by which it is provided (Scott, 1999). Entertainment, rather than education, is sometimes the key to positive student evaluations, as a senior lecturer reports:

> . . . there is, therefore, a lot of pressure, when students dislike any aspects of courses immediately. For the sake of the subject review any

element of students disliking modules is bad. And sometimes when students don't like things it's because they find it challenging, or they're still learning, and I do find that really problematic. And I do think that that's sort of led to a bit of a dumbing down here, because we're frightened of what it might look like if they say they don't like issues with English language or something like that.

There are questions about whether the 'feel good factor' is conducive to intellectual growth. The emphasis on keeping students happy and in the comfort zone contradicts Said's (1994: 9) view on the role of the intellectual whom he believed should fulfil an abrasive function, challenging certainties and rigidities of thought.

> Least of all should an intellectual be there to make his/her audiences feel good? The whole point is to be embarrassing, contrary, even unpleasant.

If intellectual challenge becomes constructed as a risk, it is questionable if the quality movement has added value to the student experience. The incorporation of students into the managerialist project can be perceived as an opportunity for voice and also as a form of exploitation. The endless production of documentation for students, evaluation procedures and student consultations could also be perceived as another form of domination. Students are asked to evaluate courses, to take time off work to sit on committees, meet subject reviewers, and mentor new students. They have to live with the tension of quality audits and are often expected to represent their institutions as the authentic student voice. Students' voices and time are colonized for the purposes of continuous improvement. The emphasis on outcomes-based education is reducing their academic experiences to trades-based notions of competencies. Performativity involves students too. The sense of tribalism that often feeds collegiality has been extended to students. In the tradition of managerialism, every organizational member is responsibilized or co-opted into achieving corporate goals, as a head of department in a new university indicates:

> Students – it's been great. They've wanted to come along and take part in the process, you know we've been briefing them. We've got to know them better. That side of things has been fine. It's kept us in contact with old, you know ex-students as well, they've all come back willingly to sing our praises and stuff. So in that sense we've sort of created a mini alumni ourselves here.

A professor also describes how audits activate student loyalty:

> . . . the students took ownership of the visit as well, which was very nice, they were interested and wanted the department to do well, and were keen to help wherever possible, well, I say a small proportion of the course reps and things like that.

The head of a quality unit in a new university related a critical incident that seemed to exemplify the Foucauldian notion of regimes of power being both oppressive and creative. The students subverted the pressures and transformed them into artefact:

> This is just a lovely story; my favourite subject review ever was of the X School of Art . . . which was characterized by the incredible involvement of its students. The students tend not to be. They kind of get roped in to talk to the reviewers, and they obviously do talk to staff and whatnot before, and they have little briefing sessions. But the X because of the nature of the teaching, they're much more intimately involved with their students, and the students are very supportive. And at the end of this, the whole thing, after the reviewers had been packed off the premises, we were shown in to one of the X studios for the obligatory party, and I've been to lots of those I can tell you. But the party had been set up by the students, which was astounding, and they'd made this little film, little art film, a black and white thing, sort of screened on to the back. It was a huge great big plane just zooming up a runway, and just taking off, and flying into the distance, and they played it about three times. This was apparently subject review taking off and disappearing, you see. It was most extraordinary, and one of the guys who's put an awful lot of work in, who's now actually the head of the X school, lovely chap, got presented with this present by his students. It was a lovely huge glass jar, you know with one of those old-fashioned wax tops on, you know for pickling and things. And inside was all this paper, blue paper, all cut up. It wasn't until you actually looked at it very carefully you realized it was a SAD, a self assessment document, cut up and put up in to this jar. And it was really beautiful, it was really artistic, and I just thought that was extraordinary, and I don't think I'll ever have a subject review like that again!

An assistant registrar at an old university relates how students are reassured by consultative mechanisms being in place, even if they are not used. Part of their empowerment is to decide when to use their 'voice', rather than to perform:

> But what I do notice is an interest, on the part of students, in, as it were, being satisfied that things are being done. If I remember rightly, there's a very interesting passage, in Moodie and Eustace . . . *Power and Authority in British Universities*, and they were writing in the late 60s about students on committees, and they said very wisely, that once students had got on committees they probably wouldn't turn up, they just wanted to know that they had a voice. . . .

Student evaluation is a form of perpetual referendum. A head of department in a new university explores how this is producing a blame culture that ultimately disempowers students:

> . . . the extent to which students have begun to define the whole experience as a consumer, as a consumer choice. They have become much

more litigious. . . . At one level it's an empowering of students who previously were, I think, quite oppressed. They were de-powered in the situation. But I think that there are some fundamental contradictions in the relationship where students are engaging with learning, and almost regard the fact that if they don't learn that somehow it's a fault of the staff, or the course, or the institution, as some kind of deficit model. . . . If you don't get the knowledge, then you haven't got what you paid for.

In this analysis, students are being made passive and dependent, engaging with a product, not a process. This informant feels that this has perverted rather than improved teacher–learner relations and that higher education is now about the reproduction, rather than the production of knowledge:

> . . . students use the quality assurance process, the complaints frame-work, all of the codes of practice, and all of their rights as stake-holders. . . . What it does is to create the notion of, as a commodity to be transmitted in the most efficient manner possible, rather than a shared journey into the exploration of the frontiers of knowledge . . . I think that we are, more and more, involved in a massified higher education system of knowledge reproduction, and therefore there is a quality assurance for that reproduction, based on, you know, human capital and organizational efficiency arguments.

A reader in social policy outlines how student questioning is now more related to grades, entitlements and credentialism than to intellectual debates:

> Students are more demanding. I mean like 'Will you put your lecture notes on the internet? Give me this handout. Do this. Tell me how to do this. What should this be?' Looking for much more detailed instruc-tions. 'Tell me what's a 2i and what's a 2ii. Why haven't you given me a 2i?' Also questioning marks, asking for double marking and so on. I don't know whether that's just a general part of the whole atmosphere in academia, more pressure on students to achieve.

The entitlement culture is more about 'what can I get?' rather than 'what should I do?' She continues to explain how student evaluations represent a one-way gaze, with little opportunity for them to reflect on their role in the teacher–learner relationship:

> I've argued for a long time that there's no student evaluation of their own learning. You know they come in and say 'This is a bad teacher and they didn't give me enough of this, that, and the other'. But there's nothing that says how many times did you attend? . . . It seems to be that everybody's measuring the teaching rather than the other way round.

The changing political economy of higher education, with the influence on human capital and wealth creation reflects Lyotard's (1984: 48) view that the transmission of knowledge is no longer designed to train an elite capable of guiding a nation towards emancipation, but to supply the system with players capable of acceptably fulfilling their roles in the pragmatic posts required of institutions. Fears abound that education is being replaced by instruction and training (Coate *et al.*, 2000), and that intellectuals are being transformed into technicians, compelled to deliver skills transcontextually. This leads to concerns that universities are being asked to collude in potentially exploitative labour relations. Teaching is rapidly being perceived as a service industry (Atkins, 1999). Professional judgements are subjected to managerial prerogatives.

Quality assurance can operate rhetorically in the interests of power. The emphasis on student satisfaction can have potent moral authority. In Britain, the media have recognized the news potential of student satisfaction. The *Independent* (Abbott, 2001) conducted a survey of 40 students and found that a little more than half (57 per cent) of students claimed that the teaching that they received was good on the whole. However, Bensimon (1995: 595) suggests that 'categories such as "customer", "quality", and "satisfaction" have no fixed and intrinsic meaning, but rather their meaning is produced locally by the culture, history, mission and power relations that mark the institution'. Policy priorities and corporate cultures are impacting on student identities. A lecturer in a new university identifies how students describe themselves now in new managerialist terms of purchaser and provider:

> I think that also in the culture of, you know, legacies of Thatcherism, that education increasingly becomes seen as a product by very many of our students. And I actually had a student say to me a fortnight ago, 'We are the purchasers you know, you do have to listen to us' . . . and so I think it's kind of like a double-edged sword. You know I think it's good that students think, you know, that it is about their education and they do have input, and that they are involved in it. But I think that increasingly students now see their education as something that they get given by their lecturers.

The passivity and blame culture that this informant describes is reminiscent of Henkel's (2000: 100) observation: that the closure enforced by subject review was disempowering students:

> Concepts of quality that elevated clarity of exposition, comprehensive handout material, contained and predictable learning formats above other values were encouraging passivity and dependence in students.

The construction of students as passive recipients of wealth-creating skills and knowledge contradicts the OECD (1996) view and that of the British Government (DTI, 1998) that innovation is the driver for economic growth (Marceau, 2000).

An academic development officer in an old university argues that quality assurance has raised the significance of students in the hierarchy of interest in universities:

It's been a positive benefit in persuading, you know winning hearts and minds between departments, that students need to be moved up the pecking order a bit.

In this sense, the democracy of the consumer, or knowledge capitalism, appears to have been more successful than earlier notions of student empowerment.

Radical pedagogy or teaching and learning?

The pedagogical project has become socially decontextualized, with learners constructed as cognitive entities. Yet the quality discourse has appropriated some of the language of radical pedagogy. Feminist pedagogy's concerns with student empowerment are being re-articulated in discourses of what constitutes quality teaching and learning. For example, groupwork, problem solving, interactive approaches, rather than transmission are heavily promoted as examples of 'good practice'. On the other hand, the emphasis on predictable learning outcomes represents a form of premature closure and teacher direction that contradicts the principles of negotiation, participation and the decentring of authority. The more fluently that academics learn to write syllabuses in terms of objectives and outcomes, the more danger there is that they will take on the pedagogy those terms are part of. The closure of the terms stifle critique and contain presuppositions about education that are embedded in the terminology.

In terms of pedagogical practices, feminist discourses of empowerment are precariously positioned in the closed culture of predictable learning outcomes and teacher prescribed aims and objectives. Cameron (2000: 127) sees this paradigm shift as a move towards the enterprising approach to curriculum development. This begins by specifying 'outcomes, the skills or "competencies" a student should be able to demonstrate at the end of the course'. Regimes of teaching, learning and assessment are constellating around skills and competencies rather than knowledge and understanding. This is a departure from more traditional curriculum development which starts with identifying a body of knowledge to be transmitted. The discourse of social utility overlooks the fact that skill requirements are constantly in flux. Employment stability has been reduced. Timeserving complacency has been assaulted! Gregg and Wadsworth (1995) used Labour Force Survey data to examine how job tenure for the average worker has fallen from 7 to 4 years in the last two decades. In a rapidly changing context, just-in-time, or disposable skills and knowledges are seen as more appropriate than in-depth disciplinary knowledge. In a knowledge economy the emphasis is now on knowledge management, rather than on knowledge acquisition. Hence, there is an ongoing tension between the applied and the abstract. A professor in a new university outlines a tension between learning objectives and creativity:

I think what has changed in terms of the teaching of colleagues has been in terms of organization, in overt statements of things like learning objectives. I have to say I'm not terribly sympathetic to this kind of approach because I think it has hindered creativity and spontaneity in teaching. Or, at least, it's involved staff in a sort of sophistry where they say, 'Oh, these are the learning objectives, etc., etc.' but then they more or less carry on in the way that they would wish and then, as it were, claim that the objectives have been satisfied . . . and when I've been asked about my learning objectives, I've longed to say, 'To teach the students economics. Full stop.' I don't say that because I play the game.

This suggests that teachers and students have to enact and collude in a game that feels inauthentic to all parties. However, one informant felt that subject review had provided the opportunity to get better facilities for students with disabilities and for international students. This corresponds with Luke's (1997b) observations that quality audits can bring marginalized groups of students under the spotlight. In this context, quality is a creative and transformative space.

Voice discourse plays an important role on debates on 'the student experience' (see Moore and Muller, 1999). Again, this is a direct import from earlier ideas on radical pedagogy (see Morley, 1998). Troyna (1994) warned against the simplistic equation of empowerment and giving a voice, arguing that the former cannot be read off automatically from the latter. There are questions about what constitutes an 'authentic student voice' when briefings and selection are endemic in the methodology, and the terms of engagement are so heavily prescribed. A curriculum leader in a new university describes:

. . . a key point, which helped us do well, was the students were very positive. Of course we, we briefed them beforehand, as everybody does, but we didn't over-do it, I don't think. And they, you know, they seemed to value having a say in the process, which I guess is maybe the way higher education is going, students, you know, becoming more like customers, of course.

Externality is a central constituent of quality assurance procedures. The externality of audits provides some leverage for students. In a therapeutic sense, good attention with someone carefully listening can provide the preconditions for a range of feelings to surface. Quality managers have to ensure that students do not mistake quality audits for appeals hearings or therapy sessions. It is representation and promotion rather than disclosure that it is required. The briefing/coaching of students was also noted by a pro-vice chancellor:

I'd challenge anybody to find me a department that hasn't coached its students. If they say they don't coach and they get high scores then great. I mean they're running an extremely wonderful university. But we'll always have challenges, and what the students believe is that the reason the department can't give them everything that they want is because the university stops them. So what students will do will be to go to the reviewers and say, and complain. Because they think that they've then got strength in the arm of the department . . . and one of the first things we have to do of course, is to disabuse them of that. It changes the relationships with our students . . . I think our students learn to play the game, they've done it in schools and they understand.

A senior lecturer observes how, in her institution, some students saw the subject reviewers as ombudspersons to whom they could complain about quotidian irritations:

We had a mock review here, and the mock review didn't go terribly well, because the students, some of our overseas MA students basically thought that the process was about telling some nice people about the difficulties they were having so that these difficulties would be sorted. So on the mock review, that happened particularly with one very verbal overseas student from my group. And I just had to write to him and say 'Thank you very much for participating, you'll be jolly pleased to know you won't be required for the real one'. You know I had to sort of doctor them. And luckily I had a friend, student, on the inside, who gave us quite a lot of feedback about a couple of other students we needed to weed out. Which sounds terrible, like fixing it, but you know.

Students are more overtly perceived as carriers of power relations. Their 'voices' are being appropriated, rejected and selectively included for organizational purposes. Ostensibly, in the context of contractualism, students appear to have gained some recognition. It is still questionable as to whether this has been accompanied by an authentic redistribution of rights and entitlements, or whether these remain at the level of text. In some cases, students have been successful at strategically capitalizing on transparency and accountability to open up practices and procedures. But the rights discourse can evoke 'possessive individualism', and ignore systemic disadvantage (Blackmore, 1999: 50). There has been a process of desocialization and depoliticization. Improvements in the 'student experience' could imply an acceptance of the changing purpose of higher education and its transmutation into a speedy, utilitarian corporate university (Kenway and Langmead, 1998). Students are being co-opted into 'battery higher education' (Russell, 1993: 100). Students are being reduced to their position in the market. While students might have gained more consumer leverage in terms of turnaround time for essays etc., they could have lost more complex identities as scholars and social agents. It is the democratization of users with solicitousness employed to pacify. Students' needs and priorities are being defined, manipulated and constructed. Quality assurance could operate to make students more docile – by transforming them into consumers, they become more governable.

8

(E)quality

Quality and equality

Both feminism and quality assurance movements have attempted to deconstruct and reconstruct the academy. Both have sought for more transparency in procedures, accountability from elite professional groups and the privileging of the student experience (Morley, 1999). Both are globalized systems calling for transformation. However, it is questionable as to whether these two forces for change can form strategic alliances to challenge inequalities and social exclusions, or whether indeed they are in oppositional or indifferent relationship. The UNESCO (1998) Declaration on Higher Education included a statement that higher education 'should promote solidarity and equity', and it also included for equality of access. Fourth among the declaration's 17 missions and functions of higher education is gender equity. Theoretically, quality could provide new governance frameworks through which issues of equity can be mobilized. However, equity is frequently absent, as a category of analysis in organizational arrangements for quality assurance. Blackmore (1999) argues that this may be because, compared to technologically well resourced organizations or strong leadership, equity is not such a marketable indicator of success.

However, social inclusion is a dominant policy discourse now in several national locations. In Britain, there is a policy initiative to include underrepresented groups in higher education (HEFCE, 2001). The Dearing Report (Dearing, 1997) expressed concern about the under-representation of students from socioeconomically disadvantaged groups. European Union policy documentation has discursively linked poverty, mass unemployment and social exclusion with lack of opportunities for education and training (EC, 1993, 1995). In Britain, even with the necessary entry qualifications, people from working class backgrounds are only 70 per cent as likely to enter universities and colleges as people from professional, middle class backgrounds (Reay, 1998). Social class is currently enjoying more policy attention than gender, as quantitative representation of women undergraduate students has increased. The percentage of female undergraduates in the UK has doubled since the publication of the Robbins Report in 1963 (Brooks, 1997). However, the education system is still a pyramid, with representation of women tailing off as one approaches the pinnacle. Only 35 per cent of post-graduate research students in the UK are women. In the academic year 1997–98 10,993 doctorates were awarded in the UK, of which 3752 were awarded to women.

Quantitative change is important, but simply, counting women, black, disabled or working class students in does not represent a radical transformation of higher education. Morley, Unterhalter and Gold (2003) argue that access policies might bring about a small expansion of numbers of students in certain academic locations, but there is still the notion of a particular body of knowledge, or canon, to be transmitted to an elite student body. When social identity is acknowledged, for example, in the case of policies for enhancing participation (HEFCE, 2001), inclusion tends to be on set institutional terms and demands assimilation of new constituencies. There are dangers of a remediation ethos as the different forms of knowledge, lifestyles or practice, they bring, is rarely given epistemic recognition. Delanty (2001) argues that the mode of knowledge itself has not been transformed by democratizing interventions linked to social inclusion, citizenship and pluralization. There have been only limited attempts to close the epistemological and curricular gender gaps in higher education, for example by the development of women's studies, and feminist research methodologies (Roland Martin, 2000).

While feminism has had some impact on the academy, it has had little influence on higher education studies, with most of the influential (male and female) writers on higher education ignoring gender completely (Leonard, 2001). Scholarship on the sociology of knowledge tends to develop on a different trajectory from mainstream higher education policy studies. Theorizing difference in higher education has been left to feminists (see Morley, 1999), post-modernists (for example, Foucault, 1980), Marxists (for example, Marcuse, 1964), lesbian and gays (for example, Griffin and Andermahr, 1997; Mintz and Rothblum, 1997), anti-racists (for example, hooks, 1995; Adia *et al.*, 1996; Modood and Acland, 1998), the disability rights movement (Borland and James, 1996; Hurst, 1999) and post-colonialists (for example, Spivak, 1993). Connections have been made between knowledge, culture and power and the status of authorized knowledge. Marcuse (1964) characterized all forms of knowledge as ideological and Foucault's (1980) work has been central in linking knowledge and power. For Bourdieu (1984) cognitive structures are intrinsically linked to the field of power. In feminist scholarship there have been extensive debates about how knowledge is produced and transmitted via research methodologies and pedagogies (e.g. Lather, 1991; hooks, 1995; Stanley, 1997). Institutional sexism has been theorized in terms of the formation and governance of universities (Evans, 1995). However, counter-hegemonic scholarship does not seem to have influenced thinking about quality assurance.

Quality assurance is an example of a modernist, rationalist construction of the universal subject, whereby teachers, researchers, managers and learners are constructed as disembodied, cognitive, socially decontextualized entities. The inclusion of gender as an add-on in quality audits is often clumsy, tokenistic and arbitrary. For example, in my study, the underrepresentation of women students in engineering was commented on in a subject review, as a faculty manager in an old university relates:

> It was suggested that they weren't doing enough to encourage female representation on the courses, but, I mean, in engineering it's a hell of a job. So it was a rather unfair criticism I think. Well, they were very angry when they realized it would be docking them a point, especially the female members of staff. Bust a gut going to school, as did the male members, you know. In fact we have run an insight course for young female engineers for a decade now, to encourage that sort of thing.

It could be argued, as the faculty manager suggests, that gender participation is a bigger problem located in the wider social terrain and the culture of science. Glover (2001) notes how only 9 per cent of all personnel and 2 per cent of professors in engineering are women. It could be considered unreasonable to deduct a point in one particular audit of teaching quality when vertical and horizontal segregation are embedded in the academy.

A lecturer in English literature comments on how the rapid restructuring of the workforce for the RAE in her university meant that all equal opportunities procedures were breached and paradoxically summoned to justify the breaches:

> We appointed a research professor just before the RAE for obvious reasons as she'd got an awful lot on her CV. And it was a very, very, very controversial appointment because it was just given to her, there wasn't a shortlist, there wasn't an advertisement, it was just given to her and she came in from another institution so it wasn't even an internal promotion. And at the time we had a big department meeting about it and I said, 'We are an equal opportunities employer, we can't just have a shortlist of one.' And a man in the department said, 'But she's a woman, so where's the problem with equal opportunities?'. . . And I think that's where, you know, when the RAE comes into contact with a macho departmental culture, you know, the macho departmental culture sort of subsumes the RAE for its own purposes.

In this analysis, audits reproduce and bring to the surface power inequalities. Equity is reduced to biological identity, with no attention paid to structures and procedures.

Joining the procession

While there has been some policy recognition that exclusion of groups from certain social locations has played an essential role in the process of bestowing symbolic and cultural capital, power is neither redistributed nor problematized. If equity changes are not accompanied by a redistribution of political and economic power, there are dangers of tokenism (Young, 1990; Fraser, 1997). Entry nowadays into the academy either as a producer or consumer of academic services can simply inscribe under-represented groups in managerialist discourses. Seven decades ago, Virginia Woolf (1938: 184) asked:

> Do we want to join the procession or don't we? On what terms shall we join that procession? Above all, where is it leading us, the procession of educated men?

While the quality procession is getting longer and longer, it is unclear where it is going – particularly for women. Quality management is seen by some feminists as inherently authoritarian and naively preoccupied with orthodoxies, and socially constructed and decontextualized indicators of worth. New managerialism is perceived as reinforcing 'macho' styles of leadership, as it is very outcome-oriented, with emphasis on targets, performance, and measurement (Deem and Ozga, 2000; Lafferty and Fleming, 2000; Brooks and MacKinnon, 2001; De La Rey, 2001). A contradictory view also exists. Quality audits, particularly those focusing on teaching and learning, are seen as enabling women to enter the managerial elite in organizations, and sometimes help fulfil ideological and career aspirations concerned with influence and change agency. Luke (2001: 57/8) argues that 'working creatively and politically within dynamic contradictions can mean rearticulating and using a managerialist discourse such as QA for social justice means and ends in the interests of women'. However, for many feminists, the move into quality management can often be accompanied by the imperative to moderate radical ideals and compromise values (Deem and Ozga, 2000). A pervasive theme in the literature on gender and organizations centres on the question of whether women in management can make a difference or are they incorporated into existing regimes of power (Eggins, 1997; David and Woodward, 1998; Wyn *et al.*, 2000)? In relation to quality assurance, it could be argued that academic managers have been trapped into promoting a neoliberal economic agenda (Dominelli and Hoogvelt, 1996). Iris Marion Young (1990: 165) identifies a further trap that many members of oppressed groups often face:

> When participation is taken to imply assimilation, the oppressed person is caught in an irresolvable dilemma: to participate means to accept and adopt an identity one is not and to try and participate means to be reminded by oneself and others of the identity one is.

This study indicates that there are women who enjoy and benefit from involvement in quality procedures. They participate by consent rather than by coercion. Involvement in the management of quality can provide women with the opportunity to cast off the status of 'other' and demonstrate corporatism and their ability to make a difference in their organization. Often disciplinary areas where women proliferate are losing status. Universities, influenced by globalization, favour some disciplinary areas at the expense of others. Technologies, management and the hard sciences are seen as more relevant by students and governments than areas such as women's studies (Currie and Thiele, 2001). A lecturer in sociology relates how the quality industry is in the ascent compared to the descent of women's studies:

> . . . for some women it's been, you know a career opportunity, and I suppose I can see that, and I certainly see some of my, particularly female, colleagues, because they seem to be really good at administration. . . . But again even that's like a double-edged sword, I mean one of my very close friends and colleagues has got a promotion that now is much more of a kind of administrative role. She partly applied for that job because women's studies had been closed down at the institution where she worked.

In much of professional life, there is a thin line between opportunity and exploitation.

Quantitative signifiers and qualitative differences

The history of higher education for women, black and working class people has often been portrayed as a bitter struggle that has had to be challenged via political and legal reform and policy interventions for change (Dyhouse, 1995; Mirza, 1998; Reay, 1998). Carter, Fenton and Modood (1999) point out how only 6.6 per cent of academic staff in UK HEIs are 'not white', and more than one in four minority academics reported that they had personally experienced discrimination in job applications. One in five had experienced racial harassment from students or staff. The struggle continues after access has been achieved (Morley, 1999). Quantitative representation does not always affect qualitative change. Quality assurance does precipitate change, but does it incorporate an understanding of equity?

Quality assurance is a contradictory space. Bensimon (1995: 598) asks 'what might be the consequences for TQM for educational movements that theorize about difference?' I would also pose the question the other way round. What are the consequences for the equity movements of quality assurance technologies and practices? I believe that there are several arguments connecting quality and equality. One argument is that equity issues are not always performance indicators in quality audits. In taxonomies of effectiveness, the organizational world is presented as an orderly, rational surface, untainted by the mess and chaos of unequal power relations in which the lived world is constituted.

Quality accolades do not coincide with equality achievements. Some of the most elite research organizations in Britain, with consistently high RAE scores, also have the worst record on gender equity. For example, Cambridge did not allow women graduates full status until 1947. Today, only 6 per cent of Cambridge professors are women (compared to a national average of 10 per cent). Even at lecturer level, women only make up 15 per cent compared with 35 per cent nationally (Cole, 1999). The 'student experience' is also highly gendered in these institutions, with more male students awarded first class honours degrees (Leman and Mann, 1999).

A second argument is that quality assessment procedures are reinforcing gendered divisions of labour in the academy (Morley, 2001a). Teaching quality is female-dominated, while research quality is male-dominated. There is a morality of quality that I argue can be profoundly gendered, with women heavily responsibilized for services. There has been some sex role spillover, with women's socialized patterns of caring getting appropriated by the teaching quality movement. The psychic economy involved in quality assessment is part of a gendered care chain. Lander (2000: 136) believes that at the heart of quality is service to others. Pirsig (1974) also suggests that the notion of quality is deeply connected to caring because quality and caring are internal and external aspects of the same thing (Shields, 1999). In relation to managing the quality of teaching and learning, some women move away from the status of research activity and into the world that ties them to organizational development, new managerialism, presenteeism and responsibilization (Morley 2001a). So, while women are well represented as reviewers and managers of teaching quality, they are under-represented both as producers and reviewers of research quality. The boundaries between teaching and learning and research are highly gendered. Leonard (2001: 17) points out how, in the 2001 RAE, fewer than one in four panel members and only one in seven of the panel chairs were women, and that the panels chaired by women were responsible for allocating less than 10 per cent of RAE funding. A third argument suggests that the quality agenda can be appropriated to enhance the rights of less powerful groups, for example students with dyslexia (Luke, 1997b). In Britain, quality assessment of teaching and learning has been popular with the National Union of Students, as they believe that it has provided them with opportunities for influence and 'voice'. Marginalized groups have been brought under the auditing gaze. Externality has been an important driver for change (Glazer, 1999). Luke (1997b) argues that accountability measures, the 'institutional economies' of quality assurance, and the new contractualism can be harnessed for equity ends. Blackmore (1999: 47) suggests that 'equity can be built into all contractual arrangements. . . . Top management commitment can be gained on the grounds that equity is more 'productive'.

A further question relates to the transformatory potential of higher education itself. This is a central aspiration in countries in transition such as South Africa. Higher education is seen to be a pivotal social institution and part of a rehabilitation process, raising consciousness and contributing to changing professional and social practices. While this can sound utopian and over-ambitious, the university has sometimes been a site for the articulation of democratic and progressive values including feminism and anti-colonialism

(Morley, 1999). Social movements have impacted on the academy, yet have not seemed to have influenced current policies for quality, access and participation.

Globalizing inequality

Inequalities in higher education are globalized. While female participation rates in higher education are a major indicator of development, gender equity does not appear to be applied to employment. There is persistent evidence of horizontal and vertical segregation across national boundaries in the academy. The focus has often been on discriminatory employment practices in academic and administrative posts. The UNESCO Report on Women in Higher Education and Management in 1996 stated: 'With hardly an exception, the global picture is one of men outnumbering women on a ratio of five to one at middle management and at about twenty to one at senior management level' (quoted in Currie and Thiele, 2001). The under-representation of women in senior positions is a theme in Commonwealth research studies (Morley, Unterhalter and Gold, 2003). Wyn *et al.* (2000) note that women hold 11 per cent of full professorships in Canada. Statistics for Australian universities show that only 17.1 per cent of associate and full professors are women (Chesterman, 2002). In Sri Lanka Kalugama (1999) reports that women are concentrated in humanities and social sciences and that they occupy middle management rather than senior management roles. In South Africa, Ndugane (1999) observes that, despite the fact that race and gender were areas that the government was keen to address, the situation has not changed much since 1990 (De La Rey, 2001). Manya (2000) records how, at the University of Nairobi women account for 7.1 per cent of professors. Barry (1995) describes how, in Guinea women lecturers represent 5 per cent of the teaching staff. There are no professors and only one female associate professor. In Nigeria, women form 18 per cent of the total staff population of federal universities (Mbanefoh, 1995). In the University of Ghana women constitute 20.6 per cent of the working population and are 3.4 per cent of professors.

The statistics are similar for many European countries. Even those with sophisticated policies for equality still have low numbers of senior women in academic employment. For example, women constitute 11.7 per cent of the professoriate in Norway and 11 per cent in Sweden and 20 per cent in Finland (Husu, 2001). Women's exclusion from positions of authority in the academy in Britain has been well documented. Overall women hold 35 per cent of lecturer posts, but account for fewer than 10 per cent of professors. In the UK 68 per cent of all academics are men. However, 29 per cent of male academics are in senior positions in universities compared to 11.6 per cent of women. In numerical terms, this translates into the stark fact that 8697 professors are men and 812 are women (Halvorsen, 1998). Women academics' salaries are lower than those of men at the same academic rank

(Bett, 1999). Figures from the Higher Education Statistics Agency (HESA) show that the average female academic will earn four to five years' less salary than an average male colleague for the same number of years worked. Forty-two per cent of women academics have full-time permanent positions compared to 59 per cent of men. Women are 33 per cent more likely than men to be employed on fixed-term contracts and 550 per cent less likely to be professors (*Guardian*, 1999).

Debates continue about how the persistent inequalities can be challenged (Morley, 1999; Husu, 2001). One view is to make the academy more transparent. A senior lecturer argues that the quantitative transparency of the RAE allows 'research active' women to claim their right to promotion to senior positions.

> I mean the RAE, I mean, I know again this is not a normal view, but I know several female colleagues who were on the temporary treadmill forever. But then as soon as they had a lot of publications they started getting jobs immediately. Whereas before at an earlier stage of our careers, when we didn't have any publications, and everything was just down to sort of, you know, personal likes and dislikes at interviews, and all of a sudden we got jobs and were promoted very quickly. And I know a lot of people think the RAE disadvantages women . . . but I actually think that sometimes it is an advantage. Because places, I tend to think the more prestigious institutions are the ones with the most hidden snobbery, but they need to achieve good results in terms of the RAE like everybody else. If you've got a lot of research these days they tend to pick you even if you're not their type.

However, it appears that credentials and academic capital in women's possession mysteriously lose their value. Park's study (1992: 237) reported that:

> University women are about three times less likely to be professors than men when age and publication rate are taken into account.

Wyn *et al.* (2000) note how research productivity has a hidden curriculum too, with certain areas being perceived as outside the mainstream, for example qualitative inquiries, feminist research, research on or by women.

In my study, a senior lecturer in English notes how increasing transparency, as a consequence of a quality culture, can challenge discriminatory employment practices:

> Earlier in my career, say 1992 to 1996 where, particularly in the old university cultures there wasn't as much pressure for accountability, but when choices were made. For example about things like whether to, you know, make temporary people permanent within the work situation. Quite often my perception was that permanent jobs were going to men, and usually public school educated men who were similar to people making the decisions. There was no pressure to show criteria, or to explain the decision, or any of these things. And in some senses

I feel that I, and other women that I know actually, were sort of disadvantaged by that. I feel as my career has gone on that there has been
more sort of pressure towards having sort of criteria, having to give
good feedback, etc.

This analysis suggests that there is a technology transfer from 'good' practice in teaching and learning to quality in employment practices. Quality is
perceived as building fair institutions. The quality movement's concern
with transparency has its limits. As I have previously argued, the emphasis is
on outputs, not on inputs or enablers. The declared agenda focuses on the
student, not the employee experience. While quality audits interrogate
practices such as staff development and appraisal, they ignore procedures
for promotion and recruitment. Quality assessment looks closely at the curriculum, but not the hidden curriculum and the informal subterranean
practices that reinforce and construct gendered power relations. Informal
procedures for career development abound, and are in breach of equality
policies. In Onsongo's (2000) study of a Kenyan university 69 per cent of
women and 92 per cent of men felt that they had been encouraged to apply
for promotion. She found that 21.4 per cent of men applied for promotion
even though they did not meet the criteria. In Finland, in spite of evolved
policies and codes of practice for gender equity, a highly gendered
invitational system for promotion exists (Husu, 2000). Many women are not
invited to 'join the procession'.

Various explanatory frameworks for women's under-representation have
been developed. A common theme is how women's domestic responsibilities and their ensuing lack of mobility restricts their participation and
ascent in the professional domain (Acker, 1980). My problem with this theory
is that it relies on normalized discursive framings of women in relation to
their construction within the traditional family. All women are presumed to
be heterosexual and living in conventional nuclear families. By emphasizing
the presumed bimodal character of women's lives, their marginalization in
male-dominated fields is guaranteed. This analysis offers a rational explanation for irrational prejudice. It also overlooks gendered micropolitics. A
lecturer in English literature comments on how macho culture is relayed
micropolitically via discriminatory interaction patterns. This provides sponsorship for men and discouragement and discomfort for women:

It's very interesting the way it's done, it's not done upfront at all. It's
done entirely through barbed comments and timed laughter in the bar
basically. It took me ages to cotton on to this; for a couple of years I
used to go down to where they all eat in the bar at lunchtime and hang
out and think why am I hating this so much? Why is this so God-awful?
And after a while I realised: (a) no women go down, (b) the culture is
absolutely sexist in the extreme and also there's a huge kind of power
wash going on in those informal meetings. So once I realized that I just
stopped going and I felt better ever since, I must say. But there is
something I think about us four young women in the department who

are, we're all quietly, you know, plugging away at it but it just interests me very much that all the young men who came in at the same time as us – one's a senior lecturer, two are readers and one is applying for a senior lectureship and we've none of us even applied. And I think that must have something to do with the prevailing culture of the department, which has been reported and sort of like externally validated by these attempts at measuring our work.

The culture of measurement appears to be reinforcing macho competition. Micropolitical relays of gendered power are notoriously difficult to capture. The same people operating distorted and sometimes discriminatory practices in relation to sponsorship and distribution of resources and opportunities are charged with the responsibility for maintaining transparency elsewhere in the academy.

The gendered division of labour

Men and women in the academy often appear to be on different career trajectories. The quality movement is reinforcing this. The socially constructed indicators of career success reflect existing divisions of labour, with research at the top of the hierarchy. The two quality accounting systems in Britain are gendered and are contributing to polarized employment regimes. Women are already disproportionately concentrated in areas and institutions with the lowest levels of research funding (Lafferty and Fleming, 2000). Women, in general, apply for fewer research grants than men (Wellcome Trust, 1997). A recent survey carried out by the National Centre for Social Research discovered that women academics are less likely than men to be eligible to apply for research funding as a consequence of being on fixed-term contracts, or being in more junior posts (NCSR, 2000). There is a vicious circle – women are too busy teaching or administrating, too junior, and too precariously employed to gain major research grants. They are then ineligible to apply for senior posts, as they have no major research grants. In addition to these structural barriers, there are attitudinal barriers. In Sweden, Wenneras and Wold (1997) found that eligibility criteria were gendered, and that women needed to be two-and-a-half times more productive in terms of publications than their male counterparts to get the same rating for scientific competence.

There is a danger that women will be squeezed out of high status research work. This has implications for women's career development. The exclusion of many women from research opportunities might account for why so many get sucked into quality assurance procedures for teaching and learning. For them, this provides a welcome opportunity to be included and valued. Involvement in quality management creates career opportunities for women, while simultaneously pushing them into a career pathway strongly associated with organizational housekeeping. A lecturer in English literature discusses the 'braking' on her career:

I'm in a department of 25 full-timers, of whom six are women. There's us four junior women who are between 31 and 41 and we're none of us promoted and something has really had a sort of braking influence on all of our careers. We've all come in as quite 'hot' and quite 'sharp' and quite energetic and we're not producing at the rate that we should, in a sense, although, you know, in another way I think, why the hell should we produce in that kind of way? But we've all been pushed into the convening classes, teaching classes, taking on pastoral care. All these things which, I mean I think are terribly, terribly important but you don't see the men getting pushed into them. . . . It's absolutely all down to research and there is what I think is a very macho culture.

Women are often taking responsibility for the domestic labour of teaching and administration while more senior men are left to focus on research. Henkel (2000: 217) notes:

. . . staff, previously valued for their contribution to institutional and departmental reputations, could find themselves valued instead for shouldering teaching loads that would enable others to bring in re- search resources and make reputations.

Henkel does not attempt to gender this division of labour. A sociology lecturer in my study argues that the extensive administrative preparations for quality audits and the accompanying preoccupation with teaching and learning, requires significant amounts of self-sacrifice which is profoundly gendered:

Often it's women that are doing an awful lot of the labour, and an awful lot of the work . . . and it seems to me if people are going to misbehave in terms of kind of their commitment to work in relation to all this, then they're more likely to be men than women.

Quality assurance requirements make greedy organizations even greedier (Currie *et al.*, 2000). Data gathering invariably entails extra work for women. The preparation of base rooms, documentation and audit trails consume women's time in a way that does not necessarily serve their long-term pro- fessional interests. Smith theorized the social division of labour as far back as 1987. She highlighted how women's invisible labour promotes men's authority. Davies (1996) also wrote about women's 'adjunct' roles whereby male professionals are kept aloof and elite by armies of women who deal with all the clutter. It would appear that women's labour is being appropri- ated in the extensive preparations for quality assessment, and that this is often unrecognized and unacknowledged.

Some of my informants noted how women were being over-responsibilized with the preparation for teaching quality assessment, whereas the more prestigious preparations for research assessment are undertaken by senior men. A philosophy lecturer observes:

Well, my theory is that it's younger female members of staff that take it (teaching quality) on in the first instance . . . my impression is that research committees are made up of, primarily, male members of staff, and those who head research committees and those that put in RAE submissions. In my experience it's young female members of, junior members of staff that pick up the initial work of SPR, not realizing quite what a hell that they're getting in to.

As with many regimes of power, this had both positive and negative effects. Negative in the sense that women were being pulled away from high status research work, but positive in so far as it contributed to relationship-building in the academy – especially across academic and administrative boundaries. A senior lecturer in education comments on the sense of comradeship and war effort experienced by women working together under stressful circumstances:

> My colleagues were a couple of the administrators, women . . . we spent two days in the base room, and we made sure things were in the boxes, and we were labelling the boxes, and we, our base room was opposite our archive room, so the three of us were running in and out of the base room, retrieving stuff to put in the boxes, you know the six examples of work and stuff like that. And actually that was the nicest, nicest day I had last year. Because we had coffee, and we had chocolate biscuits, and it was just nice, and it was just fun, and we were just laughing. And were all . . . really stressed . . . and we just all had a laugh. . . . you know, we were having a go at some of the men who were the leaders who were nowhere to be seen, and basically that was a real day of comradeship and affection . . . like being part of a community.

This story, apart from celebrating the connectedness of some women, reminds me of an image that I have written about elsewhere (Morley, 2001a). Women often appear to be the organizational Morelocks – the creatures who live underground and service the 'Upper World' people (Wells, 1971). This has also been described as working in an ivory basement (Benokraitis, 1998)!

Gendering performativity

The act of inspection itself is riven with gendered implications. The lack of accountability of reviewers and the lack of a right to reply suggests that quality audits are a one-way gaze, reminiscent of pornographic objectification. The continuous improvement discourse is reminiscent of the cultural pressures on women in general to strive for perfection. It is like diets and exercise regimes. It also echoes another regulatory force, that is original sin. Women enter the academy as flawed and imperfect academics and they have to struggle to redeem themselves. Walkerdine (1989, 1990) argued that femininity is performance, and that girls are socialized to perform with diligence and conscientiousness. Women's gender socialization makes them particularly well-schooled players in quality assurance. A senior lecturer describes how she felt that she had to perfom a particular type of femininity to make herself more acceptable to the male subject reviewers:

> I feel so ashamed of myself in what I'm going to say, they were all men who came to review . . . I just sort of felt sucked up into that whole awful process, and that might say more about me than them, but I felt that it was a process that pushed you in that direction, and I felt un-pleased with myself, and soiled . . . I bought a new dress to wear for the week, you know, I would never buy a new dress for anything. And I felt, and there was a bit of me that I thought, 'all right I'm going to dress for this, and in a sense it's me putting on a mask, and doing the QAA, and doing it for a week, and presenting my embodied self as QAA-able'. And while I did that, because I felt that in a sense it was like my armour . . . and I wore lipstick, I wore lipstick, and you know I don't wear makeup, or very rarely yeah?

Performativity, in this case, is highly gendered. The language that this informant used was evocative of narratives of violence against women. Violence in organizations is often subtle and confusing (Hearn and Parkin, 2001). She felt 'soiled' by what she felt as the dishonesty of the gendered performance. Terms such as 'abusive', 'violation', 'bullying' were frequently invoked by my informants to describe the sense of invasion. Women aca-demics' precarious and predominantly junior positions in the academy make them more vulnerable to bullying, manipulation and compliance. While audit is experienced as a form of violence by some women, it is perceived as a welcome antidote to individualism by others. A senior lecturer in English speculates that women, especially young women academics, are more sup-portive of quality assurance procedures than their male counterparts:

> I do think also, that women of my age, I'm in my mid-thirties, tend to be . . . more pro the quality culture than the men of my age. A lot of my colleagues are very against it and feel that their job is just to re-search interestingly. And sometimes I do feel that the objections are pursued along the lines that this is a surveillance culture etc., etc. A lot of my experience is it's my male colleagues who say that, my younger male colleagues, and they just feel it's encroaching on their research time essentially, and they feel that their job as academics is to do research, and not to do the form filling . . . I have quite a wide network of female, you know, academic friends my age, I don't know any of them actually, that are really hostile, and a lot of them work within feminism, but I would struggle to find many men of my age who are actually at all supportive of it.

It is hard to enter into a dialogue with these observations without retreating into essentialized notions of women's dispositions. Women could be more supportive of quality because their under-representation can make them more compliant. It could also stem from a commitment to students.

Gender socialization can mean that they are more easily responsibilized to be communal, rather than individualistic. In this analysis, participation in quality preparations can be a form of role entrapment. However, it would be erroneous to represent women academics in terms of victim or angel narratives and to ignore hierarchies and power relations among women. Eagleton (1998) believes that we need a new understanding that takes into account the simultaneous experiences of pleasure, passion, constraint, and control in women's engagement with academic organizations. The academy, like any other organization is full of contradictions – structures are both fixed and volatile, enabling and constraining. There are gendered sites of opportunity and constraint.

9

Desiring Changes

Long-term effects: supply, stratification and surveillance

This final chapter considers long-term effects, desired changes and attempts to summarize the central findings of the study. Informants were asked to comment on the long-term effects of quality assurance in higher education and to offer their observations for changes that they would like to see in the future. Predictions can be summarized in terms of supply problems, organizational isomorphism versus more stratification, increased textual representation of processes, student-led demand, and ontological and epistemological concerns. Recommended changes were for more intertextuality between quality processes in the public and private sectors, with the academy learning from the mistakes, as well as the aspirations in industry. While the over-elaborate subject review finished in Britain at the end of 2001, the ethos of beratement and surveillance has continued in a new structural guise. This is proliferating internationally. In this study, it was argued that inspection and quality control should be replaced by more effective processes built into the system. There were calls for the return of trust, the strengthening of appeals and evaluation procedures and a more comparative approach to quality assurance.

Quality assurance has contributed to the reconfiguration of academic *habitus.* New discursive constellations, employment regimes and multiskilling have produced disruption, cognitive dissonance and dislocation. For some this is embraced as progress and innovation, for others it is experienced in terms of enhanced workload, occupational stress and domination. For some, quality assurance provides a fixed point of reference in a changing higher education policy context. It represents a creed, a catechism or a *modus operandi.* However, quality assurance is part of a hegemonic battle between modernity and post-modernity. For many, the methodology of QA is perceived as taking the academy backwards in terms of sophistication of analysis. Discourses in education policy documents, concerning the knowledge society of the twenty-first century, are often to be found accompanied by quality assurance discourses based on a positivistic epistemology from the nineteenth century.

Loss is becoming constitutive of current academic identity. In quality assurance, loss of autonomy for example is constructed as a consequence of fault, and is therefore ungrievable. Current loss of autonomy is becoming equated with future loss of human resources. The threat of supply is noted by a senior lecturer in economics:

> It is clear that people are leaving the subject, leaving university to do other things, or trying to protect themselves from quality assurance in one form or another. In 10 or 20 years' time, the subject in the UK will be of less international standing than it is at the moment . . . because people are leaving . . . British economists do not want to go into academia, they go out and do something else – earn lots of money in the city, or they work for economics research institutes that don't enter into the standard academic jobs. . . . People have left and everyone who has left recently we have an exit interview for all members of staff and everyone who has left has mentioned that (QA) is one of the reasons for leaving, if not a major reason.

It appears that excessive regulation combined with low salaries is making the academy an unattractive career option. A registrar in an old university notes:

> I suppose one thing to worry about slightly is that that possibly combined with the inadequacy of academic salaries may deter younger people from coming into higher education. It may not be such an attractive career as it was when you could come in and just do your teaching and research. It won't seem such an attractive profession.

The notion of an increasingly unattractive profession was prevalent in this study. A professor in a new university concedes that processes have been tightened up, but that this has been achieved on top of considerable resentment:

> Long-term effects – I think we sharpened up our procedures and policies a bit – there's a bit more 'joined upness', a bit more consistency, the quality of the materials that we give to students has improved. That's it I would say. Otherwise, it's a legacy of bile and annoyance generally. . . .

In the Kantian tradition, the university has been a site of critique. The quality movement in higher education has compromised and muted the possibilities for critical engagement with the technologies used to assure quality. It demands compliance and performativity and the endless reproduction of norms. Delanty (2001: 73) talks about the need for 'a zone of engagement between power, knowledge, politics and culture'. The university could occupy that zone. However, there are fears that intellectually able and critical staff will exit to escape unacceptable regulation and surveillance. Organizations and individuals are berated by a constantly shifting ideal. Quality assurance is perceived as an instrument of containment, in opposition to critique and intellectual creativity. A professor in an old university feels that the supply chain will continue, but with lower quality staff:

> . . . this is demoralizing; we got two new members of staff here, who started in September, and I don't think they knew what was happening, or hitting them, you know they didn't think this is what academia was all about . . . if you combine this extra hassle, bureaucracy, and all of these other costs that are involved with it, with the salaries that we offer, then inevitably it will tend to lead to a reduction in good quality staff in the future.

Paradoxically, the culture of excellence is producing mediocrity. The compliance culture and command economy in higher education threatens to produce self-policing, ventriloquizing apparatchiks, as opportunities for cultural agency are reduced. Wolf (2001: 17) asserts that 'Under-funding, uniformity and death by intrusive inspection – that is the road to ruin. The consequences are foreseeable: ill-paid and demoralized functionaries will take the place of independent and innovative scholars'. A philosophy lecturer also notes the potential reduction of staff quality:

> I think what will happen is that we'll have an awful lot of fairly mediocre lecturing staff.

For a senior lecturer in an old university, supply and human capital are racialized:

> They will have largely a non-British – I'm trying to avoid saying this in what could be interpreted as racist . . . – but with largely non-British-educated members of British economics departments in the future. That means they'll stay in this country for less time and the actual human capital we'll have invested in our economics departments will be less but they'll stay for a period of maybe five, ten or fifteen years, but they won't be thinking of spending most of their academic career in British universities . . . which means that we'll have a problem in ten or twenty years' time. People are recruiting young lecturers, they stay for five years, and then go onto another country in the world or go home or something. Whereas Brits have a high probability of staying in the long term, which sort of means you retain your human capital . . . I'm trying to say that in a non-racist manner.

The push/pull movement of human resources, or 'brain drain' via globalized opportunities means that individuals, particularly in shortage subjects, can relocate if employment conditions continue to be unacceptable. This is racialized. Education is a global trade with a globalized elite of knowledge workers. Jarvis (1999) argues that lower income countries are forced to buy the symbolic analytical skills from the West, while simultaneously trying to generate more skills in symbolic analysis in their own societies. However, once qualified, many of these people are attracted to the higher salaries in the West. The lower income countries are trapped into investing in expensive initial training in high skills and eventually losing the human capital. The importation of human resources is currently a major issue in the British public services as lower income countries are plundered for their expensively trained doctors, nurses and teachers to address supply problems here. A Western standpoint interprets this process as the loss of pure local spaces in the public services.

A further speculation on the long-term effects relates to increasing divisions and differentiation. An academic registrar in a new university comments:

> Initially I think the idea was about there being common standards, yeah? And I think that's gone out the window a little bit, you know the idea that all universities become the same in some way. It isn't going to happen, there's going to be very, very good universities, and there's going to be not-so-good universities. . . . So the effect of the QA systems, external and internal, has been to reinforce that, you know it's a much more open, explicit transparent system, in higher education.

Institutional differentiation between research and teaching universities are being reinforced. A lecturer in English literature also predicts long-term stratification:

> I think there will be an increase in stratification. We're already seeing it. We're trying to confirm ourselves as a research institution, although many of our departments don't really merit that and I think, overall, we're going to probably find ourselves as a teaching institution, which will mean, you know, lower down the totem pole and less resources and so on. So that's, I think stratification is one thing.

A vice provost holds the opposite view, predicting common standards and organizational isomorphism:

> I don't think there's any doubt that there is, in some people's minds, an agenda towards moving towards a sector in which the difference in the institutions is much less than it is now. And in which there's much more – uniformity is the word I'm struggling for. Much greater uniformity in which it is much clearer that someone who gets an Honours degree in biochemistry at the University of Aberdeen, it will be the same as if they got it at the University of Aberystwyth.

Rights will continue to be constructed as the democracy of the consumer. A lecturer in English literature notes the strengthening of consumer-led demand in a market economy:

> I think increasingly it's going to be student-demand led, or at least, student-as-consumer led. Though I think that the objective measuring of various activities and the publication of those results will probably

support the student's notion of themselves as, you know, having rights to various kinds of things. And in lots of ways I think they should have those rights but when it comes to having a right to a B grade, I don't believe in it at all. I actually spent a little while teaching in the States in a very expensive college there where they pay $30,000 a year tuition and feel they deserve A minuses because they've paid. And I don't ever want to see this country going that way. And I think that's probably part of the deal. Not because of, but supported by QAA procedures.

A professor in an old university believes that mistrust is now so embedded in the system that contract and textual representation will be the norm:

I think the effects are there for many years to come, that we will be forever amassing paper, cumulating paper in vast numbers, because there is always, around the corner, the possibility of people coming to say 'We need to see your paperwork' . . . just because it's based on a system of mistrust and that's not how we should be working, it really isn't.

Some informants were less willing to make independent predictions, framing their observations in terms of changes introduced by key agencies. A faculty manager comments on the need for agencies to undertake evaluation:

That's a difficult one because it really depends on what the QA externally impose, as it were, measures will be subject to change, they will evolve. So the effect will very much depend on the extent to which there's some kind of positive feedback process, which is a real tough one, well I mean at national level what somebody has got to be saying is 'Are the changes we've made resulting in increased quality? Or are they just resulting in higher overheads?' I mean if they are just resulting in higher overheads, and no perceptible increase in quality then we ought to change them and how do we change them? I can't really answer the question. It really depends on the people that run the process.

Cultural change in the academy has been achieved, not by revolution consultation or dialogue, but by time-hungry bureaucratic and administrative means. Current quality assurance practices seem to demand such a high degree of compliance and responsiveness that little space has been allowed for future scenario planning.

Quality otherwise

Quality assurance is a socially constructed domain of power. As a discourse, it wields the power to form and regulate through the imposition of its own terms. Workers in the academy have had to incorporate and internalize it for their professional and organizational survival. Hence, it has become difficult to contest. Quality assurance demands a self and organization berate-ment that demoralizes and disempowers. Quality assurance discursively car-ries the threat and trace of the other within it. Resistance cannot be easily declared as it implies espousal of the other side of quality, that is privilege, elitism, mystification of decision making, unreliability, and shoddiness. Opposition is not easily communicated as to oppose quality is to favour its opposite. Disempowerment is compounded by excessive volumes of work involved in preparation. The processes inflict a type of social, psychic and organizational violence and trauma. Many informants hesitated when asked about changes that they would like to see. Some were too preoccupied re-sponding to the ever-shifting systems of quality assurance to allow themselves the opportunity to think of quality otherwise. When asked about desired fu-ture changes, an academic development officer in an old university responds:

> Ooh, that's hard to say . . . I think that it probably is fairly well embed-ded in the culture now.

The TINA effect, or 'there is no alternative' was ubiquitous. A vice provost comments on the inevitability of externality:

> I think it's just inevitable – the external part is played in ensuring that the internal processes are up to snuff and then perhaps having some mechanism for going into it in detail if they aren't.

An academic development officer in an old university argues that if exter-nal inspection is inevitable, it should audit existing performance, rather than enforce performativity:

> I think probably what I would like to see happen, perhaps even more than, you know, than audits, and dipping down like I said, is probably that QA has its teams of reviewers to actually go in, and, you know by arrangement, sit in on institutional processes, as they occur, rather than jacking something up from scratch to show the QAA.

A senior lecturer also comments that quality assurance is seen more as performativity than performance in an under-funded system.

> In all we've got better playing games in the research assessment exer-cise in massive grade inflation. And in subject review, people have got much better at hiding things, so if that is the case, one, rather than looking for spending rash resources on it, if you really wanted to do it properly, you'd have to spend more resources, but those resources aren't available. . . . So on one hand I feel that we ought to be doing these quality assurance mechanisms better because people have learnt to play the games rather than get around them. So, how accountable we are is not so clear.

An assistant registrar in an old university believes that the balance of power between externally driven change and internal processes must be changed:

I think what needs to change is that the, at the moment quality assurance is fundamentally, externally driven. Institutions are finding themselves, whether they wish to or not, responding to an agenda which has
been devised externally, partly through the statutory obligations placed
in the 1992 Act on HEFCE. Partly through everything that came out of
Dearing, and the whole area has snowballed, in terms of both institutional review, and subject level review expanding way beyond what was
originally intended . . . and institutions are forced into a position of
complete reactiveness. Now my belief is that this ought to be an institution's responsibility. Institutions ought to be trusted to do it more, and
institutions ought also be given more breathing space actually, to try to
work out a kind of quality assurance strategy, where they have the
destiny of things in their own hands. . . . And to that extent institutions
should be working to very different comparitors, very different yard-
sticks, very different forms of measurement, and that's not happening
at the moment because of the externally imposed agenda.

However, the externality has a parochial feel to it. A common observation
in this study was how the academy had failed to look at QA assessments in
other sectors or in other national locations. This was also the central thesis
of Birnbaum's (2001) study of management 'fads' in higher education.
According to a faculty manager the academy has transferred quality technology from industry, but has failed to learn lessons from the private sector:

I would want to really learn the lessons of business and industry. And
really look at best practices in industry and business and try and transfer some of that to higher education quality assurance. . . . You got to
that point in industry probably three decades ago. It's pretty out-
rageous that we haven't got to that point in higher education yet. It's
probably because it's very, very difficult, because there's no lack of
intelligent people putting their minds on the subject. So I'll just add
my feeble intelligence onto that, and try and eliminate inspection and
build it into the fabric of what we do. I'm not sure how though.

A pro-vice chancellor in an old university warns against the cut and paste
approach to quality processes:

. . . will it be a patch up thing? Just taking on what industry has done
and trying to transplant it into academic life? And as a result making
life very, very much more difficult for us to talk about quality in any
meaningful way.

A faculty manager in an old university observes that quality should be
more about assurance than control:

I've spent 13 years in the aerospace industry, including military defence. So I've got a lot of experience of the Ministry of Defence and
the British Standards approach to quality assurance . . . they've been
going for the approach that perhaps HE is just starting to think about,

that is you don't inspect quality into a product, you build the quality into the process, and inspecting quality into it just wastes money. So wherever I can, I take that approach. Otherwise I think all the useful things I do, in terms of quality and HE are the ones that lead to building the quality into the process, and nothing, if I have a cynical half-hour, nothing that I do that is involved in inspection, or audit, or review, is doing anything but wasting money.

A review of the cost-effectiveness of quality assessment systems was suggested. A professor in a new university recommends a form of policy borrowing from industry and suggests that the 'Investors in People' process would be more useful and less expensive:

Subject review, I think that's had a very considerable impact upon everybody in the sector. I have to say very little of it I think is beneficial . . . I've also been very closely involved in the 'Investors in People' process. . . . That, I think, has been much more beneficial certainly at least in terms of cost/benefit approach because the amount of time, effort and energy that's gone into that is a fraction of what's been spent on subject review.

An academic registrar in a new university believes that processes need to be less driven by external inspection:

There should be a much sort of more arm's length trusting relationship as institutions become more mature at doing it for themselves.

An assistant registrar in an old university also argues against the extent of external involvement:

I'm thinking of the HEFCE consultation where they're proposing institutional audit, with drill down. And we think drill down is a very bad idea. . . . Clearly we have our own systems of review in our courses internally, and we don't see any need for a second set of externals to come down and re-do that, when they could simply look at the outcomes of our own internal mechanism, and test aspects of those out if they so wished, against other sources of evidence.

A professor in an old university fears that inspection could become even more ubiquitous:

They'll invent a system that, you know, there was one idea, and I think this is the idea going around Scotland at the moment, where they visit on a sort of every two- or three-weeks basis. I think, I'm not sure of that. But I mean I can imagine us then building, instead of building up for this one week we'd be building up continually, through every one of these visits.

A professor in an old university believes that the invasiveness of inspection creates a tension that is counter-productive to good teaching:

> There needs to be a movement away from subject review . . . this idea
> of drilling down into various subjects, and going into greater detail is
> extremely invasive, and it makes people very tense. It's actually pre-
> vented them from being good teachers because they're conscious of
> the pressures of other things around them. And my sense is that the
> best teachers are those who work in a relaxed environment, and who
> are able to communicate effectively, and well, with students. It's not to
> do with paperwork, not at all.

A philosophy lecturer argues that the emphasis needs to be shifted away
from teaching performance and towards effective learning:

> The first thing is that we need to move away from thinking about
> lecturing performance, or academic performance, and think about
> effective learning. And although that sounds a bit like student experi-
> ence, it's not, because effective learning places responsibility for the
> learning on the students, and the lecturer can but facilitate that, and
> it's not the lecturer's job to ensure that the student learns.

She also comments on the inappropriateness of academics operating
managerially. For her multiskilling and split focusing are political issues:

> We politically need to view all this talk about quality as being talk about
> management processes, and we need to stop internalizing the language
> of management.

A further political issue is the link between quality and equality. Quality
assurance discourses can both achieve and inhibit the policy objectives of
innovation and productivity to be found in the knowledge society discourses,
and the equity ideals incorporated in social justice discourses. A lecturer
in English literature believes that the conceit of transparency espoused by
audit needs to be transferred to employment conditions and career development. At the moment, she sees quality processes as a way of increasing
marginalization and bullying at work:

> I'd like to see a far wider monitoring of equal ops issues. I'd like it
> noted, you know, not as a footnote, I'd like it highlighted what the
> portion of women students, women staff, women in all categories there
> are in the departments that are being measured. What percentage of
> racial minorities – I mean we are pathetic, we have no member of staff,
> or post-grad, who is of a racial minority . . . I'd like to see a kind of
> equal opportunities auditing going on as part of both research and
> teaching because I think it has a huge impact on both of them. I'd also
> like to see other kinds of areas being monitored, like the difference in
> ages between the different kinds of staff in the department and how
> much interaction, or how much help there is, coming down to the
> unpromoted staff. . . . I'd like something put in place that meant that
> when we were going through the whole ghastly process of putting the
> submission, whether for teaching or research, in that that couldn't

then be turned into a means of persecuting the weak, which is what's happened right now . . . I mean, you could either say, 'Okay, these QA procedures can be used to pull departments together so that there aren't any marginalized any more.'

Ironically, while feedback loops and action in relation to student evaluation were heavily audited in subject review, little evaluation of the process itself was conducted. An assistant registrar in an old university comments on the insularity, the lack of reflexivity and lack of evaluation of the methodology itself:

> And this is also a trap where I think HEFCE and its new groups are heading into. We're not standing outside the whole project and looking for external comparatives. I believe strongly that we should be asking ourselves what kind of information demands are made on hospitals or schools. What kinds of systems are used in America, or Japan? . . . I would actually like to see a proper moratorium, a proper evaluation.

Emphasis on the student experience in subject review was embedded in a rights discourse. This was not extended to organizations. The head of academic standards in an old university would like to see a more robust appeals procedure:

> I think there should certainly be a formal appeal mechanism, because I think without that it just discredits the system. We've seen in *The Times Higher* a lot where universities have had a severe report from the QAA, they've complained, and the QAA's kind of half retracted it, or not retracted it and then gone back a little later and said 'Well it wasn't really that bad' this kind of thing. I think that just discredits the system.

The head of quality assurance in a new university would like to see the return of trust:

> Sometimes I feel the QAA's . . . attitude was, you know, to distrust all academics. It was all about 'We distrust academics so these are the things that we are doing to make sure that our distrust is not justified' a terrible way to proceed. I'd love to see more trust coming back.

A head of department in a new university wants to see an end to evangelical certainty and more attention paid to epistemological uncertainty. He believes that the academy is in mourning for an ideal – a lost other – which probably never existed:

> In terms of what I would like to see, well it's hard to be anything other than 'golden ageist' and of course the golden age wasn't a golden age. It had its own contradictions and problems. . . . So I think what I would like to see is a much more open-ended debate about the nature of quality. Because I don't think the concept of quality is going to go away, it's a kind of genie out of the bottle thing. I'd like to see it much

more around notions of quality enhancement. I'd see the induction into the uncertainty principle, more centre stage, where what you're doing is working with a series of provisional hypotheses about how one can do things better, and see quality enhancement, because we're all trying to be better practitioners, if you like, rather than simply evangelize a particular enthusiasm about what is identified as good practice. I'd like to see it recognized as a, a much more ephemeral concept, what was quality under Thatcher is not quality under Blair. I mean the whole definition migrates. And yet every time an organization sets down the criteria for quality you'd think that the holy grail had been discovered and it could somehow be cast in stone, handed down as tablets from the mountain by Moses or whatever. And so you have this you know because you have an historical perspective, that definitions of quality are constantly overturned.

Constant change, unpredictability, instability and disequilibrium are part of social and organizational life (Cutright, 2001). The quantitative, linear rationality of quality systems contrasts starkly with the range of qualitative engagements that I have encountered in this study. For some, quality assessment has transformative potential and is perceived as part of the democratizing process in which students and other stakeholders have a more formalized structural position in relation to organizational development and the maintenance of professional standards. For others, quality assessment is unstable, unreliable and undesirable. In this analysis, some aspects of higher education are perceived as non-narratable and cannot be tied to the conceit of transparency. Furthermore, quality assessment produces normative aspirations in the midst of considerable diversity. For another group, quality is both positive and negative, as a head of department observes:

> I mean there are some bits of quality I don't mind, you know this is the multi-accentuality of sign isn't it?

The multi-accentuality of the sign was a leitmotif in this study. Because quality is discourse, it is polysemic and multi-dimensional. The narrative grammar of quality is characterized by articulations of ambivalence. Some members of the academy occupy a liminal position – operating within and outside quality assurance. For some, quality assurance has provided new paradigms for thinking about academic work and new career opportunities. For others, it is about suspicion, mistrust and the management of processes, rather than standards, with considerable wastage and frustration involved. As a new disciplinary technology it has exacerbated old or introduced new power relations. The imposition of interpretation and scoring on multiple academic realities has created potential for major misrecognition and inequalities. As such it has been a form of symbolic violence. A question is whether there is a less corrosive way of assuring quality, and whether current systems can be evaluated consultatively, with an expansion of the conceptual language of quality. Can the significant theoretical capital possessed by the academy be applied to the development of structures and procedures that operate with, rather than in opposition to academic processes? Can there be an informed debate that includes a range of stakeholders, but particularly those who are responsible for delivering quality services? Can we start to think in terms of quality otherwise?

References

Abbott, D. (2001) Satisfaction guaranteed (well, almost). *Independent*, 24 October.

Acker, S. (1980) Hierarchies, jobs, bodies: a theory of gendered organizations, *Gender and Society*, 4(2): 139–58.

Acker, S. (1996) Doing good and feeling bad: the work of women university teachers, *Cambridge Journal of Education*, 26: 401–22.

Acker, S. and Webber, M. (2000) Pleasure and danger in the lives of academics. Paper presented at the Annual Meeting of the American Educational Research Association, New Orleans, April.

Adams, D. (1998) Examining the fabric of academic life: an analysis of three decades of research on the perceptions of Australian academics about their roles, *Higher Education*, 36: 421–35.

Adams, D. (2000) Views of academic work, *Teacher Development*, 4(1): 65–78.

Adia, E., Roberts, D. and Allen, A. (eds) (1996) *Higher Education: The Ethnic Minority Student Experience*. Leeds: HEIST.

Aglietta, M. (1979) *Theory of Capitalist Regulation: The US Experience*. London: Verso.

Alderman, G. (1996) Audit, assessment and academic autonomy, *Higher Education Quarterly*, 50(3): 178–92.

Altbach, P. (ed.) (1999) *Private Prometheus: Private Higher Education and Development in the 21st Century*. Westport, CT: Greenwood.

Althusser, L. (1971) Ideology and ideological state apparatuses, in L. Althusser (ed.) *Lenin and Philosophy and Other Essays*. New York: Monthly Review Press.

Angelo, T. (2000) Doing academic development as though we value learning most. Transformative guidelines from research and practice, in R. James, J. Milton and R. Gabb (eds) *Cornerstones of Higher Education Research and Development in Higher Education*. Australia: HERDSA.

Apple, M.W. (2000) Between neoliberalism and neoconservatism: education and conservatism in a global context, in N.C. Burbules and A. Torres (eds) *Globalization and Education*. New York: Routledge.

Argyris, C. and Schön, D. (1974) *Theory in Practice: Increasing Professional Effectiveness*. San Francisco, CA: Jossey Bass.

Argyris, C. and Schön, D. (1978) *Organisational Learning: A Theory of Action Perspective*. Reading, MA: Addison-Wesley.

Association of University Teachers (AUT) (1993) *Bursting at the Seams*. London: AUT.

Association of University Teachers (AUT) (1996) *Efficiency Gains or Quality Losses?: How Falling Investment Affects Higher Education's Capacity to Contribute to the UK's Economic Success.* London: AUT.

Association of University Teachers (AUT) (1998) *Pressure Points – A Survey into the Causes and Consequences of Occupational Stress in UK Academic and Related Staff.* London: AUT.

Atkins, M.J. (1999) Oven-ready and self-basting: taking stock of employability skills, *Teaching in Higher Education*, 4(2): 267–80.

Audit Commission (1984) *Audit Commission for England and Wales: Report of Accounts for Year Ended 31 March 1984.* London: HMSO.

Avis, J., Bloomer, M., Esland, G., Gleeson, D. and Hodkinson, P. (1996) *Knowledge and Nationhood.* London: Cassell Education.

Bacchi, C. (2000) Policy as discourse: what does it mean? Where does it get us?, *Discourse: Studies in the Cultural Politics of Education*, 21(1): 45–57.

Baimbridge, M. (1998) Institutional research performance 1992–1996: a tale of two sectors, *Journal of Further and Higher Education*, 22: 69–78.

Baker Miller, J. (1976) *Towards a New Psychology of Women.* Harmondsworth: Penguin.

Ball, S. (1990a) Management as moral technology: a Luddite Analysis, in S. Ball (ed.) *Foucault and Education.* London: Routledge.

Ball, S. (1990b) *Politics and Policy Making in Education: Explorations in Policy Sociology.* London: Routledge.

Ball, S. (1994) *Education Reform – a Critical and Post-Structuralist Approach.* Buckingham: Open University Press.

Ball, S. (1998) Performativity and fragmentation, in J. Carter (ed.) *Postmodern Schooling.* London: Routledge.

Ball, S. (2000) Performativities and fabrications in the education economy. Towards the preformative society?, *The Australian Educational Researcher*, 27(2): 1–23.

Ball, S., Vincent, C. and Radnor, H. (1997) Into confusion: LEAs, accountability and democracy, *Journal of Education Policy*, 12(3): 147–64.

Ball, S., Maguire, M. and Macrae, S. (2000) Worlds apart – education markets in the post-16 sector of one urban locale 1995–98, in F. Coffield (ed.) *Differing Visions of a Learning Society.* Bristol: The Policy Press.

Ball, S., Davies, J., David, M. and Reay, D. (2002) 'Classification' and 'judgement': social class and the cognitive structures of choice of Higher Education, *British Journal of Sociology of Education*, 23(1): 51–72.

Barnetson, B. and Cutright, M. (2000) Performance indicators as conceptual technologies, *Higher Education*, 40(3): 277–92.

Barnett, R. (2000) *Realizing the University.* Buckingham: SRHE/Open University Press.

Baron, H. (2000) Riding the crest of a trough, *Teacher Development*, 4(1): 145–60.

Barrow, M. (1999) Quality management systems and dramaturgical compliance, *Quality in Higher Education*, 5(1): 27–36.

Barry, D. (1995) Women's participation in higher education in Guinea, *Women in Higher Education in Africa.* Dakar: UNESCO Regional Office.

Baty, P. (2002) Fury as Hodge calls the shots, *Times Higher Education Supplement*, 22 February.

Baudrillard, J. (1998) *The Consumer Society.* London: Sage.

Bauman, Z. (1987) *Legislators and Interpreters.* Cambridge: Polity Press.

Bauman, Z. (1998a) *Globalization: The Human Consequences.* Cambridge: Polity Press.

Bauman, Z. (1998b) *Work, Consumerism and the New Poor.* Buckingham: Open University Press.

Bauman, Z. (2001a) *The Individualized Society.* Malden, MA: Polity Press.

Bauman, Z. (2001b) *Community: Seeking Safety in an Insecure World.* Cambridge: Polity Press.

Becher, T. (1989) *Academic Tribes and Territories: Intellectual Enquiry and the Cultures of Disciplines.* Milton Keynes: SRHE/Open University Press.

Becher, T. and Trowler, P. (2001) *Academic Tribes and Territories: Intellectual Enquiry and the Cultures of Disciplines.* Buckingham: SRHE/Open University Press.

Beck, U. (1997) *The Reinvention of Politics: Rethinking Modernity in the Global Social Order.* Cambridge: Polity Press.

Beckett, F. (2001) Wheel of fortune, *Guardian,* 1 May.

Beilharz, P. (ed.) (2001) *The Bauman Reader.* Oxford: Blackwell.

Benjamin, J. (2000) The Oedipal riddle, in P. Du Gay, J. Evans and P. Redman (eds) *Identity: A Reader.* London: Sage in association with The Open University.

Benokraitis, N. (1998) Working in the ivory basement: subtle sex discrimination in higher education, in L. Collins, J. Chrisler and K. Quina (eds) *Arming Athena: Career Strategies for Women in Academe.* London: Sage.

Bensimon, E. (1995) TQM in the Academy: a rebellious reading, *Harvard Educational Review,* 4: 593–611.

Berdahl, R. (1990) *British Universities and the State.* New York: Arno Press.

Bernstein, B. (1996) *Pedagogy, Symbolic Control and Identity.* London: Taylor and Francis.

Berry, C. (1999) University league tables: artefacts and inconsistencies in individual rankings, *Higher Education Review,* 31(2): 3–10.

Bett, M. (1999) *Independent Review of Higher Education Pay and Conditions: Report of a Committee Chaired by Sir Michael Bett.* London: The Stationery Office.

Billing, D. and Thomas, H.G. (1998) Quality management and organisational structure in higher education, *Journal of Higher Education Policy and Management,* 20(2): 139–59.

Billing, D. and Thomas, H. (2000) Evaluating a transnational university quality assessment project in Turkey, *Journal of Studies in International Education,* 4(2): 55–68.

Birnbaum, R. (2001) *Management Fads in Higher Education.* San Francisco, CA: Jossey Bass.

Blackmore, J. (1999) Localization/globalization and the midwife state: strategic dilemmas for state feminism in education?, *Journal of Education Policy,* 14(1): 33–54.

Blackmore, J. (2000) Globalization: a useful concept for feminists rethinking theory and strategies in education?, in N. Burbules and C. Torres (eds) *Globalization and Education: Critical Perspectives.* London: Routledge.

Blackmore, J. and Sachs, J. (2001) Women leaders in the restructured and internationalized university, in A. Brooks and A. McKinnon (eds) *Gender and the Restructured University.* Buckingham: SRHE/Open University Press.

Blase, J. (ed.) (1991) *The Politics of Life in Schools.* Newbury Park, CA: Sage.

Bologna Declaration (1999) www.unige.ch/cre (accessed July 2001).

Borland, J. and James, S. (1999) The learning experiences of students with disabilities in higher education, *Disability and Society,* 14(1): 85–101.

Bottery, M. and Wright, N. (1997) Impoverishing a sense of professionalism: who's to blame?, *Educational Management and Administration,* 25(1): 7–25.

Bourdieu, P. (1981) Men and machines, in K. Knorr-Cetina and A.C. Cicourel (eds) *Advances in Social Theory and Methodology: Towards an Integration of Micro- and Macro-Sociologies.* London: Routledge and Kegan Paul.

Bourdieu, P. (1984) *Distinction.* London: Routledge and Kegan Paul.

Bourdieu, P. (1996) *The State Nobility: Elite Schools in the Field of Power.* Cambridge: Polity Press.

Bourdieu, P. (1998) *Acts of Resistance.* Cambridge: Polity Press.

Bowden, R. (2000) Fantasy higher education: university and college league tables, *Quality in Higher Education*, 6(1): 41–59.

Brennan, J. and Shah, T. (2000) *Managing Quality in Higher Education.* Buckingham: SRHE/Open University Press.

Brennan, J., El-Khawas, E. and Shah, T. (1994) *Peer Review and the Assessment of Higher Education Quality: An International Perspective.* London: Quality Support Centre.

Brigham, S. (1993) TQM: ten lessons we can learn from industry, *Change*, 25: 42–8.

Brimblecombe, N., Ormston, M. and Shaw, M. (1996) Gender differences in teacher response to school inspection, *Educational Studies*, 22(1): 27–40.

Broadfoot, P. (1998) Quality standards and control in higher education: what price life-long learning?, *International Studies in Sociology of Education*, 8(2): 155–80.

Brooks, A. (1997) *Academic Women.* Buckingham: SRHE/Open University Press.

Brooks, A. (2001) Restructuring bodies of knowledge, in A. Brooks and A. MacKinnon (eds) *Gender and the Restructured University: Changing Management and Culture in Higher Education.* Buckingham: SRHE/Open University Press.

Brooks, A. and MacKinnon, A. (eds) (2001) *Gender and the Restructured University: Changing Management and Culture in Higher Education.* Buckingham: SRHE/Open University Press.

Brown, R. (2000) The new UK quality framework, *Higher Education Quarterly*, 54(4): 323–42.

Brown, M. and Ralph, S. (1998) Change-linked stress in British teachers. Paper presented to the British Educational Research Association Conference, September, Queen's University, Belfast.

Burbules, N. (2000) Does the internet constitute a global educational community?, in N. Burbules and C. Torres (eds) *Globalization and Education: Critical Perspectives.* London: Routledge.

Burbules, N. and Torres, C. (eds) (2000) *Globalization and Education: Critical Perspectives.* London: Routledge.

Burke, P. (2002) *Accessing Education: Effectively Widening Participation.* Stoke-on-Trent: Trentham.

Butler, J. (1994) Gender as performance: an interview with Judith Butler, *Radical Philosophy*, 67: 32–9.

Butler, J. (1997a) *The Psychic Life of Power: Theories in Subjection.* Stanford, CA: Stanford University Press.

Butler, J. (1997b) *Excitable Speech: A Politics of the Performative.* London: Routledge.

Butler, J. (2000) *Contingency, Hegemony, Universality: Contemporary Dialogues on the Left / Judith Butler, Ernesto Laclau and Slavoj Žižek.* London: Verso.

Callender, C. and Kemp, M. (2000) *Changing Student Finances: Income, Expenditure and the Take-up of Student Loans Among Full and Part-time Higher Education Students in 1998/9.* London: Department for Education and Employment.

Cameron, D. (2000) *Good to Talk.* London: Sage.

Cameron, D. (2001) 'Mission impenetrable', *Critical Quarterly*, 43(2): 99–103.

Cameron, K. and Ettington, D. (1988) Conceptual foundations of organizational culture, in J.C. Smart (ed.) *Handbook of Theory and Research.* New York: Agathon Press.

Carter, J., Fenton, S. and Modood, T. (1999) *Ethnicity and Employment in Higher Education.* London: Policy Studies Institute.

Case, P., Case, S. and Catling, S. (2000) Please show you're working: a critical assessment of the impact of OFSTED inspection on primary teachers, *British Journal of Sociology of Education*, 21(4): 605–21.

Castells, M. (1996) *The Rise of the Network Society: Economy, Society and Culture*, Vol. 1. Oxford: Blackwell.

Chesterman, C. (2002) Women's executive development in Australian higher education, in G. Howie and A. Tauchert (eds) *Gender, Teaching and Research in Higher Education: Challenges for the 21st Century*. Aldershot: Ashgate.

Chomsky, N. (1998) *Conversation with Carlos Alberto Torres, MIT, Massachussetts, 9 October*, cited in Burbules and Torres (2000) *Globalization and Education: Critical Perspectives*. London: Routledge.

Cizas, A. (1997) Quality assessment in smaller countries: problem and Lithuanian approach, *Higher Education Management*, 9(1): 43–8.

Clark, B. (1987) *The Academic Life*. Princeton, NJ: Carnegie.

Clark, B. (1996) Substantive growth and innovative organisation, *Higher Education*, 32: 417–30.

Clarke, J. and Newman, J. (1997) *The Managerial State*. London: Sage.

Clegg, S. (1999) Professional education, reflective practice and feminism, *International Journal of Inclusive Education*, 3(2): 167–79.

Clegg, S. (2001) Expertise, Professionalism and Managerialism: Trouble Relationships in Contemporary Higher Education? Inaugural Lecture, Sheffield Hallam University.

Clouder, L. (1998) Getting the 'right answers': student evaluation as a reflection of intellectual development, *Teaching in Higher Education*, 3(2): 185–95.

Coaldrake, P. (2000) Rethinking academic and university work, *Higher Education Management*, 12(3): 7–30.

Coate, K., Court, S., Gillon, E., Morley, L. and Williams, G. (2000) *Academic and Academic Related Staff Involvement in the Local, Regional and National Economy*. London: Association of University Teachers Institute of Education, University of London.

Cole, P. (1999) To what extent is the culture of a university department supportive of equal opportunities for women?, *International Studies in Sociology of Education*, 8(3): 271–97.

Court, S. (1996) The use of time by academic and related staff, *Higher Education Quarterly*, 50(4): 237–60.

Cowen, R. (1996) Performativity, post-modernity and the University, *Comparative Education*, 32(2): 245–58.

Cullingford, C. (ed.) (1999) *An Inspector Calls*. London: Kogan Page.

Currie, J. and Newson, J. (eds) (1998) *Universities and Globalisation*. London: Sage.

Currie, J. and Thiele, B. (2001) Globalization and gendered work cultures, in A. Brooks and A. McKinnon (eds) *Gender and the Restructured University: Changing Management and Culture in Higher Education*. Buckingham: SRHE/Open University Press.

Currie, J., Harris, P. and Thiele, B. (2000) Sacrifices in greedy universities: are they gendered?, *Gender and Education*, 12(3): 269–91.

Currie, J., Thiele, B. and Harris, P. (eds) (2001) *Gendered Universities in Globalized Economies: Power, Careers and Sacrifices*. Lexington, MA: Lexington Books.

Cutright, M. (ed.) (2001) *Chaos Theory and Higher Education: Leadership, Planning, and Policy*. New York: P. Lang.

David, M. and Woodward, D. (eds) (1998) *Negotiating the Glass Ceiling: Careers of Senior Women in the Academic World*. London: Falmer Press.

Davies, C. (1996) The sociology of professions and the profession of gender, *Sociology*, 30: 661–78.

Day, C. (1997) Teachers in the twenty-first century: time to renew the vision, in A. Hargreaves and R. Evans (eds) *Beyond Educational Reform*. Buckingham: Open University Press.

De Groot, J. (1997) After the ivory tower: gender, commodification and the 'Academic', *Feminist Review*, 55 (Spring): 130–42.

De la Rey, C. (2001) Women and Management in Higher Education in South Africa. Paper presented at the ACU/IoE Seminar on Managing Gendered Change in Selected Commonwealth Universities, Johannesburg, South Africa, February.

Dean, J. (1995) What teachers and headteachers think about inspection, *Cambridge Journal of Inspection*, 25(1): 45–52.

Dearing, R. (1997) *Higher Education in the Learning Society (The Dearing Report)*. London: National Committee of Inquiry into Higher Education.

Dearlove, J. (1997) The academic labour process: from collegiality and professionalism to managerialism and proletarianisation?, *Higher Education Review*, 30: 56–75.

Deem, R. (1998) 'New Managerialism' and higher education: the management of performance and cultures in universities in the United Kingdom, *International Studies in Sociology of Education* 8(1): 47–70.

Deem, R. (2001) Globalisation, new managerialism, academic capitalism and entrepreneurialism in universities: is the local dimension still important?, *Comparative Education*, 37(1): 7–20.

Deem, R. and Ozga, J. (2000) Transforming post-compulsory education? Femocrats at work in the Academy, *Women's Studies International Forum*, 23(2): 153–66.

Delanty, G. (2001) *Challenging Knowledge: The University in the Knowledge Society*. Buckingham: SRHE/Open University Press.

Deming, W. (1986) *Out of the Crisis: Quality, Productivity and Competitive Position*. Cambridge: Cambridge University Press.

DES (Department of Education and Science) (1991) *Higher Education: A New Framework*. London: HMSO.

DES (Department of Education and Science) (1993) *Realising Our Potential: A Strategy for Science, Engineering and Technology*. London: HMSO, Cm 2250.

Dhillon, P. and Standish, P. (eds) (2000) *Lyotard: Just Education*. London: Routledge.

Dill, D. (1995) Through Deming's eyes: a cross-national analysis of quality assurance policies in higher education, *Quality in Higher Education*, 1(2): 95–110.

Dill, D. (2001) The regulation of public research universities: changes in academic competition and implications for university autonomy and accountability, *Higher Education Policy*, 14(1): 21–35.

Dominelli, L. and Hoogvelt, A. (1996) Globalization, contract government and the Taylorization of intellectual labour in academia, *Studies in Political Economy*, 49: 71–100.

Douglas, M. (1966) *Purity and Danger: An Analysis of Concepts of Pollution and Taboo*. London: Routledge and Kegan Paul.

Douglas, M. (ed.) (1992) *Risk and Blame: Essays in Cultural Theory*. London: Routledge.

Dreyfus, H. and Rabinow, P. (1982) *Michel Foucault: Beyond Structuralism and Hermeneutics*. Brighton: Harvester Press.

DTI (1998) *Competitive Futures: Building the Knowledge Driven Economy*. London: Department of Trade and Industry (DTI).

Du Gay, P. (1994) Making up managers: bureaucracy, enterprise and the liberal art of separation, *British Journal of Sociology*, 45(4): 655–74.

Duke, C. (1997) Towards a lifelong curriculum, in F. Coffield and B. Williamson (eds) *Repositioning Higher Education*. Buckingham: SRHE/Open University Press.

Dyhouse, C. (1995) *No Distinction of Sex? Women in British Universities 1870–1939*. London: UCL Press.

Eagleton, M. (1998) Reading between bodies and institutions, *Gender and Education*, 10: 343–9.

EC (European Commission) (1993) *White Paper: Growth, Competitiveness, Employment: The Challenges and the Way Forward into the Twenty First Century*. Luxembourg: Office for the Official Publications of the European Commission.

EC (European Commission) (1995) *White Paper: Education and Training: Teaching and Learning: Towards the Learning Society*. Luxembourg: Office for the Official Publications of the European Commission.

EC (European Commission) (1997) *European Co-operation in Quality Assurance in Higher Education*. Luxembourg: Office for the Official Publications of the European Commission.

Edwards, R. (1993) *Mature Women Students*. London: The Falmer Press.

Eggins, H. (ed.) (1997) *Women as Leaders and Managers in Higher Education*. Buckingham: SRHE/Open University Press.

Eraut, M. (1994) *Developing Professional Knowledge and Competence*. London: Falmer.

Eraut, M., Morley, L. and Cole, G. (1998) *Standards and Vocational Qualifications in Continuing Professional Development*. London: QCA.

Etzkowitz, H. and Leydesdorff, L. (eds) (1997) *Universities in the Global Economy: A Triple Helix of University, Industry, Government Relations*. London: Cassell Academic.

Evalueringscenteret (1999) *Evaluation of European Higher Education: A Status Report*. Copenhagen: European Commission/Centre for Quality Assurance.

Evans, M. (1995) Ivory towers: life in the mind, in L. Morley and V. Walsh (eds) *Feminist Academics: Creative Agents for Change*. London: Taylor and Francis.

Farish, M., McPake, J., Powney, J. and Weiner, G. (1995) *Equal Opportunities in Colleges and Universities*. Buckingham: SRHE/Open University Press.

Fillitz, T. (2000) Academia; same pressures, same conditions of work?, in M. Strathern (ed.) *Audit Cultures: Anthropological Studies in Accountability, Ethics, and the Academy*. London: Routledge.

Finch, J. (1997) Power, legitimacy and academic standards, in J. Brennan, P. De Vries and R. Williams (eds) *Standards and Quality in Higher Education*. London: Jessica Kingsley.

Fisher, S. (1994) *Stress in Academic Life: The Mental Assembly Line*. Buckingham: SRHE/Open University Press.

Floud, R. (2001) Universities are sinking under inspection load, *Times Higher Education Studies*, 23 March.

Foucault, M. (1972) *The Archaeology of Knowledge*. London: Routledge.

Foucault, M. (1979a) Governmentability, *Ideology and Consciousness*, 6: 5–22.

Foucault, M. (1979b) *Discipline and Punish*. New York: Vintage.

Foucault, M. (1980) In C. Gordon (ed.) (1980) *Power-knowledge: Selected Interviews and Other Writings, 1972–1977/Michel Foucault*. Brighton: Harvester Press.

Fraser, N. (1997) *Justice Interruptus: Critical Reflections on the 'Postsocialist' Condition*. New York: Routledge.

Frazer, M. (1997) Report of the modalities of external evaluation of higher education in Europe, *Higher Education in Europe*, 22(3): 349–401.

Fredericks, M., Westerheijden, D. and Weusthof, P. (1994) Effects of quality assurance in Dutch higher education, *European Journal of Education*, 29: 101–18.

Fuller, S. (1999) Making the university fit for critical intellectuals: recovering from the ravages of the postmodern condition, *British Educational Research Journal,* 25(25): 583–95.

Fulton, O. (1996) The academic profession in England on the eve of structural reform, in P. Altbach (ed.) *The International Academic Profession.* Mento Park: Carnegie Foundation.

Gefou-Madianou, D. (2000) Disciples, discipline and reflection, in M. Strathern (ed.) *Audit Cultures: Anthropological Studies in Accountability, Ethics, and the Academy.* London: Routledge.

Gellert, C. (ed.) (1993) *Higher Education in Europe.* London: Jessica Kingsley.

Gewirtz, S., Ball, S.J. and Bowe, R. (1995) *Equity, Markets and Choice.* Buckingham: Open University Press.

Gibbons, M., Limoges, C., Nowotny, H. *et al.* (1994) *The New Production of Knowledge: Science and Research in Contemporary Societies.* London: Sage.

Gibbs, G. (1995) The relationship between quality in research and quality in teaching, *Quality in Higher Education,* 1(2): 147–57.

Gibbs, G. (1997) A teaching and learning strategy for higher education. Unpublished report to the HEFCE. Milton Keynes: Centre for Higher Education Practice, The Open University.

Gibbs, G., Habeshaw, T. and Yorke, M. (2000) Institutional learning and teaching strategies in English higher education, *Higher Education,* 40(3): 351–72.

Giddens, A. (1984) *The Constitution of Society: Outline of the Theory of Structuration.* Cambridge: Polity Press.

Giddens, A. (1990) *The Consequences of Modernity.* Cambridge: Polity Press.

Giddens, A. (1991) *Modernity and Self-Identity.* Cambridge: Polity Press.

Glazer, J. (1999) *Shattering the Myths: Women in Academe.* Baltimore, MD: John Hopkins University Press.

Glover, J. (2001) Women and Scientific Employment. Paper presented at the ATHENA Project Conference, Royal Institution of Great Britain, 25 September.

Goffman, E. (1968) *Stigma: Notes on the Management of Spoiled Identity.* London: Penguin.

Goffman, E. (1972) *Interaction Ritual: Essays on Face-to-face Behaviour.* Harmondsworth: Penguin.

Goleman, D. (1996) *Emotional Intelligence: Why It Can Matter More Than IQ.* London: Bloomsbury.

Goode, E. and Ben-Yehuda, N. (1994) *Moral Panics: The Social Construction of Deviance.* Cambridge, MA: Blackwell.

Gorostiaga, X. (1999) In search of the missing link between education and development, in P. Altbach (ed.) *Private Prometheus: Private Higher Education and Development in the 21st Century.* Westport, CT: Greenwood Press.

Gregg, P. and Wadsworth, J. (1995) *Feeling Insecure.* London: Employment Policy Institute.

Griffin, G. and Andermahr, S. (ed.) (1997) *Straight Studies Modified: Lesbian Intervention in the Academy.* London: Cassell.

Guardian (2001) Trial by ordeal, 30 January: 12.

Guardian (1999) Class acts, *Guardian Higher Education,* 9 March: i.

Gudeman, S. (1998) The new captains of information, *Anthropology Today,* 14(1): 1–3.

Guile, D. (2001) MA Seminar at the University of London Institute of Education, 13 March.

Habermas, J. (1971) The university in a democracy: democratization of the university, *Toward a Rational Society*. London: Heinemann.

Habermas, J. (1992) The idea of the university – learning processes, *The New Conservatism: Cultural Criticism and the Historians' Debate*. Cambridge: Polity Press.

Hall, S. and Du Gay, P. (ed.) (1996) *Questions of Cultural Identity*. London: Sage.

Halsey, A.H. and Trow, M.A. (1971) *The British Academics*. London: Faber and Faber.

Halvorsen, E. (1999) *Gender Analysis of the Higher Education Statistics Agency Data 1996/7*. London: Association of University Teachers.

Hamilton, D. (1998) The idols of the market place, in R.W. Slee, G. Weiner and S. Tomlinson (eds) *School Effectiveness for Whom? Challenges to the School Effectiveness and School Improvement Movements*. London: Falmer Press.

Handy, C. (1993) *Understanding Organisations*. Harmondsworth: Penguin.

Harari, O. (1993) Ten reasons why TQM doesn't work, *Management Review*, 82(1): 33–8.

Harley, S. and Lowe, P. (1998) *Academics Divided: The Research Assessment Exercise and the Academic Labour Process*. Leicester: Leicester Business School.

Hart, W.A. (1997) The qualitymongers, *The Journal of the Philosophy of Education Society of Great Britain*, 31(2): 295–308.

Hassard, J. and Parker, M. (1993) *Postmodernism and Organisations*. London: Sage.

Hatcher, C. (1998) Making the enterprising manager in Australia: a genealogy, *School of Cultural and Political Studies, Faculty of Education*. Australia: Queensland University of Technology.

Health and Safety Executive (HSE) (1998) *Annual Report and Accounts 1997/1998*. London: HSE.

Hearn, J. and Parkin, W. (2001) *Gender, Sexuality and Violence in Organizations: The Unspoken Forces of Organization Violations*. London: Sage.

HEFCE (Higher Education Funding Council for England) (1992) *Quality Assessment*. Circular 10/92. Bristol: HEFCE.

HEFCE (1993) *The Review of the Academic Year (Flowers Report)*. London: HEFCE.

HEFCE (2000) *Interactions Between Teaching, Research and Other Activities: Report to the HEFCE Fundamental Review of Research and Funding Policies*. London: HEFCE.

HEFCE (2001) *Strategies for Widening Participation in Higher Education: A Guide to Good Practice*. Bristol: HEFCE.

HEFCE (2002a) *Information on Quality and Standards in Higher Education. Final Report of the Task Group*. Bristol: HEFCE.

HEFCE (2002b) *2001 Research Assessment Exercise: The Outcome*. Bristol: HEFCE.

Henkel, M. (1999) The modernisation of research evaluation: the case of the UK, *Higher Education*, 38: 105–22.

Henkel, M. (2000) *Academic Identities and Policy Changes in Higher Education*. London: JKP.

HEQC (1996) *Academic Standards in the Approval, Review and Classification of Degrees*. London: HEQC.

HEQC (Higher Education Quality Council) (1997) *The Graduate Standards Programme: Final Report*. London: HEQC.

Herzberg, F., Mauser, B. and Snyderman, B. (1959) *The Motivation to Work*. New York: John Wiley.

Hill, M.D. (1986) A theoretical analysis of faculty job satisfaction/dissatisfaction, *Educational Research Quarterly*, 10: 36–44.

Hodson, P.J. and Thomas, H.G. (1999) Towards an enterprise culture: will the Quality Assurance Agency help or hinder, *Higher Educational Review*, 32(1): 24–33.

hooks, b. (1995) *Teaching to Transgress*. London: Routledge.

Hughes, C. and Tight, M. (1998) The myth of the learning society, in S. Ranson (ed.) *Inside the Learning Society*. London: Cassell.

Hurst, A. (1999) The Dearing Report and students with disabilities and learning difficulties, *Disability and Society*, 14(1): 65–83.

Husu, L. (2000) Gender discrimination in the promised land of gender equality, *Higher Education in Europe*, XXV(2): 221–8.

Husu, L. (2001) *Sexism, Support and Survival in Academia: Academic Women and Hidden Discrimination in Finland*. Helsinki: University of Helsinki.

Imai, M. (1986) *Kaizen (Ky'zen): The Key to Japan's Competitiveness*. New York: Random House.

Jackson, N. and Lund, H. (eds) (2000) *Benchmarking for Higher Education*. Buckingham: SRHE/Open University Press.

Jackson, B. and Marsden, D. (1962) *Education and the Working Class: Some General Themes Raised by a Study of 88 Working-class Children in a Northern Industrial City*. London: Routledge and Kegan Paul.

James, R. (2000) Quality assurance and the growing puzzle of managing organisational knowledge in universities, *Higher Education Management*, 12(3): 41–59.

Jarvis, P. (1999) Global trends in lifelong learning and the response of the universities, *Comparative Education*, 35(2): 249–57.

Jarvis, P. (2000) The changing university: meeting a need and needing to change, *Higher Education Quarterly*, 54(1): 43–67.

Jenkins, P. (1999) *Synthetic Panics: The Symbolic Politics of Designer Drugs*. New York: New York University Press.

Johnson, N. (1994) Dons in decline, *20th Century British History*, 5: 370–85.

Kaufman, R. (1988) Preparing useful performance indicators, *Training and Development Journal*, September: 80–3.

Kalugama, P.S. (1999) Is this an example of gender discrimination? An analysis of higher educational management and administration in Sri Lanka. Unpublished MA dissertation, University of London, Institute of Education.

Keegan, M. (2000) *E-Learning: The Engine of the Knowledge Economy*. New York: Morgan Keegan.

Keller, G. (1992) Increasing quality on campus: what should colleges do about the TQM mania?, *Change*, May–June: 48–51.

Kemp, E., Storey, J. and Sisson, K. (1996) Managing the employment relationship in higher education: quo vadis?, in R. Cuthbert (ed.) *Working in Higher Education*. Buckingham: Open University Press.

Kenway, J. and Langmead, D. (1998) Governmentality, the 'now' university and the future of knowledge work, *Australian Universities' Review*, 41(2): 28–31.

Kickert, W. (1995) Steering at a distance: a new paradigm in public governance in Dutch higher education, *Governance: An International Journal of Policy and Administration*, 8(1): 135–57.

Knight, P. and Trowler, P. (2000) Editorial, *Quality in Higher Education*, 6(2): 109–14.

Kogan, M. and Hanney, S. (2000) *Reforming Higher Education*. London: Jessica Kingsley.

Kramer, R. and Tyler, T. (eds) (1996) *Trust in Organizations*. London: Sage.

Lacy, F.J. and Sheehan, B.A. (1997) Job satisfaction among academic staff, *Higher Education*, 34: 305–22.

Lafferty, G. and Fleming, J. (2000) The restructuring of academic work in Australia: power, management and gender, *British Journal of Sociology of Education*, 21(2): 257–67.

Laing, R.D. (1965) *The Divided Self: An Existential Study in Sanity and Madness.* Harmondsworth: Penguin Books.

Lander, D. (2000) A provocation: quality is service, *Quality in Higher Education*, 6(2): 135–41.

Lather, P. (1991) *Feminist Research in Education: Within/Against.* Waurn Ponds: Deakin University.

Laurillard, D. (1980) Validity of indicators of performance, in D. Billing (ed.) *Indicators of Performance.* Guildford: SRHE.

Lawson, A. (1998) Culture and utility: phrases in dispute, in D. Jary and M. Parker (eds) *The New Higher Education: Issues and Directions for the Post-Dearing University.* Stoke-on-Trent: Staffordshire University Press.

Leckey, J. and Neill, N. (2001) Quantifying quality: the importance of student feedback, *Quality in Higher Education*, 7(1): 19–32.

Lee, M. (1999) Corporatization, privatization, and internationalization of higher education in Malaysia, in P. Altbach (ed.) *Private Prometheus: Private Higher Education and Development in the 21st Century.* Westport, CT: Greenwood Press.

Lee, F. and Harley, S. (1998) Economics divided: the limitations of peer review, in D. Jary and M. Parker (eds) *The New Higher Education: Issues and Directions for the Post-Dearing University.* Stoke-on-Trent: Staffordshire University Press.

Leman, P. and Mann, C. (1999) Gender differences in students' performances in examinations: the Cambridge University project, in P. Fogelberg, J. Hearn, L. Husu and T. Mankkinen (eds) *Hard Work in the Academy: Research and Interventions on Gender Inequalities in Higher Education.* Helsinki: Helsinki University Press.

Leonard, D. (2001) *A Women's Guide to Doctoral Studies.* Buckingham: Open University Press.

Lim, D. (2001) *Quality Assurance in Higher Education: A Study of Developing Countries.* Aldershot: Ashgate.

Lingard, B. (2000) It is and it isn't: vernacular globalization, educational policy, and restructuring, in N. Burbules and C. Torres (eds) *Globalization and Education: Critical Perspectives.* London: Routledge.

Lingard, B. and Blackmore, J. (1997) Editorial – the 'performative' state and the state of educational research, *The Australian Educational Researcher*, 24(3): 1–20.

London School of Economics (LSE) (2001) *Draft Resolution to LSE Academic Board*, 14 March.

Lucas, L. and Webster, F. (1998) Maintaining standards in higher education?: a case study, in D. Jary and M. Parker (eds) *The New Higher Education.* Stoke-on-Trent: Staffordshire University Press.

Luke, C. (1997a) Feminist pedagogy theory in higher education: reflections on power and authority, in C. Marshall (ed.) *Feminist Critical Policy Analysis: A Perspective from Post-secondary Education.* London: Falmer Press.

Luke, C. (1997b) Quality assurance and women in higher education, *Higher Education*, 33: 433–51.

Luke, C. (2001) *Globalization and Women in Academia: North/West – South/East.* Mahwah, NJ: Lawrence Erlbaum.

Luke, A. and Luke, C. (2000) A situated perspective on globalization, in N. Burbules and C. Torres (eds) *Globalization and Education: Critical Perspectives.* London: Routledge.

Lukes, S. (1974) *Power: A Radical View.* London: Macmillan.

Lyotard, J. (1984) *The Postmodern Condition.* Manchester: Manchester University Press.

Macrae, S., Maguire, M. and Ball, S. (1997) Whose 'learning' society? A tentative deconstruction, *Journal of Education Policy*, 12(6), 499–509.

Major, L.E. (2001) A watchdog bitten, *Guardian*, 27 March: 9.

Malina, D. and Maslin-Prothero, S. (ed.) (1998) *Surviving the Academy: Feminist Perspectives*. London: The Falmer Press.

Mallea, J. (1999) *International Trade in Professional and Educational Services: Implications for the Professions and Higher Education*. Paris: OECD/Centre for Educational Research and Innovation (CERI).

Manicas, P. (1998) Higher education at risk, *Futures*, 30(7): 651–6.

Manya, M.O. (2000) Equal opportunities policy (gender). A means to increasing the number of female senior managers and decision-makers at the university of Nairobi. Unpublished MA dissertation, University of London Institute of Education.

Marceau, J. (2000) Australian universities: a contestable future, in T. Coady (ed.) *Why Universities Matter: A Conversation about Values, Means and Directions*. Sydney: Allen and Unwin.

Marcuse, H. (1964) *One-dimensional Man*. London: Routledge and Kegan Paul.

Marcuse, H. (1969) *An Essay on Liberation*. Boston: Beacon Press.

Marginson, S. (1997) Competition and contestability in Australian higher education, *Australian Universities Review*, 40(1): 5–14.

Marginson, S. (1999) After globalization: Emerging politics of education, *Journal of Education Policy*, 14(1): 19–31.

Marginson, S. (2000) Rethinking academic work in a global era, *Journal of Higher Education Policy and Management*, 22(1): 23–35.

Margolis, E. (ed.) (2001) *The Hidden Curriculum in Higher Education*. New York: Routledge.

Mbanefoh, N. (1995) Women's participation in higher education in Nigeria, in *Women in Higher Education in Africa*. Dakar: UNESCO Regional Office.

McBurnie, G. (2001) Leveraging globalization as a policy paradigm for higher education, *Higher Education in Europe*, 26(1): 11–26.

McDonough, P.M., Antonio, A.L., Walpole, M. and Perez, L. (1997) *College Rankings: Who Uses Them and With What Impact*. Chicago, IL: AERA Annual Meeting.

McInnis, C. (2000) Changing academic work roles: the everyday realities challenging quality in teaching, *Quality in Higher Education*, 6(2): 143–52.

McNay, I. (1997) *The Impact of the 1992 RAE on Institutional and Individual Behaviour in English Higher Education*. Bristol: HEFCE.

McNay, I. (1998) The RAE and after: 'you never know how it will turn out' perspectives, *Policy and Practice in Higher Education*, 2(1): 19–22.

McRobbie, A. (1994) *Post-Modernism and Popular Culture*. London: Routledge.

McWilliam, E., Hatcher, C. and Meadmore, D. (1999) Developing professional identities: remaking the acdemic for corporate times, *Pedagogy, Culture and Society*, 7(1): 55–72.

Meadmore, D. (1998) Changing the culture: the governance of the Australian pre-millennial university, *International Studies in Sociology of Education*, 8: 27–45.

Middlehurst, R. (2000) *The Business of Borderless Education*. London: CVCP/HEFCE.

Middleton, C. (2000) Models of state and market in the 'modernization' of higher education, *British Journal of Sociology of Education*, 21(4): 537–53.

Miller, H. (1998) Managing academics in Canada and the UK, *International Studies in the Sociology of Education*, 8: 3–26.

Mintz, B. and Rothblum, E. (ed.) (1997) *Lesbians in Academia: Degrees of Freedom*. New York: Routledge.

Mirza, H.S. (1998) Black women in education: a collective movement for social change, in T. Modood and T. Acland (eds) *Race and Higher Education*. London: Policy Studies Institute.

Modood, T. (1993) The number of ethnic minority students in British higher education: some grounds for optimism, *Oxford Review of Education*, 19(2): 167–82.

Modood, T. and Acland, T. (eds) (1998) *Race and Higher Education: Experiences, Challenges and Policy Implications*. London: Policy Studies Institute.

Moodie, G. and Eustace, R. (1974) *Power and Authority in British Universities*. London: Allen and Unwin.

Moore, R. and Muller, J. (1999) The discourse of 'voice' and the problem of knowledge and identity in the sociology of education, *British Journal of Sociology of Education*, 20(2): 189–205.

Morley, L. (1995) Measuring the muse: creativity, writing and career development, in L. Morley and V. Walsh (eds) *Feminist Academics: Creative Agents for Change*. London: Taylor and Francis.

Morley, L. (1997) Change and equity in higher education, *British Journal of Sociology of Education*, 18(2): 229–40.

Morley, L. (1998) All you need is love: feminist pedagogy for empowerment and emotional labour in the Academy, *International Journal of Inclusive Education*, 2(1): 15–27.

Morley, L. (1999) *Organising Feminisms: The Micropolitics of the Academy*. London: Macmillan.

Morley, L. (2001a) Subjected to review: engendering quality in higher education, *Journal of Education Policy*, 16(5): 465–78.

Morley, L. (2001b) Producing new workers: quality, equality and employability in higher education, *Quality in Higher Education*, 7(2): 131–8.

Morley, L. (2002) Comedy of manners: quality and power in higher education, in P. Trowler (ed.) *Higher Education Policy and Institutional Change*. Buckingham: SRHE/Open University Press.

Morley, L. and Rassool, N. (1999) *School Effectiveness: Fracturing the Discourse*. London: Falmer Press.

Morley, L., Unterhalter, E. and Gold, A. (2003) Enterprise culture, equity and gendered change in Commonwealth higher education, in G. Williams (ed.) *The Enterprising University: Reform, Excellence and Equity*. Buckingham: SRHE/Open University Press.

Morrow, R. and Torres, C. (2000) The state, globalization, and educational policy, in N. Burbules and C. Torres (eds) *Globalization and Education*. London: Routledge.

Moses, I. (1986) Promotion of academic staff, *Higher Education*, 15: 33–7.

NCSR (National Centre for Social Research) (2000) *Who Applies for Research Funding?* London: National Centre for Social Research.

Ndungane, P. (1999) Women academics in research in humanities and social sciences at universities in South Africa. Unpublished MA dissertation, University of London, Institute of Education.

Neave, G. (1998) The evaluative state reconsidered, *European Journal of Education*, 33(3): 265–84.

Newman, F. and Couturier, L. (2002) Trading public good in the higher education market, *The Observatory on Borderless Education*. www.obhe.ac.uk (accessed January 2002).

Newton, J. (2000) Feeding the beast or improving quality? Academics' perceptions of quality assurance and quality monitoring, *Quality in Higher Education*, 6(2): 153–63.

NIACE (1993) *Learning to Succeed.* London: Heinemann.

Nias, J. (1996) Thinking about feeling: the emotions in teaching, *Cambridge Journal of Education,* 26(3): 293–306.

Nicholls, G. (2002) *Developing Teaching and Learning in Higher Education.* London: Routledge/Falmer.

Nisbet, R. (1971) *The Degradation of Academic Dogma: The University in America, 1945–70.* London: Heinemann.

Nixon, J., Beattie, M., Challis, M. and Walker, M. (1998) What does it mean to be an academic? A Colloquium, *Teaching in Higher Education,* 3(3): 277–98.

OECD (1996) *Employment and Growth in the Knowledge-Based Economy.* Paris: OECD.

O'Neill, O. (2002) *A Question of Trust.* Reith Lectures. http://www.bbc.co.uk/radio4/reith2002/schedule.shtml (accessed January 2003).

Onsongo, J. (2000) Publish or perish? An investigation into academic women's access to research and publication in Kenyan universities. Unpublished MA dissertation, University of London, Institute of Education.

O'Reilly, D., Cunningham, L. and Lester, L. (eds) (1999) *Developing the Capable Practitioner.* London: Kogan Page.

Oshagbemi, T. (1988) *Leadership and Management in Universities.* Berlin: Walter de Gruyter.

Oshagbemi, T. (1996) Job satisfaction of UK academics, *Educational Management and Administration,* 24: 389–400.

Oswald, A. (2001) Kick teaching inspectors out of universities, *The Sunday Times,* 1 April: 15.

Ozga, J. (1998) The entrepreneurial researcher: re-formations of identity in the research marketplace, *International Studies in Sociology of Education,* 8(2): 143–53.

Ozga, J. and Walker, L. (1999) In the company of men, in S. Whitehead and R. Moodley (eds) *Transforming Managers.* London: UCL Press.

Park, A. (1992) Women, men, and the academic hierarchy: exploring the relationship between rank and sex, *Oxford Review of Education,* 18(3): 227–39.

Pattern, J. (1993) Only quality can save universities, *The Times,* 6 December.

Pels, P. (2000) The trickster's dilemma: ethics and the technologies of the anthropological self, in M. Strathern (ed.) *Audit Cultures: Anthropological Studies in Accountability, Ethics and the Academy.* London: Routledge.

Perellon, J. (2001) The development of quality assurance policy in higher education. A comparative analysis of England, the Netherlands, Spain and Switzerland. Unpublished PhD thesis, Institute of Education, University of London.

Peters, T. and Waterman, R. (1982) *In Search of Excellence.* Sydney: Harper and Row.

Pirsig, R. (1974) *Zen and the Art of Motorcycle Maintenance.* London: Bodley Head.

Polster, C. (2000) The future of the liberal university in the era of the global knowledge grab, *Higher Education,* 39: 19–41.

Polster, C. and Newson, J. (1998) Don't count your blessings: the social accomplishments of performance indicators, in J. Currie and J. Newson (eds) *Universities and Globalization: Critical Perspectives.* London: Sage.

Power, M. (1994) *The Audit Explosion.* London: Demos.

Power, M. (1997) *The Audit Society.* Oxford: Oxford University Press.

Prichard, C. (2000) *Making Managers in Universities and Colleges.* Buckingham: SRHE/Open University Press.

Priestley, J.B. (1965) *An Inspector Calls.* London: Heinemann Educational.

Pugsley, L. (1998) Throwing your brains at it: higher education, markets and choice, *International Studies in Sociology of Education,* 8: 71–90.

QAA (2001) *Quality Assurance in UK Higher Education: Proposals for Consultation.* Gloucester: Quality Assurance Agency.

Ramsden, P. (1998) Out of the Wilderness, *The Australian*, 29 April.

Randall, J. (2001) Belief System, *Guardian*, 15 February.

Randle, K. and Brady, N. (1997) Managerialism and professionalism in the 'Cinderella service', *Journal of Vocational Education and Training*, 49: 121–39.

Readings, B. (1996) *The University in Ruins.* Cambridge, MA: Harvard University Press.

Reay, D. (1998) 'Always knowing' and 'never being sure': familial and institutional habituses and higher education choice, *Journal of Education Policy*, 13(4): 519–29.

Reay, D. (2000) 'Dim dross': marginalised women both inside and outside the Academy, *Women's Studies International Forum*, 23(1): 13–22.

Reay, D., Davies, J., David, M. and Ball, S. (2001) Choices of degree or degrees of choice? Class, 'race' and the higher education choice process, *Sociology*, 35(4): 855–74.

Reed, M. and Hughes, M. (eds) (1991) *Rethinking Organisations.* London: Sage.

Reich, R. (1991) *The Work of Nations: Preparing Ourselves for 21st Century Capitalism.* London: Simon and Schuster.

Riesman, D. (1998) *On Higher Education: The Academic Enterprise in an Era of Rising Student Consumerism.* New Brunswick: Transaction.

Rifkin, J. (1995) *The End of Work.* New York: G.P. Putnam's Sons.

Rizvi, F. and Lingard, B. (2000) Globalization and education: complexities and contingencies, *Educational Theory*, 50(4): 419–26.

Robertson, R. (1992) *Globalization.* London: Sage.

Robertson, J. and Bond, C.H. (2001) Experiences of the relation between teaching and research: what do academics value?, *Higher Education Research and Development*, 20(1): 5–19.

Roland Martin, J. (2000) *Coming of Age in Academe.* London: Routledge.

Rowland, S., Byron, C., Furedi, F., Padfield, N. and Smyth, T. (1998) Turning academics into teachers?, *Teaching in Higher Education*, 3(2): 133–41.

Rowley, J. (1995) Student feedback: a shaky foundation for quality assurance, *Innovation and Learning in Education*, 1(3): 14–22.

Rowley, D., Lujan, H. and Dolence, M. (1998) *Strategic Choices for the Academy.* San Francisco, CA: Jossey Bass.

Russell, C. (1993) *Academic Freedom.* London: Routledge.

Russell, L. (2002) Private correspondence, email to L. Morley, 7 March.

Ryan, A. (2001) Stalin had to die too, *The Times Higher Education Supplement*, 30 March.

Ryan, Y. (2002) Emerging indicators of success and failure in borderless higher education. *The Observatory on Borderless Higher Education.* www.obhe.ac.uk (accessed February 2002).

Sabel, C.F. (1984) *Work and Politics: The Division of Labor in Industry.* Cambridge: Cambridge University Press.

Sadlak, J. (1998) Globalization and concurrent challenges for higher education, in P. Scott (ed.) *The Globalization of Higher Education.* Buckingham: SRHE/Open University Press.

Said, E. (1994) *Representations of the Intellectual: The 1993 Reith Lectures.* London: Vintage.

Samuelowicz, K. (2001) Revisiting academics' beliefs about teaching and learning, *Higher Education*, 41(3): 299–325.

Scheffler, I. (1965) *Conditions of Knowledge.* Chicago, IL: Chicago University Press.

Scott, P. (1995) *The Meanings of Mass Higher Education*. Buckingham: SRHE/Open University Press.

Scott, P. (1998) Massification, internationalisation and globalization, in P. Scott (ed.) *The Globalization of Higher Education*. Buckingham: SRHE/Open University Press.

Scott, S. (1999) The academic as service provider: is the customer 'always right'?, *Journal of Higher Education Policy and Management*, 21(2): 193–202.

Scott, P. (2000) Globalisation and higher education: challenges for the 21st century, *Journal of International Studies in International Education*, 4(1): 3–10.

Segal Quince Wicksteed (1999) *Providing Public Information on the Quality and Standards of Higher Education Courses: Report to DENI, HEFCE, HEFCW, QAA, SHEFCE*. Cambridge: Segal Quince Wicksteed.

Senge, P. (1990) *The Fifth Discipline: The Art and Practice of the Learning Organization*. New York: Doubleday.

Sennett, R. (1998) *The Corrosion of character: The Personal Consequences of Work in the New Capitalism*. New York: Norton.

Shaw, J. (1995) *Education, Gender and Anxiety*. London: Taylor and Francis.

Sheehan, B.A. and Walsh, A.R. (1996) *The Academic Profession in Australia*. Canberra: DEETYA, AGPS.

Shields, P.M. (1999) Zen and the art of higher education maintenance, *Journal of Higher Education Policy and Management*, 21(2): 165–72.

Shore, C. and Selwyn, T. (1998) The marketisation of higher education: management, discourse and the politics of performance, in D. Jary and M. Parker (eds) *The New Higher Education*. Stoke-on-Trent: Staffordshire University Press.

Shore, C. and Wright, S. (1999) Audit culture and anthropology: neo liberalism in British higher education, *Journal of the Royal Anthropological Institute*, 557–75.

Shore, C. and Wright, S. (2000) Coercive accountability: the rise of audit culture in higher education, in M. Strathern (ed.) *Audit Cultures: Anthropological Studies in Accountability, Ethics, and the Academy*. London: Routledge.

Silver, H. (1993) *External Examiners: Changing Roles*. London: CNAA.

Singh, M. (2001) Re-inserting the 'public good' into higher education transformation. Paper presented at the SRHE Conference 'Globalisation and Higher Education: Views from the South', March, Cape Town, South Africa.

Sitkin, S. and Roth, N. (1993) Explaining the limited effectiveness of legalistic remedies for trust/distrust, *Organization Science*, 4(3): 367–92.

Skeggs, B. (1995) Women's studies in Britain in the 1990s: entitlement culture and institutional constraints, *Women's Studies International Forum*, 18(4): 475–85.

Slaughter, S. and Leslie, L. (1997) *Academic Capitalism: Politics, Policies and the Entrepreneurial University*. Baltimore, MD: John Hopkins University Press.

Smith, D. (1987) *The Everyday World as Problematic: A Feminist Sociology*. Milton Keynes: Open University Press.

Sommer, J. (1995) *The Academy in Crisis: The Political Economy of Higher Education*. New Brunswick: Transaction.

Spivak, G.C. (1993) *Outside in the Teaching Machine*. New York: Routledge.

Stanley, L. (ed.) (1997) *Knowing Feminisms*. London: Sage.

Strathern, M. (1997) 'Improving ratings': audit in the British university system. *European Review*, 5(3): 305–21.

Strathern, M. (ed.) (2000a) *Audit Cultures: Anthropological Studies in Accountability, Ethics and the Academy*. London: Routledge.

Strathern, M. (2000b) The tyranny of transparency, *British Educational Research Journal*, 26(3): 309–21.

Swift, J. (1785) The adventures of Captain Gulliver in a voyage to the islands of Lulliput and Brobdingnag, *Gulliver's Travels*. London: Osborne & Griffin.

Talib, A. and Steele, A. (2000) The Research Assessment Exercise: strategies and trade-offs, *Higher Education Quarterly*, 54(1): 68–87.

Tapsall, S. (2001) 'All aboard' the borderless education bandwagon, *Open Learning*, 16(1): 35–46.

Taylor, F.W. (1911) *The Principles of Scientific Management*. New York: Harper and Brothers.

Taylor, J. (2001) The impact of performance indicators on the work of university academics: evidence from Australian universities, *Higher Education Quarterly*, 55(1).

THES (*The Times Higher Education Supplement*) (1994) Sad life of the alienated academics: UK scholars sing blues, *The Times Higher Educational Supplement*, pp. 1–2.

THES (1999) 5 February.

THES (2000) 4 August: 1.

THES (2001) 30 March.

Thompson, E.P. (1970) *Warwick University Ltd.* Harmondsworth: Penguin.

Thompson, G. (1998) Does higher necessarily mean better?, in D. Jary and M. Parker (eds) *The New Higher Education: Issues and Directions for the Post-Dearing University*. Stoke-on-Trent: Staffordshire University Press.

Tight, M. (2000) Do league tables contribute to the development of a quality culture? Football and higher education compared, *Higher Education Quarterly*, 54(1): 22–42.

Tomlin, R. (1998) Research league tables: is there a better way?, *Higher Education Quarterly*, 52: 204–20.

Touraine, A. (1971) *The May Movement: Revolt and Reform*. New York: Random House.

Travers, C.J. and Cooper, C.L. (1996) *Teachers Under Pressure*. London: Routledge.

Triesman, D. (2001) Keynote address to the AUT Annual Women's Conference, London, 8 March.

Troman, G. (2000) Teacher stress in the low trust society, *British Journal of Sociology of Education*, 23(3): 331–53.

Trow, M. (1994) Managerialism and the academic profession, *Higher Education Policy*, 7(2): 11–18.

Trow, M. (1996) Comparative reflections on diversity in British higher education, *Higher Education Digest*, 26: 16–23.

Trowler, P. (1998) *Academics Responding to Change: New Higher Education Frameworks and Academic Cultures*. Buckingham: SRHE/Open University Press.

Troyna, B. (1994) Blind faith? empowerment and educational research, *International Studies in Sociology of Education*, 4(1): 3–24.

UCAS (1998) Get AHEAD: access to higher education, applicants and their decisions, *Guardian* and UCAS Report.

UNESCO (1995) *Policy Paper for Change and Development in Higher Education*. Paris: UNESCO.

UNESCO (1998) *Towards an Agenda for Higher Education: Challenges and Tasks for the 21st Century Viewed in the Light of the Regional Conference*. Paris: UNESCO.

Vidovich, L. and Slee, R. (2001) Bringing universities to account? Exploring some global and local policy tensions, *Journal of Education Policy*, 16(5): 431–53.

Walker, M. (ed.) (2001) *Reconstructing Professionalism in University Teaching*. Buckingham: SRHE/Open University Press.

Walkerdine, V. (1989) Femininity as performance, *Oxford Review of Education*, 15(3).

Walkerdine, V. (1990) *Schoolgirl Fictions*. London: Verso.

Watson, D. and Bowden, R. (1999) Why did they do it? The Conservatives and mass higher education, 1979–97, *Journal of Education Policy*, 14(3): 243–56.

Wellcome Trust (1997) *Women and Peer Review: An Audit of the Wellcome Trust's decision-making on grants*. London: The Wellcome Trust.

Wells, H.G. (1971) *The Time Machine*. London: Heinemann.

Wenneras, C. and Wold, A. (1997) Nepotism and sexism in peer review, *Nature*, 387, 22 May: 341–3.

White, S.K. (1986) Foucault's challenge to critical theory, *American Political Science Review*, 80(2): 419–31.

Whitehead, S. (1997) The gendered transition of educational management. Paper presented at the Gender and Education Conference, University of Warwick, April.

Whittington, G. (1997) The 1996 Research Assessment Exercise, *British Accounting Review*, 29: 181–97.

Wilcox, B. and Gray, J. (1994) Reactions to inspection: a study of three variants, *Cambridge Journal of Education*, 24: 245–59.

Williams, R. (1976) *Keywords*. London: Fontana.

Williams, G. and Blackstone, T. (1974) *The Academic Labour Market: Economic and Social Aspects of a Profession*. Amsterdam: Elsevier.

Williams, G. and Blackstone, T. (1983) *Response to Adversity*. Guildford: Society for Research into Higher Education.

Wolf, M. (2001) Mediocrity flourishes when an inspector calls, *Financial Times*, 16 April.

Womack, P. (1999) Ac-cen-tchuate the positive, *CCUE NEWS (Council for College & University English)*, 10, Winter: 3–5.

Woolf, V. (1938) *Three Guineas*. London: Hogarth Press.

Woolgar, S. (ed.) (1988) *Knowledge and Reflexivity: New Frontiers in the Sociology of Knowledge*. London: Sage.

World Bank (1994) *Higher Education: The Lessons of Experience*. Washington, DC: World Bank.

Wyn, J., Acker, S. and Richards, E. (2000) Making a difference: women in management in Australian and Canadian faculties of education, *Gender and Education*, 12(4): 435–47.

Yeatman, A. (1995) Interpreting contemporary contractualism, in J. Boston (ed.) *The State Under Contract*. Wellington: Bridge Williams Books.

Yeaxlee, B. (1929) *Lifelong Learning*. London: Cassell.

Yorke, M. (1999) Assuring quality and standards in globalised higher education, *Quality Assurance in Higher Education*, 7(1): 14–24.

Young, I.M. (1990) *Justice and the Politics of Difference*. Princeton, NJ: Princeton University Press.

Young, I.M. (2000) *Inclusion and Democracy*. New York: Oxford University Press.

Index

Academic Audit Unit, 18
access agendas, 118
accountability
    and autonomy, 53–7
    and costs of quality audits, 63–4
    and equity, 151
    globalization of, 19
    and new managerialism, 48, 51,
        53
    and peer review, 121
    and students, 134, 145
    and trust, 69–70
    UK government policies, 16–17
accountability, vii, 14, 53–7
accreditation
    and the ILT, 30
    and quality assurance, 19
    and US online universities, 9–10
action research, 8
Adams, D., 27, 51, 78
adhocracy, 15
Africa, Sub-Saharan, 9
alienation, 71
    and job satisfaction, 76–8
Althusser, L., 88
Angelo, T., 63
anxiety
    and job satisfaction, 76
    and stress, 82
appeals procedures, 118, 169
Apple, M.W., 128
Argyris, C., 49
aspiration, 50

assessment
    and the ILT, 29–34
    international, 18–21
    peer review/assessment, 111–22
    RAE (Research Assessment Exercise),
        17, 21–6
    research productivity, 21–6
    scores and league tables, 34–41
    standards, benchmarks and
        qualifications frameworks, 41–6
    and subject review, 128
    teaching and learning, 26–9
    see also self-assessment
Association of University Teachers see
    AUT (Association of University
    Teachers)
audit
    culture, 53–7
    procedures, 57
    quality audits
        costs of, 63–4
        and increased workloads, 95
        and peer review, 111, 113
        and stress, 85–6, 87
        and women, 149
    society, 93
    success in, 88, 89
    trails, 49, 127, 156
Australia
    incentive funding in, 27
    job satisfaction, 78
    quality assurance in, 51
        costs of, 63

studies of learning and teaching, 27
Workplace Industrial Relations
    Survey, 79
Austria, 20
AUT (Association of University
    Teachers), 17, 29, 99
surveys
    and occupational stress, 78
    and working hours, 93
autonomy
    and accountability, 53–7
    loss of, 161
    and performativity, 73–4
autopsy model of quality, 138

Baker Miller, J., 55
Ball, S., 49, 53, 73, 76, 106
Barnetson, B., 54, 58
Barnett, R., 14
Barrow, M., 73–4
Bauman, Z., 9, 83, 92–3, 118
Becher, T., 40, 134
Beck, U., 6
Ben-Yehuda, N., 6
benchmarking, 41–6
Benjamin, J., 55
Bensimon, E., 130, 142, 150
Berdahl, R., 56
Bernstein, B., 43
best practice
    changing criteria for, 128
    and peer review, 112–13
best value, 14
bias, and peer review, 117
binary divide, 123–6
Birnbaum, R., 166
Blackmore, J., 55, 136, 146, 151
blame culture, 89–90
    and student evaluation, 140–1, 142
    and subject review, 89–90
Blase, J., 105–6
Bologna Declaration (1999), 8–9, 42
borderless higher education, 4, 8, 9–10
boundaries
    and benchmarks, 43, 45
    and the binary divide, 123
    and micropolitics, 106–7, 108–9
    and peer review, 116
    and students, 134
Bourdieu, P., 81, 147

Brennan, J., 19, 111
British Council, 21
bullying, quality processes as
    increasing, 168–9
Burbules, N., 1, 4
burnout, professional, 85
Butler, J.P., 71, 72, 88

Cambridge University, 124, 150–1
Cameron, D., 72, 143
Canada, 12, 152
career development
    and the gendered division of labour,
        155–7
    and research productivity, 28, 29
change, 160–71
    agencies, 164
    and performance indicators, 59–60
    resistance to, ix, 87–8
    theory, 50
changing employment regimes, 91–104
chaos, and globalization, 1
Chomsky, N., 92
citizenship, and the learning society,
    11
Clark, B., 49
class *see* social class
Clegg, S., 31, 49
CNAA (Council for National Academic
    Awards), 16, 18
    and the binary divide, 123, 124
cognitive dissonance, 71, 160
collegiality, 107–11
    and peer review, 122
    and students, 139
Commonwealth research studies, 152
competencies, and student evaluation,
    139, 143
complaints by students, 133–5, 138
compliance, 161
    culture of, 52, 87–8, 99, 162
consumerism
    and the learning society, 11
    and the professionalization of
        university teachers, 29–30
    students as consumers, 128–45,
        163–4
consumerism, viii
continuous improvement, 13–14
    and new managerialism, 47, 48

contractualism, 134
  and equity, 151
Cooper, C.L., 79
corporate training, 10
corporatism, 7
corporatization agenda, 7
costs, of quality assurance, 60–6, 167
CPD (continuing professional
      development), 8, 12
creativity
  and learning objectives, 143–4
  measuring, 57–60
  and quality assurance, 162
  and the RAE, 24
credentialism, viii, 8, 29
critical feedback, 88–9
critique, the university as a site of, 161–2
cultural capital, 11, 68, 75, 149
curriculum
  and benchmarking, 42–3
  development, and quality assurance,
      17
  see also hidden curriculum
customer care, 14
  and students, 133–7
customer-driven packaged learning, 12
Cutwright, M., 54, 58
CVCP/Universities UK, 18

danger
  quality assurance as an area of, 68
  students as a site of, 133–4
Davies, C., 156
De Groot, J., 76
Dearing Committee Report (1997), 16,
      27, 131
  and the ITL, 29
  and social inclusion, 146
Deem, R., 3, 48
Delanty, G., 53, 100, 131, 147, 161
democracy, as an economic concept,
      128
democratizing discourses, 10–12
  and accountability, 53
Denmark, 19
disabilities, students with, 144
disciplinary areas, and women, 150
disciplinary knowledge, 7
  and benchmarking, 43–4
  and the binary divide, 125

disciplinary power, and peer review,
      120–1
discourse
  performativity and the power of,
      70–5
  quality assurance, 160–1, 164–5, 168
dislocation, 160
distance learning, 4, 8, 12
  private sector, 9–10
divisions of labour
  and collegiality, 107
  gendered, 151, 155–7
  and split focusing, 100
domination
  imposition of quality as, 51
  and peer review, 121, 122
  and the psychic economy of quality,
      68
  and rights of appeal, 118
Dominelli, L., 48, 72, 73, 121
Douglas, M., 69

Eagleton, M., 159
Eastern European countries, 9, 10–11,
      19
educatainment and student evaluation,
      137–43
effective learning, 168
efficiency, and new managerialism, 48
elitism, and the binary divide, 126
emotional labour, 67, 87, 134
emotions
  and the psychic economy of quality,
      67
  and quality procedures, x
employment regimes
  changing, 91–104
  Foucauldian analysis of, 48
empowerment
  student, 130, 143, 144
  and success in audits, 89
empowerment, viii
enhanced reflexivity, 132–3
entitlements, and student evaluations,
      141
epistemology, 128, 161
equal opportunities procedures, 148
equality, 146–59
  globalizing inequality, 152–5
  and peer review, 121

and quality, 146–8, 168–9
see also gender
equity, and autonomy, 54
ethnicity, and the market economy,
    136
European Union, 3
    and lifelong learning, 11
    and quality assurance, 19
    and social exclusion, 146
evaluation, educatainment and student
    evaluation, 137–43
evidence-based methodology, 127
evidence-based practice, 14
excellence
    and accountability, 54
    culture of, ix
    and mediocrity, 130, 162
    and new managerialism, 48
exclusion *see* social exclusion/inclusion
external examiners system, 15
externality, 54, 144, 151, 165

family life, and the long hours' culture,
    95–6
feedback
    critical, 88–9
    loops, 169
    and new managerialism, 49
    and student evaluation, 137–8
feminism
    and micropolitics, 105, 106
    and pedagogy, 143
    research methodologies, 147
feminism, x, 126, 151
Fillitz, T., 20
Finland, 152, 154
Fisher, S., 80
Fleming, J., 79
flexible workforce, 48
Floud, R., 39, 81–2
for-profit (private) universities, 4,
    9–10
Fordism/neo-Fordism, 1, 78
Foucault, Michel, 4, 13, 51, 92, 106,
    147
franchising, 10
Fraser, N., 72
Frazer, M., 20
Fredericks, M., 19–20
Fuller, S., 9, 100–1

funding
    crisis in, 17
    higher education funding councils in
        the UK, 16
    incentive funding for learning and
        teaching, 27
    and quality discourse, 71–2
    research, 22–3, 155
    World Bank report on, 4
Further and Higher Education Act
    (1992), ix, 16, 18

Gefou-Madianou, D., 20
gender
    and autonomy, 55
    gendered division of labour, 151,
        155–7
    inequalities, and student evaluations,
        138
    and the learning society, 12
    and the long hours' culture, 95
    and the market economy, 136
    numbers of female undergraduates,
        146–7
    and performativity, 157–9
    and quality assurance, ix
    see also women
Germany, 78
Gewirtz, S., 71
Ghana, 152
Gibbons, M., 7
Gibbs, G., 28
Giddens, A., 53–4, 71, 82
globalization, 1–4, 76
    of accountability, 19
    features of, 1
    and human capital, 162–3
    impacts on higher education, 2–4
    and inequality, 152–5
    views on, 2
'glocalization', 3
Glover, J., 148
Goffman, E., 73
Gold, A., 147
Goleman, D., 67
good practice
    concept of, 31, 170
    transfer from to quality, 154
Goode, E., 6
granularization, 48

Greece, 10, 20
greedy institutions, 93, 156
Gregg, P., 143
Gudeman, S., 27
guilt
  and academic stress, 82
  and increasing workloads, 93–4
  and the psychic economy of quality,
    87, 88
Guinea, 152

Habermas, J., 100, 131
Handy, C., 65
Hatcher, C., 76
Hayek, F. von, 59
health effects, of academic stress, 86–7
HEFC (Higher Education Funding
    Council), 15
  costs of quality assurance, 60
HEFCE (Higher Education Funding
    Council for England), 22, 27,
    169
  and cost-effectiveness, 62
hegemony, and performativity, 73
Henkel, M., 23, 26–7, 53, 69, 77, 142,
    156
HEQC (Higher Education Quality
    Control), 18
  establishment of, 16
  Graduate Standards Programme, 5
  and overseas franchising, 10
Herzberg, F., 77
HESA (Higher Education Statistics
    Agency), 153
hidden curriculum, 51, 137
  and performativity, 75
  and research productivity, 153
  and split focusing, 100
  and transparency, 154
Higher Education: A New Framework, 16
Higher Education Inspectorate, 16
Hodge, Margaret, 18
Hong Kong, 10, 78
Hoogvelt, A., 48, 72, 73, 121
human capital
  and race, 162
  theory, 11, 136
human costs, of quality assurance,
    64–5, 86–7
human rights, and quality assurance, 54

identity
  and alienation, 76
  and autonomy, 54
  and naming, 88
  professional, 67–9, 91
ILT (Institute of Learning and
    Teaching), 16, 29–34
imagery, and the psychic economy of
    quality, 74–5
impression management, 61
information loops, and new
    managerialism, 49
inspection
  and control, 166–7
  costs of, 60–1
  criticisms of, 167–8
  gendered implications of, 157
institutional audit, 17–18
intellectual labour, and new
    managerialism, 48
interdisciplinary approaches, and
    benchmarks, 43
internationalism
  and benchmarking, 42
  and quality assurance, 18–21
intertextuality, 160
'Investors in People' process, 167
isomorphism, 160
  and benchmarks, 44
  organizational, 163
ivory basement work, 157

James, Oswain, 130
James, R., 7, 51, 63
Japan, 9, 13
Jarvis, P., 4, 162–3
job satisfaction, 28, 76–8
Johnson, N., 75
just-in-case production of
    documentation, 94
just-in-time knowledge, 4, 14

Kalugama, P.S., 152
Kaufmann, R., 58
Kenya, 154
  University of Nairobi, 152
knowledge
  and the binary divide, 125–6
  management, 143
  new sites of, 8–10

professionals as knowledge workers, 91–3
technocratic instrumental view of, 128
see also disciplinary knowledge
knowledge capitalism, 143
the knowledge economy, ix, 6–8
knowledge society, 4, 158

labour market training, higher education as, 7
Lacy, F.J., 77
Lafferty, G., 79
Laing, R.D., 83
Lander, D., 151
Latin America, private universities in, 9
Laurillard, D., 58
Lawson, A., 75
league tables, 34–41
  and academic stress, 81–2
learning *see* teaching and learning
learning organisation, 49
learning society, the, and benchmarks, 44
learning society, the, ix, 11–12
Lecky, J., 137
Leonard, D., 151
Leslie, L., 3
lifelong learning, and benchmarks, 44
lifelong learning, ix, 8, 12
Lim, D., 21
liquification, 8–10
London School of Economics, 122
long hours' culture, 93–9
loss, 161
Luke, A., 2
Luke, C., 2, 144, 149
Lyotard, J., 8, 72, 141

McInnis, C., 27, 78, 100
McRobbie, A., 6
McWilliam, E., 76, 89, 128
Malaysia, 10
management
  academic, viii
  processes in higher education, 47
  women in, 149–50
managerial accountability, 53
managing quality, 47–66
  accountability, 53–7
  new managerialism, 47–53

Marcuse, H., 131, 147
marginalization, quality processes as increasing, 168–9
Marginson, S., 137
market accountability, 53
markets, borderless, 9–10
massification
  and academic standards, 130
  and increased workloads, 99
  and the risk society, 5
massification, ix, 6
Mauritius, 21
Meadmore, D., 130
media
  and league tables and scoring, 39
  and student satisfaction, 142
metaphors of quality assurance, 63–4, 82–3
methodology
  of quality assurance, 126–8, 160
  and scores and league tables, 36, 40–1
micropolitics, 105–28
  and the binary divide, 123–6
  and collegiality, 107–11
  defining, 105–6
  and the everyday life of power, 105–7
  gendered, 154–5
  and peer review, 111–22
Middleton, C., 58
Miller, H., 49
misrecognition, 170
mistrust, 164, 170
modernization, and quality assurance, viii, 126–8
Moldova, 9
moral panics
  and the risk society, 5–6
  and students, 130
Morley, L., 147
Morrow, R., 4
Moses, I., 28
multiskilling, 160, 168
  and increased workloads, 99
  and occupational stress, 78
  and professional identity, 68
  and professionalization, 91
  and the RAE, 24

naming and shaming, 87–90
National Centre for Social Research, 155
Ndugane, P., 152
Neill, N., 137
neoliberalism
  and globalization, 2
  and quality management, 149
Netherlands, the, 19–20, 92
network society, 4
networks, and collegiality, 110
new managerialism
  and old organizational cultures, 47–5
  and quality discourse, 73
new sites of knowledge, 8–10
new universities, and subject review, 124
New Zealand, 73–4
Newsom, J., 7, 58–9
Newton, J., 49–50, 63–4, 82–3
Nigeria, 152
norms
  and accountability, 53–4
  and power relations, viii
  and professionalization, 92
  and the quality discourse, 70
  reproduction of, 161
Norway, 152
NPQH (National Professional Qualification for Headteachers), 8
NUS (National Union of Students), 130, 151

occupational stress, 78–87
OECD (Organization for Economic and Cultural Development), 3, 11, 142
Onsongo, J., 154
organizational culture, 88
  and new managerialism, 47–53
Oshadbemi, T., 100
Oswald, A., 70, 75
overseas franchising, 10
Ozga, J., 33

Park, A., 153
pastoral power, and peer review, 121
Patten, John, 5, 130
pedagogy, 143–5

peer review/assessment, 15, 21–2, 111–22
Pels, P., 2, 71
performance
  academic, and effective learning, 168
  and new managerialism, 48–9
performance indicators
  and equity issues, 150
  measuring creativity, 57–60
  and research productivity, 24
  and scores and league tables, 40
  and student services, 134
  and subject review scores, 36
performativity, 161, 165
  gendering, 157–9
  and the power of discourse, 70–5
  and students, 134, 139
Philippines, the, 9
Pirsig, R., 69, 151
Poland, private universities, 9
policy
  context, 1–14
  convergence, 20, 21
political technology, 51
Polster, C., 7, 58–9
positivism, 161
post-modernism, 147, 160
poststructuralism, 105
power
  and accountability, 53–4
  balance of between change and internal processes, 165–6
  and the binary divide, 125
  circuits of, and new managerialism, 49
  of discourse, 70–5
  everyday life of, 105–7
  and peer review, 120–1
  and quality assurance discourse, 164–5
  regimes, 139–40, 157
  struggles, and quality assurance, 51
  see also empowerment
Power, M., 53, 85
power relations
  and academic stress, 85–6
  and accountability, 53
  and collegiality, 107, 108
  and costs of quality assurance, 63
  gendered, ix

and new managerialism, 53
and peer review, 111, 113
and performativity, 73
and research productivity, 25, 26
and students, 137, 145
unequal, 150
power relations, viii, 170
prejudice
  and academic reputation, 40
  and the binary divide, 126
  and peer review, 117–18
  and performance indicators, 58
pride, and the psychic economy of
  quality, 87, 88
Priestley, J.B., *An Inspector Calls*, 75
private higher education, 4, 9–10
procedure versus practice binary, 132
productivity, research, 21–6, 28, 29,
  153
professional conduct, and the risk
  society, 5
professional development
  continuing (CPD), 8, 12
  and the Institute of Teaching and
    Learning, 16
  and the ITL, 33
professional identity, 67–9, 91
professional knowledge, 7–8
professionalism
  and accountability, 53, 56
  and quality assurance, 15
professionalization, viii, 8
  de- or re-professionalization, 91–3
  of university teachers, 29–34
psychic economy of quality, 67–90
  and gender equity, 151
  and job satisfaction, 76–8
  naming and shaming, 87–90
  and occupational stress, 78–87
  and performativity, 70–5
  and professional identity, 67–9
  and trust, 69–70
psychological contract, 65
public services
  and continuous improvement, 13
  funding, 92–3
  and new managerialism, 47

QAA (Quality Assurance Agency), 16,
  17, 18, 38, 50–1, 71

and academic stress, 80, 81, 83
and accountability, 54, 55–6
and the binary divide, 123, 124, 126
and collegiality, 107
and costs of quality assurance, 63
and de-professionalization, 91
and gendered performativity, 158
and increased workloads, 98
and the methodology of quality
  assurance, 128
and peer review, 115–16, 121, 122
and the psychic economy of quality,
  68, 74–5
and split focusing, 101, 103
and students, 136
and wasted time, 133
qualifications frameworks, 41–6
quality assurance
  and accountability, 53–7
  changing systems of, 59–60
  cost of, 60–6, 167
  and franchising, 10
  and globalization, 3
  international, 18–21
  methodology of, 126–8
  movement, 15–18
  and new managerialism, 47, 48, 50–3
  and professionalization, 91–3
  psychic economy of, x
  and the risk society, 5–6
  and societies in transition, 9
  and split focusing, 100–4
  see also QAA (Quality Assurance
    Agency)
quality assurance, vii–viii, ix
quality control, 17

race
  and globalizing inequality, 152
  and the learning society, 12
  and quality assurance, ix
  and supply and human capital, 162
RAE (Research Assessment Exercise),
  17, 21–6, 87
  and equal opportunities, 148
  and funding, 22–3
  and gender equity, 150–1, 153
  and peer review, 114
  scores, 34
  and split focusing, 101, 102

Ramsden, P., 49, 68, 137
Randall, John, 18, 63
Readings, B., 5, 53
Realising Our Potential, 16
reflective practice, and the ILT, 30–1
reflexivity
    'counterfeit', 76–8
    enhanced, 132–3
    lack of, 169
regulation, vii
    and benchmarks, 44
Reich, R., 3
research
    and the gendered division of labour,
        155–7
    productivity
        and academic career success, 28, 29
        and gender equity, 153
        measuring, 21–6
    and split focusing, 100–1, 102–3
    see also RAE (Research Assessment
        Exercise)
resistance, 165
    mobilizing, ix
    and new managerialism, 49, 50
    to change, ix, 87–8
responsibilization, 14
    and academic stress, 82
    and gender socialization, 159
    and the psychic economy of quality,
        68
    and teaching quality assessment,
        156–7
Reynolds Committee Report (1983),
    15–16
Riesman, D., 131
Rifkin, J., 92
rights of appeal, and peer reviews, 118
risk
    and globalization, 1
    writing risk reduction, 132–7
the risk society, 5–6
    and performance indicators, 58
    and service level agreements, 132
Robbins Report (1963), 147
Roth, N., 69
Ryan, A., 115, 133

Sadlak, J., 10
Said, E., 115, 139

salaries
    and academic careers, 161, 162
    women academics, 152–3
Scheffler, I., 7
Schon, D., 49
schoolteacher stress in Britain, 79–80
scores, 34–41
    and academic stress, 81–2
    and the binary divide, 125
    in subject reviews, 127–8
Scotland, subject review scores, 37
Scott, P., viii, 3, 9, 12, 78
Segal Quince Wickstead, 34, 136
self-assessment
    documents, 140
    and new managerialism, 49
Selwyn, T., 73, 130
Senge, P., 49
Sennett, R., 14
service level agreements, 132
Shah, T., 19
shame, and academic stress, 82–3
Shaw, J., 134
Sheehan, B.A., 77–8
Sheffield Hallam University, 124
Shore, C., 56, 73, 79, 92, 111–12, 113,
    130
signs of quality, 128
Silver, H., 15
Singapore, 10
Sitkin, S., 69
Slaughter, S., 3
Slovakia, 20
social class
    and the learning society, 12
    and the market economy, 136
    and quality assurance, ix
social exclusion/inclusion, 11, 146–7,
    148–9
    and globalization, 2
    and the learning society, 11
South Africa, 151, 152
South Korea, 9, 77
Spain, 10
split focusing, 100–4, 168
Sri Lanka, 152
standards, 6, 41–6
Steele, A., 22, 23
Strathern, M., 13, 51, 57, 111
stratification, 34, 163

stress, occupational, 78–87
students, 128–45
  briefing/coaching of, 144–5
  complaints by, 133–5, 138
  and costs of higher education, 136–7
  educatainment and student
    evaluation, 137–43
  from change agents to consumers,
    131
  growth in numbers of, ix
  and mock reviews, 145
  naming and shaming of, 90
  and pedagogy, 143–5
  spending per student, 99
  student experience, 133–7, 151, 169
  uprisings of the 1960s, 131
Sub-Saharan Africa, 9
subject review, 17, 18, 25, 160
  and academic stress, 80, 82, 84–5, 86,
    87
  and the binary divide, 124
  and blame culture, 89–90
  challenging the calibre of
    researchers, 114–15
  and collegiality, 110
  costs of, 62–3
  and gendered performativity, 158
  and the ILT, 33–4
  and increased workloads, 97
  and job satisfaction, 77
  negative experiences of, 115–16,
    127–8
  scores for, 34–5, 36, 37, 127–8
  and students, 133, 135, 138–9, 140,
    144, 145, 169
  and success in audit, 89
supply, threat of, 161–3
surveillance, vii, 158, 162
Sweden, 92, 152, 155

Talib, A., 22, 23
Taylorism, 27–8, 48
teaching, and split focusing, 100–1, 103
teaching and learning
  assessment of, 17–18
    and costs, 65, 66
    and the RAE, 25–6
  and gender equity, 151
  reinventing, 26–9
  teacher–learner relationships, 141

teamwork
  and collegiality, 109–10
  and the RAE, 23
Thailand, 9
Thompson, E.P., 131
Thompson, G., 113
Tight, M., 34
TINA effect (there is no alternative),
    120, 165
tokenism, 149
Tomlin, R., 34
Torres, C., 1, 4
Touraine, A., 131
TQA (teaching quality assessment),
    17–18, 128
  scores, 35, 37
  and students, 130, 135
TQM (total quality management),
    13
transparency
  and accountability, 56–7
  and gender equity, 153–4
  and peer review, 120
  and quality assurance, 51, 170
  and students, 145
Travers, C.J., 79
Trow, M., 87–8
Trowler, P., 55, 134
Troyna, B., 144
trust, 169
  and the psychic economy of quality,
    69–70
  and students, 135
Turkey, 21

UNESCO, 42
  Declaration on Higher Education,
    146
  Report on Women in Higher
    Education and Management,
    152
United States
  corporate training, 10
  costs of quality assurance, 63
  and lifelong learning, 12
  private universities, 4, 9–10
  and quality assurance, 19
University for Industry (UfI),
    10
Unterhalter, E., 147

violence
    and gendered performativity, 158
    language of narratives of, 83

Wadsworth, J., 143
Walkerdine, V., 157
Walsh, A.R., 77–8
war effort imagery
    and collegiality, 107–8
    and women's work, 157
Warwick University, 131
waste, and the economics of quality
    assurance, 61–2, 63
welfare, universities as recipients of, 92
Wenneras, C., 155
Whitehead, S., 36
Wold, A., 155
Wolf, M., 162
Womack, P., 70, 71
women
    discrimination against, 55
    engineering students, 148
    and gender equity, 150–1
    and the gendered division of labour,
        155–7
    and global inequality, 152–5
    and performativity, 157–9
    and quality management, 149–50
    undergraduates, 146–7
    see also gender
women managers, and the QAA,
    51
women's studies, 147, 150
Woolf, Virginia, 149
working-class students, 146, 147
workloads, increasing, 93–9
World Bank, 11, 21
    report on higher education (1994),
        3–4
Wright, C., 56, 79, 111–12, 113
Wright, S., 92
Wyn, J., 153

Young, Iris Marion, 149

The Society for Research into Higher Education

The Society for Research into Higher Education (SRHE), an international body, exists to stimulate and coordinate research into all aspects of higher eduction. It aims to improve the quality of higher education through the encouragement of debate and publication on issues of policy, on the organization and management of higher education institutions, and on the curriculum, teaching and learning methods.

The Society is entirely independent and receives no subsidies, although individual events often receive sponsorship from business or industry. The Society is financed through corporate and individual subscriptions and has members from many parts of the world. It is an NGO of UNESCO.

Under the imprint *SRHE & Open University Press*, the Society is a specialist publisher of research, having over 80 titles in print. In addition to *SRHE News*, the Society's newsletter, the Society publishes three journals: *Studies in Higher Education* (three issues a year), *Higher Education Quarterly* and *Research into Higher Education Abstracts* (three issues a year).

The Society runs frequent conferences, consultations, seminars and other events. The annual conference in December is organized at and with a higher education institution. There are a growing number of networks which focus on particular areas of interest, including:

Access	Learning Environment
Assessment	Legal Education
Consultants	Managing Innovation
Curriculum Development	New Technology for Learning
Eastern European	Postgraduate Issues
Educational Development Research	Quantitative Studies
FE/HE	Student Development
Funding	Vocational Qualifications
Graduate Employment	

Benefits to members

Individual

- The opportunity to participate in the Society's networks
- Reduced rates for the annual conferences
- Free copies of *Research into Higher Education Abstracts*

- Reduced rates for *Studies in Higher Education*
- Reduced rates for *Higher Education Quarterly*
- Free copy of *Register of Members' Research Interests* – includes valuable reference material on research being pursued by the Society's members
- Free copy of occasional in-house publications, e.g. *The Thirtieth Anniversary Seminars Presented by the Vice-Presidents*
- Free copies of *SRHE News* which informs members of the Society's activities and provides a calendar of events, with additional material provided in regular mailings
- A 35 per cent discount on all SRHE/Open University Press books
- The opportunity for you to apply for the annual research grants
- Inclusion of your research in the *Register of Members' Research Interests*

Corporate

- Reduced rates for the annual conferences
- The opportunity for members of the Institution to attend SRHE's network events at reduced rates
- Free copies of *Research into Higher Education Abstracts*
- Free copies of *Studies in Higher Education*
- Free copies of *Register of Members' Research Interests* – includes valuable reference material on research being pursued by the Society's members
- Free copy of occasional in-house publications
- Free copies of *SRHE News*
- A 35 per cent discount on all SRHE/Open University Press books
- The opportunity for members of the Institution to submit applications for the Society's research grants
- The opportunity to work with the Society and co-host conferences
- The opportunity to include in the *Register of Members' Research Interests* your Institution's research into aspects of higher education

Membership details: SRHE, 76 Portland Place, London W1B 1NT, UK Tel: 020 7637 2766. Fax: 020 7637 2781. email: srhe@mailbox.ulcc.ac.uk
world wide web: http://www.srhe.ac.uk./srhe/
Catalogue: SRHE & Open University Press, Celtic Court, 22 Ballmoor, Buckingham MK18 1XW. Tel: 01280 823388. Fax: 01280 823233. email: enquiries@openup.co.uk

THE QUEST FOR QUALITY
SIXTEEN FORMS OF HERESY IN HIGHER EDUCATION

Sinclair Goodlad

During the last two decades, universities in the United Kingdom and elsewhere have been under unprecedented pressure to deliver value for money. The word 'quality' has become political shorthand for what is required. Yet, although a large bureaucratic apparatus has been built up in the quest for quality, there seems to be very little agreement about what quality actually is. This book seeks to fill this gap.

Sinclair Goodlad asks: why is it so difficult to define quality; what are the key issues that should be addressed; and what action can and should be taken in the absence of any agreed definition of quality? In so doing, he examines a number of issues concerning the basic stuff of higher education – curriculum, teaching methods, research, college organization – that go deeper than the administrative shell that is the usual focus of the quality debate. At the same time he offers examples and case studies in which broad issues regarding good practice are earthed in particularities. Throughout, his provocative notion of 'heresies' offers grist for discussion wherever the aims, purposes and practices of higher education are being examined.

The Quest for Quality sets out the basis for a systematic approach to higher education, and is an important book for anyone who has a serious interest in what modern universities should be and do.

Contents
Introduction – Approaches to the study of higher education – Curriculum – Teaching Methods – Research – College organization – From student to system – Appendix: the sixteen forms of heresy – References – Index.

144pp   0 335 19350 1 (paperback)

BEYOND ALL REASON
LIVING WITH IDEOLOGY IN THE UNIVERSITY

Ronald Barnett

> A major work . . . provocative, unsettling and profoundly challenging. I think it should be prescribed reading for all vice-chancellors.
>> Colin Bundy, Director of the School of Oriental and African Studies,
>> University of London

> Ron Barnett's latest book lives up to, and possibly exceeds, the high standards he has set himself in his previous books – which are now established as the premier series of reflective books on higher education.
>> Peter Scott, Vice-Chancellor, Kingston University

Beyond All Reason argues that ideologies are now multiplying on campus and that, consequently, the university as a place of open debate and reason is in jeopardy. The book examines, as case studies, the ideologies of competition, quality, entrepreneurialism and managerialism. All of these movements have a positive potential but, in being pressed forward unduly, have become pernicious ideologies that are threatening to undermine the university.

Ronald Barnett argues that it is possible to realize the university by addressing the ideals present in the idea of the university, and so developing positive projects for the university. These 'utopian ideologies' may never be fully realized but, pursued seriously, they can counter the pernicious ideologies that beset the university. In this way, it is possible for the idea of the university to live on and be practised in the twenty-first century.

Beyond All Reason offers a bold optimistic statement about the future of universities and offers ideas for enabling universities to be 'universities' in the contemporary age. It will be of interest and value not just to students of higher education but also to vice-chancellors, administrators, academics generally and those who care about the future of universities.

Contents

Introduction – Part 1: The end of the matter – The ends of reason – A complex world – The states of higher education – The end of ideology? – Part 2: Pernicious ideologies – 'The entrepreneurial university' – Anything you can do – Never mind the quality – 'The academic community' – Part 3: Virtuous ideologies – Communicating values – Engaging universities – Uniting research and teaching – Reasonable universities – Prospects – Appendices – Notes – Bibliography – Index – The Society for Research into Higher Education.

c.192pp   0 335 20893 2   (Paperback)   0 335 20894 0   (Hardback)

FOR A RADICAL HIGHER EDUCATION
AFTER POSTMODERNISM

Richard Taylor, Jean Barr and Tom Steele

This is a timely and a challenging work. The contemporary debate about the purposes of higher education needs to be refocused: on the transmission of values as well as the utility of skills; on its emancipatory as well as its instrumental roles in modern society. This book should be read by students and their teachers, as well as by policy-makers and their pay-masters.

David Watson, Director, University of Brighton

This is a forceful restatement of the classic 'Left' analysis of both the shortcomings, and radical potential, of higher education. In an age of soft-focus sound-bite New Labour politics such a restatement is badly needed. The authors take no prisoners in their critique of postmodernism as an empty and conformist discourse that inhibits radical action. Not everyone will agree with this book, but everyone should read it.

Peter Scott, Vice-Chancellor, Kingston University

Higher education is being transformed, not least because of its rapid expansion. What should be the priorities, objectives and purposes of this new higher education? Much current policy development for universities and colleges is implicitly based on postmodernist ideas. *For a Radical Higher Education* explores these postmodernist approaches through social and political theory, philosophy, cultural studies and feminism, and proposes radical alternatives. It argues that, although postmodernism has provided useful insights and corrections to other frames of reference, it leads often to a reactionary and conformist position. Its emphases on relativism, consensus and apolitical cynicism in relation to all progressive perspectives, effectively gives support to those who see higher education increasingly incorporated into technicism and free market cultures. In contrast, this book argues for a revitalized and radical university, characterized by critical, sceptical enquiry, tolerance, and a commitment to humanistic, egalitarian politics.

Contents
Part 1: Introduction – The postmodernist position on higher education – Part 2: Contexts – Postmodernism and politics – Revaluing the enlightenment: The university and the educated public – Universities as epistemological communities – Part 3: Policy development in higher education – The policy context – Contested concepts of lifelong learning – Community, globalization and learner autonomy – Professionalism and vocationalism – Part 4: Conclusion – Radical perspectives for the new higher education – Bibliography – Index – The Society for Research into Higher Education.

192pp   0 335 20868 1   (Paperback)   0 335 20869 X (Hardback)